To Lord clinton - Davis,

With regards,

Amnon Rubinstein

Jerusalem, June 13, 2001

FROM HERZL
TO RABIN

FROM HERZL TO RABIN

The Changing Image of Zionism

AMNON RUBINSTEIN

HM
HOLMES & MEIER
New York / London

Published in the United States of America 2000
by Holmes & Meier Publishers, Inc.
160 Broadway • New York, NY 10038

This book has been printed on acid-free paper.

Chapters 1, 2, 3, and 8 have appeared in a somewhat different version
in *The Zionist Dream Revisited,* published by Shocken Books (New York, 1984).

Chapter 11 and part of Chapter 4 were translated by Rachel Avital. Chapter 8
was translated by Martin Friedlander.

Library of Congress Cataloging-in-Publication Data

Rubinstein, Amnon.
    From Herzl to Rabin : The Changing Image of Zionism / Amnon Rubinstein.
        p. cm.
    Includes bibliographical references (p.) and index.
    ISBN 0-8419-1048-7 (alk. paper)
    1. Zionism—History. 2. Zionism—Israel. 3. Judaism and the state.
    4. Arab-Israeli conflict. 5. Israel—Politics and government. I. Title.

DS149 .R818 2000
320.54'095694—dc21

                                                                00-020444

Manufactured in the United States of America

As this book is being published,
peace negotiations are being held between Israel,
on the one hand, Syria and the Palestinians, on the other.
No matter what the outcome will be—and the author's
view is clearly outlined in this book—the dilemmas
discussed here will not disappear.

For four years I served as a cabinet member under
Prime Minister Yitzhak Rabin and was witness to the
ship of state's change of course, which took place
during the Oslo process. I was privileged to see
how a single leader of a divided society made
painful decisions which, we all realize now,
were of historical importance.
Rabin paid with his life for his
wisdom and courage.
I dedicate this book to his memory.

TABLE OF CONTENTS

FOREWORD

Zionism as an idea is the founding pillar of the state of Israel. Yet, what is Zionism, where is it headed, will it continue to define the state of Israel, and in what sense?

Amnon Rubinstein has poignantly illustrated, in an open-minded, profound, and clear manner, the profile of Zionism from its inception till today, against the background of the turmoil and events of the twentieth century and their fateful impact on the Jewish people.

The Zionist idea is neither fixed nor sealed, but rather open and vibrant, reflecting an aspiration for national and spiritual redemption, yet filled with tensions between exile and homeland; secular and holy; East and West; democracy and religions; humanism and nationalism; fanaticism and tolerance—all these are a constant source of heated dispute.

The realization of the Zionist vision has always been accompanied by a tragic conflict with the Arab world, and the future of the state of Israel rests on its resolution. Achieving peace and security is therefore the ultimate Zionist objective. A flourishing Israel, in an environment of peace, will mark Zionism's greatest triumph. This will not be the finishing line but a fresh start. From this point on the state of Israel will be able to channel its full potential toward cultural creativity, economic prosperity, and social justice.

Indeed, even in peacetime, Israel will have to maintain and bolster its deterrent abilities, as the nature of the region dictates. However, Israel's uniqueness is in our perpetual yearning for peace; our constant pursuit of excellence, morality, and social justice; our self-demand and aspiration to be *a light unto the nations. Not a nation that will dwell in solitude and not be reckoned among the nations,* but Israel that takes its place in the dynamic world of the twentieth century as the vanguard to human progress—among the best of the world's free nations.

Zionism is an idea, a movement, and a fulfillment of historic justice, which has, by virtue of its achievements, created a reality that transcends the initial vision, notwithstanding faults and errors. The 100-year-old Zionist drama, which returned the Jewish people to the forefront of history, is unparalleled to that of any nation.

Amnon Rubinstein observes the Zionist experience and analyses it with a critical fine-tooth comb, yet with both love and empathy. His book is an intriguing and fascinating voyage into the Zionist soul with a concerned insight. He deeply identifies with Zionism, with a universal and liberal view, out of concern for our society's image. He cautions against the dangerous trends that have developed in Israeli reality, and at the same time he expresses his deep faith in the uniqueness of the Jewish people and the future of the state of Israel. Rubinstein is at his peak as he brilliantly defends the Zionist stand against its post-Zionist and anti-Zionist opponents, proving the righteousness and justice of Zionism.

With the advent of the second century of Zionism, the book *From Herzl to Rabin* is a milestone and a guide. It is the supreme route for Israel, with all its warning and guiding signs. This is the central path for renewal and renaissance, toward achieving Zionism's ultimate goals.

EHUD BARAK

PREFACE

Zionism is, these years, under fierce attack from both the right and the left. The right wing factions are rewriting the history of Zionism to depict the movement as an assertion of Jewish power that defied the Arabs and is at permanent war with the Palestinians. At the other extreme, the most radical of the new school "revisionist" historians would like Israel to cease being a Jewish state and become the state of "all its citizens," even if such a radical change in Israel's self-definition would lead, almost inevitably, to the loss of its Jewish character. Until now, those who speak for the mainstream of Zionism have been mostly counterpunching against the arguments from the right and the left, often largely with strident anger, but no new, positive presentation of mainstream Zionism has appeared. Amnon Rubinstein has performed the great and necessary service of explaining the mainstream of Zionism for our own day. He is admirably equipped for the task, for Rubinstein has served the Zionist idea and its creation, the state of Israel, in almost every conceivable capacity. Rubinstein is a practicing lawyer and a scholar of the law who rose to the deanship of the law school of Tel Aviv University. He is a major political figure who has served in several cabinets and who remains a prominent member of Israel's parliament, the Knesset. He is an intellectual who leads a secular life but is not alien to the synagogue. He is a frequent commentator on all of the major issues of Israel's life. Rubinstein's essays and books are eagerly and widely read, with respect for his courage and reasonableness.

What is most admirable in Rubinstein's new account of modern Zionism from its beginning to the present is that he does not try to plaster over the difficulties that Israeli society must still confront. Rubinstein is a Zionist. He glories in the transformation of a people, which had little power in its own hands a century ago, into one that is a major force in the Middle East. He emphasizes Israel's sovereignty. He is proud of those who founded the new Zionist settlement in Palestine a century ago, and who worked successfully to create a "new Jew," to be secular, nationalist, and unafraid of the anti-Semites. But Rubinstein knows that Zionism created unsolved conflict with the Palestinians and he is intensely aware of the ongoing quarrels between the religious believers and the secular Jews in Israel. Both as a lawyer and as a Zionist thinker, Rubinstein knows that the basic internal Jewish quarrel in Israeli society—how Israel can be at once democratic *and* a Jewish state—will not be solved by any clever, verbal formulas.

Rubinstein does not tell us of his intellectual antecedents, but what is present in almost every page of this book is the spirit of the Talmud and the Whig tradition in British politics in thought. Both the ancient rabbis and the eighteenth century Whigs knew that any ideological principle taken to its very end leads to bigotry and to persecution. Some problems, especially the large ones, cannot be solved by ideological means, they have to be lived with, precisely because solutions are far worse than untidy pragmatic accommodation.

This book has reminded one reader, the author of this preface, of a remark by Herzl's successor as leader of the Zionist movement who lived long enough to become the first president of the state of Israel, Chaim Weizmann. He asserted that the trouble with the Arab-Israel quarrel is that it is not a quarrel between right and wrong: It is a quarrel of two rights. What Weizmann meant is that the right of the Jewish people to return to its land was valid, but it was fair, and true, for the Palestinian Arabs to assert that it was wrong to make them into a minority in the land in which they had lived for many centuries. Weizmann knew that these two principles could only live at peace through pragmatic accommodation. The rabbis of the Talmud were fond of asserting that two conflicting views between which they could not decide were both "the words of the living God." And here, too, they tried to find some accommodation in real life.

This book belongs to both traditions. I suspect that when its author reads these words, he will immediately accept that he belongs among the Whigs. Probably, after a moment of reflection, he will agree that he is, also, very much an heir of the rabbis of the Talmud. At any rate, this is a book in which both the new Zionism, and the ancient Jewish traditions which it was reasserting, are given an equally learned and a sensitive hearing. Rubinstein has written a book that is an "easy read," because he is a fine writer, but this book should then be read again, with great care, to savor what is between the lines and to learn from this deep and necessary account of Zionism after one hundred years.

ARTHUR HERTZBERG
January 24, 2000

FROM HERZL
TO RABIN

INTRODUCTION: BASEL AND JERUSALEM

On Saturday, August 28, 1897—an especially hot day—the synagogue in Basel was bustling with worshipers. It wasn't every day that the smallish Swiss city was the focus of so much attention. Throughout the small Jewish community and along the streets of the city, preparations for the First—and maybe last—Zionist Congress were busily under way. Jews of all kinds were everywhere to be found: enthusiastic students from Russia and Berlin, rabbis and businessmen, professors from German universities, shopkeepers, intellectuals and poets, farmworkers and members of the moneyed classes. They came from Algiers and Bucharest, Odessa and London, Paris and Katowice, and each in his own way was eagerly anticipating the frenetic buzz of surging emotions, intellectual debate, hopes and apprehensions. Would a new gospel emerge from Basel? Or would the First Zionist Congress be another quickly forgotten episode, like the other hopelessly doomed attempts by Jewish organizations to ameliorate the situation of the Jews?

Yet there was a specific reason for the charged atmosphere in the synagogue: Dr. Theodor Herzl—the journalist, author, and playwright who had caused a storm the previous year when he published a thin booklet called *Der Judenstaat,* a man who was the object of admiration, opposition, or ridicule wherever he went—was coming to the synagogue and would rise to the altar to bless the Torah. Assimilated Herzl, whose bar mitzvah ceremony in a Budapest synagogue was his last dim memory of anything Jewish, wraps himself in a prayer shawl and recites the blessing in a foreign tongue—Hebrew.

On September 9, settled back in Vienna following the Congress, with the excitement, cheers, and calls of "Long Live the King" receding into memory, Herzl reminisced and wrote in his diary:

> In view of the religious concerns, on the Sabbath before the Congress I attended temple. The community leaders called me up to the Torah. Mr. Marcus Bamirren, brother-in-law of my friend Barr from Paris, had taught me the blessing, which I had learned by heart. And when I rose to the altar, I was more deeply moved than at any moment of the Congress

1

itself. I was simply overwhelmed by the few words of the Hebrew blessing.[1]

There was something else unique about that Sabbath in the Basel synagogue: Dr. Max Nordau, an assimilated Jew who had achieved great fame through a series of controversial books, who was well known throughout Europe as a declared atheist, also appeared in the synagogue. He wrote to his family this account of the visit:

> As soon as I arrived here this morning I began searching for Herzl. I hired a coach and rode to the synagogue, where I met him. I had altogether forgotten it was the Sabbath, and found myself right in the middle of prayers. And here was Herzl, standing there, wrapped in a prayer shawl. . . . They wanted to honor me with a blessing—reading a section of the Torah—but I refused, and escaped as soon as I could, mortified.[2]

The following day is completely different. In the main hall of the city casino, in an atmosphere of celebration and excitement, with the delegates—acceding to Herzl's request—wearing frock coats, including Nordau, who opposed the dictate to no avail, speeches are delivered, amid thunderous applause. Herzl is everywhere, controlling the proceedings as both director and producer, ironing out all the details, ruling on parliamentary procedures, gleaning from his experience as a Viennese newspaper correspondent at the Palais Bourbon, seat of the National Assembly in Paris.

Nordau, an adherent of extreme individualism and an ardent opponent of nationalism, speaks to the gathered assembly extemporaneously, talking of the troubles of the Jews and the need to deliver them from destruction. Both of them—the two assimilated Jews whose great deviation from traditional Judaism was underscored in synagogue only one day before—are speaking of the same Jewish

---

1. Theodor Herzl, *Divrei Hayamim* (Diaries), vol. 2 (Jerusalem, 1960–1961), 26.
2. Ana Nordau, *Max Nordau* (New York: The Nordau Committee, 1943), 129.

people that they now serve as spokesmen, prophets, priests, and commanders.

Herzl addresses the Congress:

> Zionism has already brought about something remarkable, heretofore regarded as impossible: a close union between the ultramodern and the ultraconservative elements of Jewry. The fact that this has come to pass without any undignified concessions on the part of either side, without intellectual sacrifices, is further proof, if such proof is necessary, of the national entity of the Jews. A union of this kind is possible only on a national basis.[3]

As he utters these words, is he thinking back to his meeting at the hotel with a delegation of rabbis participating in the Congress—a small, albeit important, minority—and of his synagogue visit of the day before? Is he considering the world of eastern European Jewry, represented by Jews from czarist Russia? Before him is a cross section of this diverse people—different from one another in language, culture, lifestyle, and religious outlook. Bidden by Herzl, they have gathered in Basel to consider the plight of a homeless, landless people, dispersed throughout the world. They are bound together by the Jewish problem—which itself takes on different forms from one place to the next. The common denominator is the universal Jewish need for deliverance from tribulation, rescue from the general state of malaise and individual shame—the need to become a nation, to be equal in a society of equals.

The writer and philosopher Ahad Ha'am—skeptical observer that he is, also reacts to the events in Basel:

> Of all the lofty goals Zionism has set for itself, there is only one that is now within reach; it is the moral objective of freeing ourselves of the slavery of the inner being, from the crushed human spirit caused by assimilation. We must bolster our national unity by working together on all aspects of our nation's existence, until we are fully prepared for a life of dignity and liberty—in the days to come.[4]

---

3. Arthur Herzberg, ed., *The Zionist Idea* (New York: Harper Torchbooks, 1966), 227.
4. Ibid., 83.

The Jews assembled in Basel wish to be unique among the nations—to be a people for whom morality and rule of law are inseparable. Herzl puts it this way:

> Let everyone find out what Zionism really is, Zionism which was rumored to be a sort of millennial marvel—that it is a moral, lawful, humanitarian movement, directed toward the long-yearned-for goal of our people.[5]

Several days before the Congress convened, on August 24, with the threat of ridicule and mockery weighing heavily upon him as always, Herzl had made this entry in his diary, while en route by train to Basel:

> The only flock I really lead consists of youths, beggars and blowhards. As far as the others, some are simply riding on my coattails. Others are resentful and jealous, and have broken faith with me, or back away when they see very little tangible result from their efforts. Only a handful are enthusiastic and pure of motive; still, this corps will certainly be enough for the job. At the first sign of success, this ragtag band will overnight be transformed into a properly organized camp. We'll have to see what the near future brings.[6]

But by August 30, the mood has shifted:

> There's no need for me to write yesterday's history; now there are others to write it.

His colleagues at the Neue Freie Presse in Vienna jocularly receive him as the "King of the Jews." Regaining his strength after his arduous labors, and with the emotional upsurge of the event abating, Herzl finds the prophetic words that will reverberate through modern Jewish history. He makes this entry in his diary on September 3:

> If I can sum up the Basel Congress in one sentence—which out of caution I will not utter in public—it is this: In Basel I

5. Ibid., 230.
6. Ibid., 17.

laid the foundations for a State of the Jews. If I said this out loud today, the response would be laughter on every front. Perhaps in another five years—fifty more years at most— everyone will know it to be true. The state will be founded first and foremost by virtue of the people's wish for nation- hood. You can go so far as to say that even the will of a sin- gle individual, if sufficiently strong, could make the difference. The geographical territory is only the material underpinning; the state exists as much in the abstract as it does in the material sense. In Basel, then, I created this abstract object, which is therefore invisible to the vast majority, perceived only in the most subtle manner. Ever so slowly, I tugged on their heartstrings, introducing them to a state of mind of statehood, implanting within them the idea that they were attending the National Assembly.[7]

Herzl writes these words at a time when the Zionism he conceived and founded—in spite of the enthusiastic passions of the Congress— is still a marginal and esoteric phenomenon.

The Congress is a wellspring from which only a thin trickle flows. Zionism has no political support to speak of: There is no indication whatsoever that the Sultan in Constantinople might entertain the dreams—others would call them hallucinations—of the Viennese journalist; the world's wealthiest Jews and the vast majority of reli- gious leaders are either opposed or ambivalent. As compared with the major movements of Judaism of the period—assimilation, Orthodoxy, reformation, revolution—the wellspring seems almost parched.

There is excitement within the Jewish communities—especially in eastern Europe—although there is much opposition as well. Not only are the ultra-Orthodox opposed to Zionism, but so are some Jewish Russian intellectuals and the revolutionaries on the Left. Important newspapers report on the Basel event—some in a positive light, some in a dismissive attitude diluted with animosity. The German embassy in Berne sends the German kaiser a detailed report on what the Jews are up to in Basel. In the margins of the document, Kaiser Wilhelm II writes: "I am all in favor of the kikes going to

---

7. Ibid., 20.

Palestine. The sooner they take off, the better. I shan't put any obstacle in their way."[8]

Fifty years after Herzl made these entries in his diary, the Jewish state came into being. It was not quite as he had envisioned it. Rather than being sanctioned by anti-Semites, the state came into being only after the bulk of European Jewry was exterminated—by members of the same Kultur that Herzl so greatly admired. They did not come on luxury ocean liners with bands playing classical music in the background, as envisaged by Herzl, but in broken-down boats, some of which sank or were sunk along the way. They came not in peace, as prophesied in Basel, but amid the bloodshed and gunfire of the War of Independence and other wars to come.

Almost one hundred years after Herzl made his remarks on the morality and rule of law inherent in Zionism, the prime minister of the State of Israel, Yitzhak Rabin, was assassinated by a religious zealot. He carried out his evil design in the name of the Jewish faith and religious law, bolstered by the counsel of his spiritual leaders. He shot a man whose crime was to tenaciously cling to the idea of peace. At the time of the murderer's sentencing, Supreme Court justice Eliezer Goldberg said:

> We have heard the appeal, which we hereby reject on this day, the twentieth day of Tamuz, the anniversary of the death of Herzl. It was he who envisioned the State. The possibility that a Jewish leader of the future state of the Jews would be murdered by a Jew certainly never entered his mind. This is not anything the founders of our nation imagined would happen upon gaining independence. Even our generation, which is fully aware of the gap between vision and reality, has a difficult time believing that such a foul deed could occur in Israel. Reality has dealt a cold, hard slap in the face of the founders and their descendants. The Prime Minister of the State of Israel was in fact murdered by the appellant.[9]

8. Amos Elon, *Herzl* (New York, Rinehart & Winston, 1975), 245.
9. Criminal Appeal 3126/96, *Yigal Amir v. the State of Israel,* Dinim Elyon (1996), vol. 44, 396.

In August 1949 the remains of Herzl were transferred to Israel and reinterred in Jerusalem, atop the hill that bears his name. At the time, Mount Herzl was a barren hill on the outskirts of Jerusalem, a divided and feeble city with a hostile border encircling it. It was the capital of a country under siege, which could barely cope with the waves of refugee immigrants arriving on its shores from east and west.

On November 6, 1996, when Yitzhak Rabin was laid to rest across from Herzl's grave, the scene was entirely different. Jerusalem had grown into a large city, and around Mount Herzl, to the north and south, one could see evidence of the accelerated rate of development that was engulfing Israel, its capital no exception. In the autumn light of Jerusalem, one could look out over the city and its suburbs, the former border, the towers and minarets, the parks and wooded areas, the new technological parks and Yad Vashem—the Holocaust memorial. From the summit of Mount Herzl, those attending the ceremony could see Jerusalem—still emotionally divided between Jews and Arabs, and between Jews and Jews, still not a City of Peace—but a great city, exhilarating in its unique beauty, the capital of the state of the Jews: a prosperous and powerful country that launches satellites into space and ships its industrial exports to markets around the globe.

There, across from Herzl's tomb—a unique man, who has over time become just a name—the leaders of the world gathered. There were kings and presidents, prime ministers and princes, military leaders and intellectuals. An assemblage of people as had never before been found in Jerusalem, even in its ancient days of glory. Heads of Arab states were there as well: the president of Egypt, the king of Jordan, representatives of the Palestinian Authority, and delegations from Morocco, Tunisia, Oman, and Qatar. Many were in tears. Yitzhak Rabin was dead. A Jewish prime minister had been assassinated. By a Jew. In the name of Judaism. One hundred years after the event in Basel.

1

Zionism and the Quest for a New Jewish Identity

In 1905, after Dr. Theodor Herzl's sudden death, a stunned grief descended upon the fledgling Zionist organization, moving a young Russian Jew to publish an obituary commemorating the founder of Zionism. Years later that young man, Ze'ev (Vladimir) Jabotinsky, would acquire some posthumous international fame as the original teacher and mentor of Israeli prime minister Menachem Begin. But, at the time, Jabotinsky was one of many young and ardent Russian Jews whose conversion to Zionism manifested itself in a total attachment to Herzl.

Not content with cliché eulogies, Jabotinsky, in his obituary, tried to explain the unique impact that the author of *Der Judenstaat* had on the Jews. The all-consuming adoration, the total subjugation to Herzl's personality could not be explained in ordinary political terms.

According to Jabotinsky, Herzl's importance was related to the inherent difficulty accompanying the birth of the new nation Zionism sought to bring about. The difficulty lay in the fact that the new type of Jew was unknown to any of the Zionist founders. "A nation, which lives a normal national life on its land," wrote Jabotinsky, "is replete with stereotypes representing a characteristic national image."[1] Among the nations of the earth are

1. Ze'ev (Vladimir) Jabotinsky, *Ktavim Tzioni'im Rishonim* (Early Zionist writings) (Jerusalem, 1949), 97–100.

types immediately recognizable as typically Russian or English or German. But, with us, continued Jabotinsky, there is no such characteristic type. "What we see around us among Jews is merely the outcome of arbitrary action perpetrated by others." This prevalent Jew, the Yid, as he is pejoratively called by the Gentiles, does not reflect a proud national past but embodies the very negative traits from which Zionism seeks to redeem the Jews. "Only after removing the dust accumulated through two thousand years of exile, of *galut*, will the true, authentic Hebrew character reveal its glorious head. Only then shall we be able to say: This is a typical Hebrew, in every sense of the word."

The portrait of such a future Hebrew cannot be visualized but merely deduced by juxtaposing him against the prevalent Diaspora few. The words Jabotinsky used are incisive:

> Our starting point is to take the typical Yid of today and to imagine his diametrical opposite . . . because the Yid is ugly, sickly, and lacks decorum, we shall endow the ideal image of the Hebrew with masculine beauty. The Yid is trodden upon and easily frightened and, therefore, the Hebrew ought to be proud and independent. The Yid is despised by all and, therefore, the Hebrew ought to charm all. The Yid has accepted submission and, therefore, the Hebrew ought to learn how to command. The Yid wants to conceal his identity from strangers and, therefore, the Hebrew should look the world straight in the eye and declare: "I am a Hebrew!"

Such a liberated Jew, such a future Hebrew, explained Jabotinsky, was Theodor Herzl. His personality, his demeanor, his majestic appearance embodied everything that Jews were not but sought to be. It was this element that struck such a strong chord in the collective Jewish mind and that explained why Herzl's death sent such deep shock waves throughout the Jewish world.

We shall see how this simplistic dichotomy is undergoing a radical transformation among those very proud Hebrew sons for whom the Zionist Fathers longed with such fervor.

But at the beginning, Zionist literature abounded with this very posture: The old-time Jew contrasted with the newly born Hebrew;

the Diaspora Jew with the native Sabra; the Yid of yesteryear with the resurrected Maccabee, the inferior Jew with the super-Jew.

The message was loud and clear: The Hebrew, the new super-Jew, represents everything that has traditionally been associated with the Gentiles, the goyim, the other side. In contrast, the dominant traits of the Diaspora Jew, our "miserable stepbrother," to use David Ben-Gurion's phrase, were to be discarded.

In the post-Holocaust era, it is embarrassing to read Zionism's founders' disparaging evaluation of European, galut, Jewry. Their poverty is reviled, their helplessness despised, their virtues ignored.

Zionism did not usher in this attitude. Nineteenth-century Hebrew and Yiddish literature, the first manifestations of a nonreligious Jewish culture in eastern Europe, vilified Jewish existence within the Pale of Settlement, the "parasitical" occupations that marred it and its sickening submission to brute force and oppression. Zionism, especially in eastern Europe, was founded on this total rejection of Jewish existence in galut but, unlike its forerunners, indicated a way out. Zionism is not content with returning the Jewish people to its lost sovereignty and never-forgotten homeland; it also seeks to be the midwife who helps the Jewish people give birth to a new kind of man. This revolution—no less than the political craving for independence—is the very basis of Zionist philosophy and explains its seeming paradoxes. Yes, the Jews are despised and lead an inferior life; no, it is not their inherent fault, as the anti-Semites charge: Circumstance alone is responsible for their plight. Thus, Nachman Syrkin, one of the founding ideologists of the Zionist labor movement, wrote: "Puny, ugly, enslaved, degraded and egoistic is the Jew when he forgets his great self; great, beautiful, moral and social is the Jew when he returns to himself and recognizes his own soul."[2]

Normality means the redemption of the individual as well as the normalization of the people. The Return to Zion is coupled with a metamorphosis of the Jew into a new man. The Jew would become a "goy" in the double meaning that this word has in Hebrew, signifying both "Gentile" and "nation." Once this rebirth takes place, the traumas of the past will be forgotten. To be a goy means to be healthy; healthy nations, healthy people are not obsessed with issues

2. B. Katzenelson, ed., *Ktavim* (Writings) (Tel Aviv, 1939), 59.

of existence and survival. Moshe Leib Lilienblum, one of the founders of the pre-Herzlian "Lovers of Zion" movement in Russia, indicated the dimensions of this transition: If the Jews are going to be a normal goy (nation), they should know how such normal goyim behave:

> Mixed marriages and foreign culture are not strange to a healthy people. Such people swallow everything and digest everything. And occasionally, the foreign things they take in, turn into a source of life. A healthy people are oblivious to the fear of death and do not have to be on guard in order to ensure their survival.[3]

"To be a goy" was, therefore, the dominant theme of Zionist philosophy in its formative period. The idea was so forceful that it united the warring factions and parties. On everything else Zionists differed: "Territorialists," ready to consider territories outside Palestine as a "night shelter" for the hard-pressed Jews, clashed with "Zionists of Zion," who regarded any substitute for the ancestral homeland—including the notorious British offer to settle Jewish refugees in Uganda—as high treason; "practical Zionists," who believed in practical steps to implement Zionism, railed against those who believed mainly in political and international action; Labor Zionists, who saw the return to Zion inextricably intertwined with a socialist-universal mission, fought against the Zionist Right, which gave precedence to the national cause. Even the very basic idea of a Jewish state did not escape dispute, and much doubt was cast on its soundness and practicality. One idea, one craving, one urge, enjoyed a veritable consensus: to be a new people; to escape the role that history had imposed on the Jews; to become, in Herzl's words, "a wondrous breed of Jews which will spring up from the earth."[4]

---

3. Y. Becker and S. Shpan, *Mivchar Ha'massah Ha'ivrit* (Selected Hebrew essays) (Tel Aviv, 1945), 68–70.
4. Theodor Herzl, "The Jewish State (1896)," in Arthur Hertzberg, ed., *The Zionist Idea* (New York: Harper Torchbooks, 1966), 225. Herzl's *Judenstaat* means "State of the Jews" and not Jewish state, but he agreed to both the English and French translations of Jewish state and Etat Juif. Only recently, the Herzlian term was used in a new translation by Hank Overberg; see *The Jews' State: A Critical English Translation* (New York: Jason Aronson, 1997).

Indeed, Jewish existence in exile was regarded as lying outside history. Both Ben-Gurion and Jabotinsky, incorrigible opponents, denied the legitimacy of Jewish history in galut. Ben-Gurion said:

> Since our last national tragedy—the suppression of the Bar Kochba rebellion by the Romans—we have had "histories" of persecution, of legal discrimination, of the Inquisition and the pogroms, of dedication and martyrdom, but we did not have Jewish history anymore, because a history of a people is only what the people create as a whole, as a national unit, and not the sum total of what happens to individuals and to groups within the people. For the last fifteen hundred years, we have been excluded from world history, which is made up of the histories of nations.[5]

Even the religious Zionists, aware as they were of the historic continuity that gave meaning to Jewish survival even in exile, subscribed to these extreme sentiments. Thus S. H. Landau, founder of Hapoel Hamizrachi, the religious Labor movement that gave rise to the National Religious Party, wrote:

> Israel in exile ceased to be a nation or, to be exact, a living nation. . . . A people lacking a land of their own whose natural life force has dried up is not a nation. Parasitism, conscious or unconscious, becomes its second nature—parasitism of the individual and of the community.[6]

This was the driving power behind the Zionist call for revolution against passivity, against tradition, against all which, at the time, was synonymous with Jewishness.

But in addition to this Zionist consensus there was a deep division regarding the very essence of the new Jewish society to be created in Palestine. This division demonstrated the difference between the Jews who came into Zionism via the route of a failed emancipation and the Jewish communities of eastern Europe living under the yoke

---

5. "Die Geuleh" (The redemption) (1917), quoted by Y. Gorni in *Hatzionut*, ed. D. Carpi, vol. 2 (Tel Aviv, 1971), 77.
6. A. Fishman, *Hapo'el Ha'mizrachi* (Tel Aviv, 1979), 162.

of an authoritarian czarist regime, from which emancipation was conspicuously absent.

Needless to say, the attempt to reach a consensus papered over such inherent divisions; the crucial issue of religious belief and all that it entailed was shunned. Such was the desire to escape the humiliation of life among hostile Gentiles that it even produced, in 1906, a strange phenomenon: Herzl, frustrated by his failed attempts to persuade the sultan of the Ottoman Empire to grant a charter to the Jews, grasped a vague British offer to establish a Jewish homeland in Uganda—the famous Night Shelter. This offer nearly rent asunder the fledgling movement between "territorialists," whose main purpose was saving Jews, and "Zionists of Zion," who refused to consider another homeland. It is instructive that while the secular Chaim Weizmann stood up as Herzl's main opponent, the religious group supported the Uganda solution, divine promises notwithstanding.

Herzl himself personified this chasm between East and West. His attachment to Judaism was minimal, his knowledge of things Jewish nebulous, consisting mainly of childhood memories of a Budapest synagogue. As a European and as a civilized man, anti-Semitism aroused anger and disgust in him. When he gradually came to discover the unfathomable depth and intensity of the new-old sickness, he was driven to the idea of a Jewish state. Yet his very philosophy remained European, secular and liberal. He sought to heal the ugly wound that afflicted the Jews and marred the enlightened face of Christian Europe: hence, his stubborn insistence on the need for international recognition and cooperation with enlightened Gentiles in carrying out the Return to Zion. That recognition, Herzl argued, should be expressed through a charter enabling the Jews to return to their homeland. The granting of the charter by the enlightened nations of Europe would constitute the one event revolutionizing relations between Jews and Gentiles. The creation of a Jewish commonwealth, a progressive society based on the European model, would symbolize the end of anti-Semitism. Recognition was imperative not only because of obvious demands of political expediency but also because of the need to put an end to the tragic friction between Jews and Christians.

Because assimilation was impossible and did not solve the issue of Jewish existence in an antagonistic Christian environment, Herzl rejected its very notion:

We have sincerely tried everywhere to merge with the national communities in which we live, seeking only to preserve the faith of our fathers. It is not permitted us. In vain we are loyal patriots, sometimes superloyal; in vain do we make the same sacrifices of life and property as our fellow citizens; in vain do we strive to enhance the fame of our native lands in the arts and sciences or their wealth by trade and commerce. In our native lands where we have lived for centuries we are still decried as aliens, often by men whose ancestors had not yet come at a time when Jewish sighs had long been heard in the country. The majority decide who the "alien" is; this, and all else in the relations between peoples, is a matter of power.[7]

This is the substitute to an idea Herzl had before converting to Zionism: a mass conversion to Christianity in order to put an end, once and for all, to Jewish suffering. Because he realized that such a conversion was impossible, he reached the inescapable conclusion: Without giving up Jewish identity, the new solution serves a parallel approach—entering the family of nations not through a side entrance for individuals but through the main gate—as an equal and respectable quest.

In this respect, Herzl was a spokesman for a whole generation of acculturated, assimilated Jews who found their way to Jewish nationalism. For him, as for other founders of Zionism, anti-Semitism was the prime mover; but as soon as the urge to combat it took the form of a national solution, a new pride in their half-forgotten, vaguely sensed Jewish heritage set in.

This pride notwithstanding, there was precious little Jewishness in Herzl's writings. The new Maccabee who would inhabit the utopian future state was not really different from the cultivated European—that figure of reason and progress whose love and acceptance Jews like Herzl sought in vain.

Herzl's colleague in the First Zionist Congress, Max Nordau, shared these attitudes. Nordau himself was a product of Jewish assimilation. Before his conversion by Herzl to Zionism, he had already acquired a reputation throughout Europe as an atheist thinker, an iconoclast author, and a sharp critic of European

---

7. Herzl, "The Jewish State (1896)," 209.

manners and morals. Like Herzl's, his education was basically
Germanic, his outlook cosmopolitan. Like Herzl, he lost contact
with Judaism and watched with shock the old anti-Semitic monster
raise its menacing head. Like Herzl's, his new attachment to Jewish
nationalism was neither motivated nor accompanied by a return to
Judaism. In his moving address to the First Zionist Congress in Basel
in 1897, he described the plight of the emancipated Western Jews—
talented, ready to serve their beloved countries, humiliated, and
rejected by their Christian neighbors. This plight, Nordau stressed,
should not be an exclusively Jewish concern:

> To Jewish distress no one can remain indifferent—neither
> Christian nor Jew. It is a great sin to let a race, whose abil-
> ity even its worst enemies do not deny, degenerate into
> intellectual and physical misery. It is a sin against them and
> it is a sin against the course of civilization, to whose
> progress Jews have made, and will yet make, significant
> contributions.[8]

For Herzl and Nordau, anti-Semitism was a plague affecting both
Jew and Gentile, but it also explained where the evil was and how it
could be uprooted. For the Jews, it served as a reminder of their
unique position: They shared not merely a common faith but also a
common fate. Herzl's conclusion—"we are a people—one people"—was totally realistic: "Prosperity weakens us as Jews and
wipes out our differences; only pressure drives us back to our own;
only hostility stamps us ever again as strangers." Willingly or
unwillingly, the Jews remain one: "Affliction binds us together, and,
thus united, we suddenly discover our strength."

Upon this diagnosis, Herzl wrote his prescription for the Jewish
illness, and his remedy is captivating in its simplicity: The new Jews
will establish an exemplary society characterized by tolerance and
social justice, and they shall not forget "the ways of the world."
They shall acquire the same international habits and customs that
enable the world to have "English hotels in Egypt and on Swiss
mountain tops, Viennese cafés in South Africa, French theaters in

---

8. Max Nordau, "Speech to the First Zionist Congress," in Arthur Hertzberg, ed., *The
Zionist Idea* (New York: Harper Torchbooks, 1966), 241.

Russia, German operas in America, and the world's best Bavarian beer in Paris."[9]

The Jews, in short, will finally become true Europeans. They will, for instance, forsake the peddler trades that had so infuriated the anti-Semites. Herzl did not rebel against this anti-Semitic stereotype. Modern European experience proves, he wrote in *Der Judenstaat*, that through modern marketing techniques and department stores, it would be possible to prevent in the future Jewish state the renewal of the hated Jewish trades. Thus the Jews' own state would rid both Europe and the Jews of their problems. The Jews will be able to occupy all appropriate trades and professions without enraging their threatened Christian rivals. They will settle on the land and cultivate it without incurring the wrath of the Christian farmer, without the envy and antagonism that frustrated all attempts to turn Jews into farmers in Europe. The state of the Jews will therefore be a mini-Switzerland in the heart of the Middle East. It will be, as Herzl titled his famous booklet *Der Judenstaat,* a state of the Jews, hardly a Jewish state.

In Herzl's utopian novel, *Altneuland,* which depicts an imaginary journey to the new state, as well as in the Zionist writings of Max Nordau, who did not forsake his militant atheism upon his conversion to Zionism, the recurrent theme is the integration of the Jew into Western civilization. Whereas he was barred from entrance to this world through emancipation and tolerance, he will enter it through the new gate: full participation founded not on a personal justice but on a national, sovereign equality.

In the political climate of *fin de siècle* Europe, the renewal of Jewish political independence seemed—certainly to Western Zionists—the embodiment of the spirit of modernity and progress. They understood that anti-Semitism is criminal because, among other evils, it precludes Jews from participating in, and contributing to, a progressive Western society. Their immigration to a territory of their own, in which their national identity combines with a liberal progressive spirit, would remove this obstacle.

This analysis throws light on the universal nature of the Herzlian approach: The establishment of a state for the Jews and their emigration out of Europe were compatible with the interests of the

---

9. Theodor Herzl, *The Jewish State* (New York: Herzl Press, 1970), 110.

family of enlightened nations. The Western world would rid itself of a painful problem and would acquire another civilized offshoot state, which would incorporate its highest values. Zionism is not only a Jewish revolution; it is, to quote Herzl, "simply the peace-maker"; it proclaims peace between Jews and Gentiles, between Judaism and Christianity.

It is, of course, easy to deride, with the benefit of hindsight, such simplistic attitudes and to criticize Herzl and many of his colleagues for failing to appreciate the enduring vigor of traditional Jewish civilization and failing to fathom the depths of those ancient roots that nourish anti-Semitism. Indeed, as we shall see, such criticism was leveled at Herzl at the time by other Zionists. Nevertheless, it was this very simplistic attitude—a product of a European non-Jewish environment—that translated into political action the age-old yearning for Zion and that forged an organizational tool destined to save many Jews from persecution and extinction.

Herzl's declaration that the Jews are a people, that there is an international benefit in giving them a land of their own, and that Zionism offered a total solution to both Jews and Gentiles was responsible for taking Zionist ideas out of the amateurish circles of the "Lovers of Zion" movement and placing them squarely in the focal center of Jewish and international attention. Without such a simplistic attitude—again, typically non-Jewish—without couching the Jewish problem in universal and international terms, it is doubtful whether a Zionist movement would have been established or whether massive Jewish immigration into Palestine would have replaced the trickle of pious Jews and devoted pioneers that preceded Herzl's initiative.

However, Herzl's and Nordau's idea of what "normalization" meant did not pass unchallenged. Herzl's secular, Western concept of the new Jewish society was anathema to many who were unwilling or unable to forsake what they regarded as their Jewish raison d'être.

Herzl's most awesome opponent was the Hebrew author Asher Zvi Ginsberg, who, under the pen name Ahad Ha'am, periodically delivered literary broadsides against the Western, Europeanized concept of Jewish nationalism. In a series of vitriolic critiques, Ahad Ha'am demolished Herzl's *Altneuland:* "Anyone examining this book will find that in their state the Jews have neither renewed nor added anything of their own. Only what they saw fragmented among the enlightened nations of Europe and America, they imitated and put together in their new land." And Ahad Ha'am added sardonically that Herzl denied the Jews even the credit for uniting these fragments into a new whole—even that art was a result of circumstance, not talent. Inasmuch as they founded their state without "the agony of heritage," they were in a position to pick and choose the best from everywhere—because, as Herzl put it, they were especially qualified for this task by their economic and cosmopolitan expertise.[10]

This typical clash between Herzl and Ahad Ha'am reflected, to a large extent, the wide divergence between the emancipated Western Jews who entered Zionism via the corridor of frustrated assimilation and the Jewish masses of eastern Europe living under the authoritarian yoke of anti-Semitic regimes. In western Europe, Jews experienced, for a short time, the sweet taste of equal rights; they participated in the seemingly rational and secular new era with an eagerness fed by generations of cultural deprivation. In the East, masses of impoverished Jews lived in the isolation of their crowded Pale of Settlement, subject to perennial persecution and periodic violence.

In the West, a great majority of the Jews shook themselves free of the Jewish tradition that had shaped their forefathers' world. They sought to obliterate their former "otherness" and merge into the host societies through secularization, assimilation, reform synagogues, intermarriage, and conversion. The speed with which they acted—within one or two generations they had moved from ghettos to the very heart of European civilization—attested to their urge to cast off the yoke of a tradition that many regarded as irrelevant in the new era of progress and enlightenment.

In the East, too, the ghetto walls were beginning to crack. The vast majority of Jews living in Poland, czarist Russia, and Rumania belonged to Yiddish-speaking, Orthodox, and self-contained communities. But there were the Maskilim—the enlightened and secularized men of letters—and there was even some initial Jewish response to a halfhearted czarist attempt at Russification of the Jews. There were the few who broke through the Pale of Settlement into Russian society and acquired "non-Jewish" professions. There

---

10. Ahad Ha'am, *Kol Kitvei* (Collected writings) (Tel Aviv, 1947), 313–320.

was some hope of a better, more progressive Russia, and there was, of course, a growing rebellion among the young against the Jewish Orthodox establishment. The emergence of a new Jewish proletariat and the opening of some secular schools to Jews ushered in a sense of an impending turning point that would bring Russia closer to Western standards. Instead, Russia reverted to a series of pogroms, beginning in 1881 after the assassination of Czar Alexander II, which ended any hope that the czarist regime would emulate the West in granting some measure of equal rights to the Jews.

Thus, Eastern Jews witnessed a rejection similar in some respects, yet more brutal and violent, to that which drove Herzl and other Western Jews toward Zionism. In both parts of Europe, the Jewish intelligentsia encountered a double rejection. The traditional, boorish anti-Semitism was compounded and made more horrible by the acquiescence of the intellectuals in the West and the socialist revolutionaries in the East. But in the East, the rejection was inherently different from that which came to be associated with the Dreyfus affair in the West. For the Jewish communities of Russia, Poland, and Rumania—the great bulk of Jews from which Zionism would draw its main strength—emancipation was a distant dream, but Judaism was a present, palpable reality. For the eastern European Zionists, the synagogue was not a vague memory of childhood days but a reality against which they rebelled. Yet, Jewish culture, with its rich tradition of prayers and folklore, was familiar. The Hebrew language did not sound strange and foreign. Many learned it as the language of the new Jews. Yiddish was spoken by almost all. As well as being their ancestral homeland, Eretz Israel (the Land of Israel) was familiar from the Bible, the prayer book, and the fledgling modern Hebrew literature.

For the eastern European Zionist, Judaism, as such, could not be glossed over with the benign and patronizing attitude that was the hallmark of emancipated Jews in the West. Judaism itself was an issue. Zionism served—like the Revolution, like the secular-socialist and anti-Zionist Bund—a collective psychological need. It was not merely a corridor through which a higher and more successful integration into European society could be achieved.

In eastern Europe, the search for a new meaning or substitute to Jewish life, for new Jewish or secular values was a direct outcome of the absence of all that characterized western European Jewry: legal equality, a reformed version of Judaism, a secular culture whose benefits Jews could experience and whose values they would want to acquire. In the East, the Jews were thrown straight from the claustrophobic existence of the *shtetl* into the arms of either Zionism or revolution. For young Jews, Zionism filled the gap formed by the revolt against the Orthodox father on the one hand and the disappointment with the Russian revolutionary brother on the other. The constant, painful friction between young Zionists and the strong rabbinical establishment and the tradition it represented contrasted sharply with the distant calm with which the assimilated Jews of France, Germany, Austria-Hungary, and England regarded the religious issue. Indeed, it was this combat with traditional Judaism that gave birth in eastern Europe to both the budding Hebrew secular literature and those wondrous Jewish idealists who gave their lives for the Revolution. It also gave Zionism its special soul.

Herzl wanted to solve the plight of the Jews. But, as Ahad Ha'am phrased it, there was also the plight of Judaism, which could no longer be contained within the shackles of traditional religion and which had to find viable alternatives or disappear by attrition. Thus, all the major trends that were destined to influence the State of Israel were born in eastern Europe: socialist Zionism, religious Zionism, the revival of Hebrew, Palestine as a spiritual center. All these, in various ways, sought to give a substantive answer to a question to which Herzl was oblivious. It is this phenomenon that also explains an apparent paradox in Zionist history: The Western Zionists, headed by Herzl, whose Jewish background was so meager, did not find any difficulty in coexisting with the religious Zionists. In progressive Western society, due respect is to be paid to faith. But the religious issue infuriated the eastern European Zionists, who were divided between an observant minority and a rebellious secular majority.

Herzl could easily accept the religious demand that the Zionist organization desist from all "cultural work"; by definition, it would put an emphasis on secular value. But for leaders like Chaim Weizmann, a rebel against his own shtetl upbringing, the issue was of crucial importance and reason enough to break with Herzl and to form, at the Second Zionist Congress, his own separate faction. For Herzl, religion had its place; the rabbis were to be respected but confined to their religious sphere, like soldiers to barracks, as is the custom of a modern progressive state. In the East, as Weizmann wrote Herzl, the rejection of religion among the youth reached such proportions that young Jews were venting their anger by desecrating Torah scrolls. In the West, such preposterous behavior could not be contemplated by those who advocated reason and tolerance.

That the Jews had a religion of their own was, by itself, compatible with the Zionist wish for normalization. After all, there were national churches in European countries, such as Greece, Rumania, Bulgaria, and Russia; there were the Anglicans and the German Lutherans; and even the universal faiths acquired in many countries a distinct national expression. Moreover, toward the end of the nineteenth century, a tendency developed to view religion as part of that national spirit that allegedly characterizes every people. This new *Zeitgeist,* this romantic-nationalist view, contrasted sharply with the more universal and rational approaches that had prevailed in the first half of the nineteenth century and had enabled the Jews to acquire their new equality. According to this romantic view, which won many admirers in Germany, every people has its own manifest destiny and its own national "soul," and, consequently, its religion too must express these special attributes. If rational universalism was going to make way for this new brand of nationalism, the Jews could easily claim their own ancient faith as a national asset par excellence. Indeed, years before the advent of Zionism, Moses Hess, the socialist philosopher and onetime collaborator of Marx and Engels, wrote that the existence of their own distinctive religion proved that the Jews were a people entitled to national independence. The existence of this both national and universal religion merely confirmed his view that the Jews were truly the first authentic nation. Thus, in Western Zionists' eyes, the existence of a Jewish faith was not incongruous with the desire of the Jewish people to be a nation like all other nations.

Max Nordau, who combined ardent Zionism with fiery atheism, brought this nationalist attitude to its extreme conclusion. Asked about the future of the Sabbath in the Jewish state, he did not exclude its optional replacement by the more universal Sunday, as is the custom of the Gentiles. Ahad Ha'am, who regarded the Jewish Sabbath as the incarnation of the Jewish spirit, was flabbergasted and infuriated by such ideas, and from his Odessa home he directed at Nordau words of fury and scorn:

Not one word escaped the mouth of this Zionist sage which would testify that his heart rebels against the cancellation of the Sabbath, because of its historical and national value. The whole question, in his eyes, is purely religious, and therefore he excludes himself from any direct commitment. He, the freethinker, will have his own appropriate day of rest, bereft of any religious, intent, and he does not care whether the Sabbath, the Queen of Judaism, exists or not.[11]

Ahad Ha'am was convinced that eastern European Zionists, including freethinkers, "will feel, like me, as if a cold northern wind invaded their hearts and threw ice on their most sacred feelings."

There were, of course, other voices within Russian Zionism. In typical fashion, some of them carried the Herzlian idea to its extreme, almost fanatical, conclusion. One of these, Jacob Klatzkin, born within the Russian Pale of Settlement and later editor of *Die Welt,* the official organ of the Zionist organization, railed against the eastern European need for "Jewish content." For Klatzkin, Zionists like Ahad Ha'am represented a galut mentality and would be responsible, if successful, for frustrating the very idea of national renaissance: "It is no accident that Zionism arose in the West and not in the East. Herzl appeared among us not from the national consciousness of a Jew but from a universal human consciousness. Not the Jew but the man in him brought him back to his people."[12]

Klatzkin claimed that the basic intention of Zionism was "to deny any conception of Jewish identity based on spiritual criteria." This is the real revolution. This is the world-destroying and world-building movement that is diametrically opposed to the eastern European attitude. That attitude, having "none of the heroism of revelation," viewed Zionism as a continuation of Jewish history and "draws its energies directly from the sources of Judaism."

Klatzkin represented an extremist view, both in the way he depicted the clash between East and West and in his denial of any element of continuation between Jewish existence and the future society of new Jews. Ahad Ha'am, too, represented only a faction of Eastern Zionists, among whom there were many ardent followers of the

---

11. Ibid., 286.
12. Jacob Klatzkin, "Boundaries (1914–1921)," in Arthur Hertzberg, ed., *The Zionist Idea* (New York: Harper Torchbooks, 1966), 326.

Herzlian view. But the clash between these two dogmatic personalities expressed the emotional upheaval sweeping the Jewish world east of Vienna. It was this world that supplied the future state of Israel with pioneers, settlers, and leaders. From them, its eastern European founders, Israel inherited its habit of continuous soul-searching concerning its identity as successor to that ancient Jewish tradition on which so many of her founders were raised and against which so many rebelled. All the problems that lie heavily on Israel's soul politic—the Jewish nature of Israel, its relations with the Diaspora and the outside world, its attachment to Jewish heritage—are the offspring of that intellectual ferment that characterized eastern European Zionism in its early heyday. The search for new values, for a contemporary gospel expressing the change in Jewish society, which would renew, or even replace, the old, crumbling, irreparable Jewish civilization of yesteryear, did not come from the salons of Western Jewry but from those for whom Zionism was the direct result of their revolt against both the father's home and the rabbi's synagogue.

This debate runs through a hundred years of Zionism. When, in the summer of 1996, after the establishment of Netanyahu's government, a meeting of secular academics was convened to speak against the rise of fundamentalist religious Judaism, the speakers reminded the audience that the majority of the deputies in the First Zionist Congress were secular.

The hidden cleavage over which Herzl built a diplomatic bridge, did not disappear. On the contrary, it became wider and more menacing.

2

The Meaning of
Normalization

In spite of all the differences within Zionism about the content of Jewish nationalism, one theme united the warring factions: the need to create a new breed of Jews in the new society destined to be established in Palestine. "Our revolution," wrote A. D. Gordon, that secular prophet of the return to the soil and the religion of work, "is the revolution of the man in the Jew."[1] That revolution has a universal human value, and through it the highest ideals of mankind will merge into a new Jewish existence.

This metamorphosis of the Jewish person will remove the defects formed by the long galut. Through this revolution, Israel will return not only to its land but also to the family of nations. Again, looking back at the strife-strewn history of Zionism, one is impressed by the consensus supporting this idea of the return of the Jews to their rightful place as human beings and as equal partners among the Gentiles of the earth. The galut is darkness, and redemption lies in this twofold revolution of the individual and of the people. Because of this craving for a return to normalcy, the great bulk of Orthodox Judaism resisted Zionism and proclaimed its message to be a heresy, a contradiction of the very tenets of Judaism. Zionism sought to transform the status of Jews among the nations from a persecuted minority awaiting the coming of the Messiah to equal partners in a secular world.

---

1. A. D. Gordon, *Ha'umma Veha'avodah* (The nation and labor) (Jerusalem, 1951), 365–367.

It required a major mental readjustment. The Jewish people—the chosen people, the people of the binding Covenant with God, who gave the world its Messianic vision—would, according to Zionist philosophy, have to reexamine these very foundation stones. The idea of a national revival for the Jews drew its initial inspiration from the successful growth of modern national liberation movements, such as the Bulgarian, the Rumanian, and the Italian, in the second half of the nineteenth century. But these national movements were bereft of any Messianic message and did not pretend to speak in the name of an exclusiveness with universal and cosmic significance. Arthur Hertzberg put this dilemma in the following words:

> Religious messianism had always imagined the Redemption as a confrontation between the Jew and God. The Gentile played a variety of roles in this drama—as chastising rod in the divine hand, as the enemy to be discomfited, or, at very least, as the spectator to pay homage at the end of the play— but none of these parts are indispensable to the plot. In the cutting edge of Zionism, in its most revolutionary expression, the essential dialogue is now between the Jew and the nations of the earth. What marks modern Zionism as a fresh beginning in Jewish history is that its ultimate values derive from the general milieu. The Messiah is now identified with the dream of an age of individual liberty, national freedom, and economic and social justice—i.e., with the progressive faith of the nineteenth century.[2]

Indeed, the change brought about by Zionism was so radical, so revisionist, that some of its implications were never expressed directly.

The first implication was a revised attitude toward anti-Semitism. Hatred of the Jews—not to mention violence against them—was, of course, regarded by all Zionists as a manifestation of evil. But if the inferiority and the abnormal status of the galut Jew explained, at least partially, the animosity toward him, this antagonism could now be seen in a new light. Because the Zionists were determined to

---

2. Arthur Hertzberg, ed., *The Zionist Idea* (New York: Harper Torchbooks, 1966), 17–18.

take their fate into their own hands and remove from a theological context their relations with the outside world, there arose a need to explain this animosity in new, rational terms. As long as galut, exile, was explainable in terms of divine punishment, reasoning about it was unnecessary. But with Zionism, galut was regarded neither as punishment nor manifest destiny but rather as a humiliating disease to be cured. Anti-Semitism was, therefore, a force not only to be reckoned with but also, to some degree, to be understood and diagnosed with a view to finding a solution: The rational response was a political remedy that would resolve the conflict between a "sick" minority and a "healthy" majority.

Indeed, Herzl's treatment of anti-Semitism in his *Der Judenstaat* was so unemotional, and occasionally even patronizing, that in a post-Auschwitz world it is difficult to digest. Herzl analyzed the inevitable clash and saw Zionism as bringing relief to both Jew and Gentile. It would also solve the problem of Jews who decided to remain behind, facilitating their complete assimilation and absorption into Christian society. Zionism removed the malignant tumor, and that tumor lay not in any personal fault but in the reality of Gentiles pitted against Jews. In anti-Semitism he saw the elements of "cruel sport, of common commercial rivalry, of inherited prejudice, of religious intolerance—but also a supposed need for self-defense."[3]

Herzl demonstrated a largesse toward anti-Semites. He planned to include "decent anti-Semites" to assist in the Zionist undertaking, "while respecting their integrity—which is important to us."

Herzl also set a precedent for future Zionist leaders by dealing with Wenzel von Plehve, the anti-Semitic czarist minister of the interior. Because Zionism sought to return the Jews as equal partners to the world scene, it would speak as equal to equal even to those whose hatred of the galut Jews was second nature. In a similar vein, Ze'ev (Vladimir) Jabotinsky, leader of the Revisionist Right, described the "objective nature" of anti-Semitism. In his testimony before the Palestine Royal Commission in 1937, after the rise of Nazism in Germany, he declared: "The cause of our suffering is the very fact of the Diaspora. It is not the anti-Semitism of men; it is,

---

3. Theodor Herzl, "The Jewish State (1896)," in Arthur Hertzberg, ed., *The Zionist Idea* (New York: Harper Torchbooks, 1966), 209. For a recent publication, see Theodor Herzl, *The Jewish State* (New York: Dover Publications, 1988).

above all, the anti-Semitism of things, the inherent xenophobia of the body social or the body economic under which we suffer."[4]

The systematic murder of six million European Jews put an end to such cool and objective indifference to anti-Semitism and anti-Semites. After the Holocaust it became impossible to resort to Herzl's phrase "decent anti-Semites." Nevertheless, the strength of the Zionist sentiment is so great that in spite of the Holocaust it continued to guide Israel's policy. In the 1950s and 1960s, many Israelis regarded as natural the new links formed between the Jewish state and those European circles whose salons were rank with the age-old anti-Semitism. In the first years of Israel's existence, one could occasionally detect a sort of latent pride: The Zionist dream became a reality because the ex-persecuted were such respectable masters that their ex-persecutors sought their company. In those years, one could have found many other similar manifestations. The new Jew, the proud Israeli, was ready to associate with his recently found equal rather than with his "miserable stepbrother," the galut Jew. And when *Time* magazine, in its first cover story on the young state on August 16, 1948, wrote that the young Israelis "run to the big-boned, blue-eyed, blond athlete type associated with anti-Semitic persecutions," this was regarded as one more proof that Herzl's "wondrous breed of new Maccabees" had indeed sprung forth.

The second implication arising from the return of the Jews to the international community related to a critical reexamination of traditional Jewish civilization. If galut was no more a preordained divine infliction and if its very essence was to be negated, then Zionism had to reevaluate Jewish history itself. Consequently, it was permissible not only to break away from the Pale of Settlement mentality and to bring down the walls of the rabbinical establishment, but also to question everything that was sacred and hallowed in Jewish tradition.

Thus, within Zionism there grew a non-Jewish, even anti-Jewish sentiment, stunning in its strength and in its longings for the pagan and the Gentile. True, this sentiment preceded Zionism, and the rebellion against traditional Judaism nourished both the Haskalah (Enlightenment) literature and the turn toward socialist and revolutionary activity among young Jews in eastern Europe. Zionism did

---

4. Evidence submitted to the Palestine Royal Commission (London, 1937), 11.

not give birth to this mood—to a certain extent it was assisted by it—but it did give it a legitimate national justification that no socialist revolution could offer. Because of Zionism, an author could write in Hebrew, with a strong sense of nationalist pride, tracts castigating Judaism for real and imaginary faults, yet retain his standing as a Jew within the community. It was permissible to cast stones at everything sacred in the father's home and to admire that which was anathema to Jews throughout the ages. *Facing the Statue of Apollo,* written in 1899 by Saul Tschernichovsky, one of the greatest Hebrew poets, is a well-known example of this new defiance. The poet describes himself facing the pagan god, "the youth-god, sublime and free, the acme of beauty!" He refers to the eternal war between the pagan god and the Jews and proclaims: "I am the first of my race to return to you." He turns away from the old God and yields to the forces of "life and courage and beauty," mourning the wild god who had "stormed Canaan in conquest" only to be "tied up with the straps phylacteries."[5]

It became permissible to advocate mixed marriages, as Lilienblum and Klatzkin had done. It was even permissible to reexamine the traditional attitudes toward Christianity and Jesus Christ. Joseph Chaim Brenner, a famous socialist Hebrew author and playwright, who was assassinated by Arabs in 1921, created a minor scandal when he wrote:

> As for myself, the Old Testament does not have that value which everybody shouts about: the Book of Books, the eternal book, the Holy Scriptures. From the hypnotism of the twenty-four books of the Bible, I have long freed myself. Many profane books, written in later periods, are closer to me and greater in my eyes; but the same importance which I find and recognize in the Bible, as remnants of ancient memories, as the embodiment of the spirit of our people and of our humanity throughout so many generations—this same importance I also find in the books of the New Testament. The New Testament too is a bone of our bones and a flesh of our flesh.[6]

---

5. Saul Tschernichovsky, *Poems,* tr. D. Kuselewitz (Tel Aviv, 1978), 91.
6. Joseph Chaim Brenner, *Kol Kitvei* (Collected writings), vol. 6 (Tel Aviv, 1927), 103–104, 117.

Even the Christian theory ascribing deity to Jesus did not deter Brenner. He failed to see any danger in it: "A person of Israel can be a good Jew, devoted to his people, despite the fact that he . . . regards the son of our people, the poor Jew, Jesus of Nazareth, with religious piety."

Such voices, though emanating from central figures within the Zionist movement, did not represent the mainstream point of view, and Brenner's dictum on the New Testament and Christ, which was merely one aspect of his frontal attack on the Jewish religion, caused a furor both inside and outside Palestine. However, that such voices existed and that they were a legitimate aspect of the Zionist reassessment of Jewish past is relevant. In fact, these anti-Jewish moods were reinforced by the new reality of the *Yishuv,* the Jewish community in Palestine.

In the special atmosphere of the Yishuv, the discrepancy between past and present, between old and new Jews, seemed palpable and irrefutable. A succinct statement of this growing sense of alienation from the past is found in "The Sermon," a famous short story written by Haim Hazaz, one of Israel's more illustrious writers, after the outbreak of World War II, when the Jews were already subject to Nazi terror. The hero of the story examines the nature of Judaism and Zionism and finally reaches the verdict, pronounced in short, cutting sentences: "Zionism and Judaism are not at all the same, but two things quite different from each other, and maybe even two things directly opposite to each other! At any rate far from the same. When a man can no longer be a Jew, he becomes a Zionist."[7]

The third implication was connected with Hazaz's verdict and concerns the relationship between the new Jews of the Yishuv and their "miserable stepbrothers" in the Diaspora.

The settlement of Palestine by a growing number of Jews enhanced two basic streams that flowed from the spring of Zionist ideology: a further alienation from the Jewish past and a further opening toward the outside world. In Palestine, in Eretz Israel, a new community of Jews was formed. From the beginning this community avoided using the term *Jew.* It was a *Hebrew* Yishuv; all of its institutions followed suit: the Histadrut was the trade union federation of the *Hebrew* workers; so were the associations of doctors,

---

7. Haim Hazaz, "The Sermon," in Joel Blocker, ed., *Israeli Stories* (New York: Schocken Books, 1962), 65.

lawyers, writers, and journalists; all were Hebrew, not Jewish. Tel Aviv was hallowed not as the first Jewish but as the first Hebrew, city. A common slogan read: "Hebrew, speak Hebrew." Yiddish was despised and often ostracized. Like the Reform communities in America, which similarly adopted the term *Hebrew,* and the assimilated French Jews, who opted for *Israelite,* the new Jews were eager to shake off the word *Jew* as a means of signifying the change taking place in their lives. But unlike the terms used by French and American Jews, *Hebrew* represented the will to create a new people—a new nation, a new goy—who live in their own land and speak their own language. The Palestinian young Hebrew was the super-Jew, and the rise of the Sabra cult accentuated this divergence between new and old.

In Palestine there had existed a small community of Orthodox Jews, the "Old Yishuv" as it came to be known, before the Zionists arrived. But from the days of the Second Aliyah, the wave of socialist pioneers who came to Palestine from pogrom-ridden Russia after 1905, the Yishuv was dominated by a strong secular element. The former rebels against father and rabbi became leaders of that Yishuv, and they led the way toward Zionist self-fulfillment. All the paraphernalia of the hated galut—Yiddish, the shtetl, the peddler trades—disappeared, and in their stead appeared the characteristics of the new Jew: Hebrew, communal settlements, manual work, a return to the soil, attachment to nature, a newly acquired rootedness. This was the new Sabra character, which was, finally, a Jewish peasant, a goyish type, characterized by a healthy earthiness. He could be recognized and identified, just as Jabotinsky, in his Herzl obituary, had wished. Yet it is interesting to note that despite this growing divergence, the Hebrew Yishuv moved toward less friction with traditional rabbinical Judaism. There were, of course, political divisions and hotly debated disputes: on the rights of women, on freedom of conscience, on the meaning of Judaism. But the explosive tension that marked the eastern European experience was gone. The old Orthodox Yishuv was marginal and lacked political power. The hegemony belonged, within a short time, to the socialist Labor movement. Father's home became remote and was transformed from a target of rebellion into a subject of homesickness. The exodus of the sons from the shtetl had diluted much of the former bitterness.

Jewishness thus meant mainly to be a Hebrew, to love the land, to be attached to nature, to give tradition a new national and social meaning. Absalom Feinberg symbolized this new attitude. One of the first Sabras, destined to die in World War I while serving the pro-British Nili spying group, he interrupted a play depicting the persecution of the Jews. "Not in Eretz Israel!" he shouted. "When we shall have beautiful olive orchards, the lifework of generations, then the people growing up in their shade will be ready to die in order to protect the trees."[8] This was the essence of the new Jews.

The lessening friction was also explicable in terms of the new reality. The nucleus of the novel society was concentrated in communal settlements far removed, physically as well as psychologically, from the religious groups. Distance breeds tolerance, and the harangues against religion were limited to writers like Brenner, who continued to castigate the galut mentality, and to work against any attempt to introduce religion into Palestine.

In the communal settlements, Jewish tradition gave birth to a new interpretation. The Sabbath became a day of rest, to be dispensed with whenever necessary. Marriage ceremonies were not always celebrated, and when they were, such formality became a mere appendage to cohabitation, a favor to faraway parents, or a half-hearted attempt to prevent a total break with the past. Occasionally, some settlements went to fanatic extremes: Anything other than the natural, healthy, and earthy was frowned upon. The poet Abraham Shlonsky described the derogatory reaction of his kibbutz comrades when they discovered that he was writing for a literary magazine, a typically Jewish cultural activity to be avoided in the new land.

The Jewish holidays acquired a new social, agricultural, or national meaning. In the Seder ceremony, the traditional Haggadah was replaced by modern writings and poems; Shavuot, the Pentecost or Festival of Weeks, which signified the giving of the Torah at Sinai, was celebrated only in its earthly, agricultural aspect: The first fruit of the season was presented in a ceremony seeking to recreate biblical scenes. Chanukah became the celebration of Maccabean heroism and Jewish liberation from a foreign yoke—and, occasionally, even signifying a class struggle. Rosh Hashanah was simply the New Year and an opportune time for self-reckoning. New holidays were

---

8. *Ktavim* (Writings) (Haifa, 1971), 154, 219.

invented: a new year for the trees; a celebration of Bar Kochba's last revolt against the Romans; Herzl's birthday; and, of course, the first of May, the international day of workers' solidarity.

There were some difficulties: What could one do about Yom Kippur, whose purely religious significance was too obvious to be tampered with? The various settlements, obviously belonging to different political movements, failed to produce a uniform response. Some, like A. D. Gordon, saw it as a day in which the individual loses his self and becomes a part of a unified whole, a limb in the body of the community, a member of a higher personality. But such theories never became part of the Zionist socialist dogma. Among the new pioneers and settlers, many, perhaps the majority, did not observe Yom Kippur. Some workers' restaurants were actually open on its holy eve. Other settlers were allowed to revert to the old ways and, out of instinct or respect for tradition, justified their "deviation." Hannah Senesh, a poet and a member of a kibbutz, who was executed after parachuting into Nazi Hungary in an attempt to organize its Jews, wrote in her diary on the eve of Yom Kippur 1941:

> I'm not fasting, because I don't feel the need. In my opinion, the only value of fasting is for the Jews in the Diaspora to express their solidarity. I feel I have other ways of expressing my ties with Judaism, and I'll forgo this one, which is completely alien to me.[9]

This divergence between the devout tradition and the new secular interpretation, between old and new Jews, is best demonstrated by a particular instance. In 1914 a mission of Orthodox rabbis, headed by the pro-Zionist Rabbi Kook, set out from its enclosed Jerusalem quarters to visit the new communal settlements in the north of the country, to learn how serious were the breaches in religious tradition and to attempt to bring back the errants to some measure of Jewishness. The odd encounter brought together two separate worlds, which only a generation ago had shared the same tradition.

---

9. Hannah Senesh, *Hannah Senesh, Her Life and Diary* (New York: Schocken Books, 1973), 115.

What the rabbis found, to their distress, was a tragic relinquishing of any semblance of religion. Their report was a litany of woes: in Hadera, "the religious situation among the workers is wild . . . they baked bread on Passover"; in Zichron Yaacov, "the teachers do their best to uproot religion from the hearts of their pupils"; in Merhavia, "there is no kosher kitchen and on Yom Kippur only fifteen out of fifty observed the fast"; in Poriah, "the young break the Sabbath and eat non-kosher food"; in Kinneret, "there is neither prayer nor fasting on Yom Kippur; bread is eaten on Passover and there is no trace of religion."[10]

There were, naturally, some rebels against this drastic transition. Reading through the Second Aliyah literature (and how abundantly these few thousand did write!) one comes across a longing for the old world ostensibly shattered beyond repair. In one of the ever-debating workers' assemblies, where Yiddish was proscribed and despised, one member who wanted to speak his mother's tongue, broke down:

> What do you want of me? I have accepted with love all the torments of this land; I broke my back in hard manual labor while starving for food; I fulfill the tenet of Hebrew self-work with devotion and dedication; I am malaria stricken. Is all this nothing in your eyes that you wish to deprive me of the language on which I grew up and to which I am attached with all my heart? Do you also want to make me dumb in this land?[11]

And occasionally a member of a kibbutz wandered into a traditional home; his heart was filled with joy and nostalgia at the reminders of the old ways: the family seated at the dinner table, the candles, the service, the challah.

But these were mere deviations from the main route that led away from galut and religion toward a brave new future. Under the sun of Canaan, in the fields of Jezreel, and on the hills of Judea, the galut seemed even more despicable, even more inferior, and its negation became a common slogan, a solid foundation on which the Yishuv

10. David Canaani, *Ha'aliyah Hasheniyah Ha'ovedet Vichassah Ladat Velamassoret* (The Second Aliyah and its attitude to religion and tradition) (Tel Aviv, 1976), 111.
11. Ibid., 87.

mentality was based. Ben-Gurion laid down the rules regarding the future attitude of Labor Zionism to the Diaspora and what it represented:

> A new yardstick will be applied to our old satchel. Anything which is great and important enough for our present road, we shall carry with us; anything which is small, rotten, and smacks of galut we shall throw away so that it will disappear with the bad heritage of the dead past, so that this past will not cast its shadow over our new soul and will not desecrate the sanctity of our redemption.

And when Ben-Gurion talked about the new Hebrew worker, the former Jew who perhaps had landed in Jaffa only a short time before, he exclaimed:

> The worker of Eretz Israel differs from the Jewish worker in Galut in his historical origin, his economic attitude, his social goals, his national destiny. . . . Not a new branch grafted to an old tradition is he; a new tree of a workers' class has grown to the Jewish people out of their new land.[12]

Anyone reading these lines—taken from a legion of similar utterances—realizes that they consciously sought to bypass large portions of Jewish history. Here was a collision between two different concepts of what "redemption" means. On one side stood secular Zionists from Left and Right—Jabotinsky as well as Ben-Gurion— who denied the validity and relevance of Jewish history from the last revolt against the Romans to the Return to Zion. On the other side stood the traditional Jewish outlook, which belittled the Jewish rebellions against the Romans and put its emphasis on the great works of scholarship created in galut. The secular view went so far as to downgrade even the Talmud and the "oral Torah," the guide by which Jews lived and which embodied their own unique legal system. Constant attempts were made to exclude its study from the Yishuv schools' curricula.

---

12. Quoted from *Hatzionut* (Zionism), ed. D. Carpi, vol. 2 (Tel Aviv, 1971), 89. The article was written in 1917.

According to the secular outlook, Zionism equaled redemption because it returned the Jewish people to their rightful place in history as an independent nation; according to the religious non-Zionist outlook, redemption remained a religious Messianic concept and Zionism, by replacing it with a secular political concept, transgressed against the divine purpose of Jewish existence.

With the growth of the Hebrew Yishuv, the emphasis on the secular concept of redemption—secular Messianism, as it was often referred to by Labor Zionists—became more pronounced. Zionism was the salvation, and salvation meant a new brand of Jews.

During the 1940s and 1950s this process yielded a strange fruit. The movement of young Hebrews, or Canaanites, became audible and active and took normalization to its extremist conclusion. Headed by Yonathan Ratosh, a gifted and innovative poet, this group sought to cut the ties uniting the Yishuv with its Jewish origins. The group was always small and lacked political organization, but its influence belied its size. It was formed in the forties, reached its zenith in the early fifties, and included some of the brightest young intellectuals in the country. Its influence was described by Baruch Kurzweil, famous literary critic and a professor at Bar Ilan University, as having created a major Israeli school of Hebrew literature.

The Canaanites' theory was confused and their reasoning muddled. They regarded Palestine and its inhabitants as one organic unity, a new Hebrew people which had to be strengthened by the imposition of Hebrew culture, intermarriage and, above all, by severing Zionist ties with Jews and the Jewish heritage. Judaism was a corruption of the pure original Hebrew spirit and, therefore, had to be eradicated. In the words of Ratosh, founder of the movement:

> Judaism, all of it, its values, the sum total of its history, is foreign to this generation of the native-born, to its young men and boys. . . . It is foreign to them because the social experience out of which and into which they grow is, by its very nature, the opposite of the Jewish experience.[13]

The appeal of the Canaanites' views to the younger generation was clear. They expressed, in strong words, attitudes and sentiments

---

13. Yonathan Ratosh, *Aleph* (periodical of the Canaanite movement), June 1951.

shared by many. Indeed, they carried Zionist doctrine to a seemingly logical end. The whole aim of the Return to Zion was to rectify the abnormality inherent in Jewish existence. It sought to solve the Jewish question by achieving normalization through creating a nation-state like all other nations. Today, some of the Canaanite utterances sound positively anti-Semitic. Again, Ratosh in his Canaanite Manifesto:

> There is no Hebrew unless he is a Hebrew, son of this land of the Hebrews, and everyone else is excluded. Anyone coming from the Jewish Diaspora is a Jew and not a Hebrew and cannot be anything but a Jew—bad or good, proud or cowardly, he is still a Jew. The Jew and the Hebrew cannot be identical and he who is a Jew cannot become a Hebrew.[14]

To replace the word *Hebrew* with *German* or *French* is to appreciate the extent of the anti-Jewish sentiment pervading the Canaanite outlook. The Canaanites were extremist and marginal, but many of their fellow travelers regarded the Zionist process as having been ended. The Hebrew child was ready to leave his parental Jewish home. The Canaanites' rejection of the traditional Jew, their infatuation with the native-born and the native land was in accord with current thinking. There has always been a narcissistic streak in the Sabra mentality; the Canaanites appealed to the vanity that characterized the native Israeli. They reviled the ghetto Jew by contrasting him with the Sabra:

> The main difference nowadays is not between the various Jewish communities overseas, but between all these communities on the one hand, and the fast-growing Hebrew younger generation manifesting itself in the Sabra type—the native-born, who is notably un-Jewish in his physique, outlook, and way of life.[15]

It is sickening to think that this rubbish was written while the Jews of Europe were being slaughtered and their remnants seeking refuge in Palestine. Yet so deeply rooted was the concept of the new

---

14. Yonathan Ratosh, *Massa Haptichah*, republished in *Reshit Ha'yamim* (Tel Aviv, 1982), 152.
15. Ratosh, *Aleph*, June 1951.

Hebrew that in the forties and fifties, this group with its anti-humanitarian, vaguely fascist sentiments was regarded by many observers as the wave of the future and caused a distinguished intellectual, Professor Ernest Simon, to cry out publicly: "Are we still Jews?"[16] The future was to prove otherwise.

The Canaanites were blind to reality—to Arab enmity, to Jewish roots—and they took the Zionist idea of normalization ad absurdum. But like all such absurd conclusions, it contained a grain of relevance. If the Jews were to be normal, they should be subject to rules that govern other immigrant, formative societies.

At the center and in the mainstream of the Yishuv, however, Zionist dogma was being reinforced by acts and deeds. The Balfour Declaration and the League of Nations' Mandate fulfilled the Herzlian vision of recognition by, and support of, the international community for Jewish national renewal. In Palestine a truly unique society of new Jews emerged, as removed from their galut parents as the Zionist writers and thinkers could wish. The Jews indeed were becoming a goy—a nation; the Jew was indeed becoming a non-Jewish goy, a semi-Gentile. So forceful was this mood that it survived even the ongoing war with the Arabs, Britain's betrayal of the Jews, and the horrors of Auschwitz—events that had a shocking impact on Zionist history.

Behind all these developments loomed a larger issue—the ever-unsolved question that dominated Zionist thought: Will the new Hebrew nation, on regaining sovereignty in its land, forsake all claims to Jewish exclusivist tradition and become a nation like every other nation? Will this process remove the foundation stone on which the house of Jewish thought was built? Will the new Jews differ from other peoples only as the French differ from the English, or will they retain some universal message, some uniqueness, some "otherness"—the heirlooms of their past—in the world they seek to join? If they are going to be a goy, what will happen to that special heritage which distinguished them from the rest of the world? If Zionism is to demolish all these past tenets bequeathed to it by Judaism, what will remain of Jewish destiny? "How," asked the atheist writer Brenner, "shall we be us without us?"

---

16. Ernest Simon, *Ha'im od Yehudim Anachnu?* (Are we still Jews?) (Tel Aviv, 1982), 9.

3

Religious versus
Secular Tensions

For generations, in fact, since they became a people, Jews saw themselves as different and separate from the "Gentiles of the earth." The Covenant between God and his people and the receiving of the Torah at Mount Sinai lay at the heart of Jewish thought, Jewish Law, and Jewish existence. This eternal Covenant lends to Jewish existence, from a religious point of view, its special status among the nations. The words of Exodus speak clearly: "If ye will hearken unto My voice indeed, and keep My covenant, then ye shall be Mine own treasure [am segula] from among all peoples" (19:5). The Covenant clothes Jews with that very sanctity that separates them from the other peoples. Chosenness depends on abiding by the Covenant and on the observance of the Law. Chosenness is that state which follows the prophecy "and ye shall be unto me a kingdom of priests and a holy nation" (19:6). Isaiah's comforting prophecy relates Israel's universal destiny with the Covenant: "I will give thee for a Covenant of the people, for a light of the nations" (42:6). The severance of the Jews from the other nations, as well as their millennial role, is attributable to the Covenant: "Ye shall be holy unto me, for I the Lord am holy and have severed you from other peoples that ye should be mine" (Leviticus 20:26).

These well-known passages explain why it is impossible, from the traditional viewpoint, to separate the idea of chosenness, of a "treasure nation" *(am segula)*, from the concept of the Covenant and the observance of Jewish religious law and how false it is to relate these

39

religious paradigms to secular values. It is futile to transplant the biblical injunctions into a secular context and support this by referring to the prophets' universal visions of social justice and peace among nations. The belief in one God and the revelation on Mount Sinai alone endowed the people of Israel with their special status among the nations.

Thus, it was unavoidable that the growth of a new secular Judaism, in a post–French Revolution world, would crack the old foundations. When faith began to disappear and the actual laws were disobeyed, the raison d'être for Jewish chosenness—which had its justification only within the confines of religion—eroded along with the decline of Jewish civilization. Furthermore, not only Judaism was being transformed by the new era. The world in which Jews lived was undergoing radical changes and was totally different from the one in which Jewish exclusiveness had developed. The pagan world, against which Judaism's monotheism shone brightly, was gone; the new civilization, based in part on Jewish moral concepts, combined advanced Christian monotheism with the ideas of equality underlying the French Revolution. Such changes affected even Orthodox canon law. Within its narrow confines, rabbis and sages began to make a distinction between the ancient pagans—against whom the religious injunctions fully prevailed—and Christians, who were recognized, because of their monotheism, as a special category.

If rigid Orthodox law could adapt its interpretations to the modern progressive era, how much more so could the young, secular, assimilated Reform Jews? After all, modern Jews in western Europe responded to emancipation by renouncing any national extrareligious claim and by delegating Judaism to the private domain. Moses Hess explained in 1862—some thirty-five years before the advent of Herzlian Zionism—that "until the French Revolution, the Jewish people were the only people in the world whose religion was at once nationalist and universalist. . . . Since the French Revolution, the French, as well as other people who followed them, have become our noble rivals and faithful allies."[1] To the Reform communities in the West, as well as the young revolutionaries in the East, chosenness,

---

1. Moses Hess, "Rome and Jerusalem," in Arthur Hertzberg, ed., *The Zionist Idea* (New York: Harper Torchbooks, 1966), 129.

in the religious Jewish sense, had lost its meaning by the time Zionism made its appearance. The spirit of ecumenical tolerance and the waves of the future socialist revolution swept aside the old concept. In the new, progressive world about to awaken, the Covenant seemed an ancient irrelevance to the growing numbers of modern Jews. In fact, toward the end of the nineteenth century the enlightened Jews were the vanguard of universal equality and ecumenical fraternity, while in major European countries new doctrines of racial superiority, of Gentile "chosenness," took root: pan-Germanism in Germany and among German-speaking minorities; pan-Slavism in czarist Russia; integral nationalism in France, the country that had formulated the universal rules of equality. Chosenness, toward the end of the century, was certainly not solely a Jewish concern.

For the Zionists, especially for those who lived in eastern Europe, the question could not be shoved aside that easily. Zionism rehabilitated the Jews not as individuals but as a collective body. What would become of the old foundations? In this new reality, how could the idea of chosenness, of the "treasure nation," find its place? Indeed, could it find a place at all? This question could not be dismissed by resorting to Ben-Gurion's avoidance of Jewish history in exile, eliminating the Talmud, and hallowing the Bible. The Book of Books, from Genesis through the prophets to the Psalms, sings the glories of the Covenant between God and his people, praises their special mission, and bewails the transgressions against the Covenant and the Law.

Secular Zionists had some inherent difficulty in delineating the place religion would occupy in the new Jewish nationalism. Despite the analogies with other national churches, Judaism is essentially different. It is a total entity covering all aspects of individual, collective, and national rules of conduct. It does not recognize any distinction between secular and religious law. It unites the people of Israel with the religion of Israel and the land of Israel. An attempt to rid Zionism of all religious underpinnings would immediately result in a set of paradoxes. What is the Sabbath? A purely religious asset that can be dispensed with, or part of a national bequest to be retained? Is circumcision—a rite to which some modern Jews objected very strongly—an act symbolizing the entrance into a nation, or merely the religious act signifying the acceptance of Abraham's

Covenant with the Lord? And the Promised Land itself—the beloved
Zion whose very name was the movement itself: Was not the Jewish
claim to it based on divine promise, which was at the core of the
very religion being discarded? Alternatively, was not the claim to
Eretz Israel an independent national right based on Jewish history?
Herzl and his Western friends, ignorant as they were of things
Jewish, were soon to appreciate the complexity involved in eliciting
a national identity from of a religion-dominated civilization. When
Zionists, who were not recognized as Jews by Jewish religious law,
sought to join the Zionist movement, the question of who was a Jew
(destined to plague the Jewish state with bitter controversies) reared
its unpleasant head. If the Jews were going to be a nation like all
nations, why should religion be the doorkeeper? Under Jewish religious law, Jewishness is governed by the concept of the Covenant. A
Jew either is born into it—by being born to a Jewish mother—or
accepts the Covenant through conversion. But how could such rules
apply to a secular, normal nation? Did it make any sense that a
movement that spoke in the name of national liberation should
insist on religious rites as credentials for joining it? Yet any deviation from religious rules automatically introduced an incorrigible
split between religious and nonreligious Zionists. Consequently,
Herzl, whose son was never circumcised, ruled against a secular definition of "Who is a Jew," a decision destined to be quoted with
affirmation seventy years later by Israel's Supreme Court.

To explain this and similar paradoxes, secular Zionists resorted to
Ahad Ha'am's interpretation of Jewish history. Ahad Ha'am resisted
all temptation to turn the Jews into merely "another nation," nor
did he seek, like Herzl and his followers, to be integrated into modern progressive society. His confidence and trust in modernity were
shaped by what he saw around him: a growing enmity toward all
Jews by both the Russian intelligentsia and the czarist regime. For
Ahad Ha'am, secularist that he was, Jewish tradition itself was
imperiled, and it was the task of Zionism to come to its rescue. That
tradition, the totality of Jewish history, had religious manifestations,
but these were merely one aspect, one form, one expression of the
Jewish national spirit. The religious aspect became naturally dominant in exile, where, in order to keep the unity of the nation, it gradually replaced other facets of the inherent national spirit. Jewish
culture was forced, as it were, into such sublimation by external

circumstance. It was this view of Jewish nationalism that enabled Zionists to incorporate major attributes of Jewish tradition and religion.

Ahad Ha'am's views were not shared by "political Zionists," who had no patience with his emphasis on spirituality and his alleged lack of sensitivity to the dire needs of suffering Jews. But there was a far wider consensus on his view of the role of religion in Jewish nationalism. Thus, Ahad Ha'am's attitude to the Bible, which lent the Book of Books a meaning transcending religion, defined its place in Zionist—and, later, Israeli—thought:

> Even the nonbeliever, if he is a national Jew, cannot regard the Holy Scriptures solely from a literary point of view, but he combines a literary and a national point of view. . . . He senses an innermost feeling which attaches him to the Bible, a feeling of special intimacy tinged by sanctity, in that a thousand invisible arteries go out from him and spawn generation, after generation reaching into the depths of distant past.[2]

Hence, the crossroads at which Zionism found itself from its early days:

> Will the sons of Israel live in their state according to their own unique spirit and give life and develop their own national assets which were bequeathed to their past, or will their state merely be another European colony in Asia, a colony which looks up to the metropolis, seeking to imitate her in every way?[3]

This view was responsible for ensuring the survival of the Zionist movement, not as a sectarian group seeking autonomy for Jews but as a widely based national movement that could unite religious and secular elements and draw on current ideas of national liberation, as well as on the main features of Jewish tradition to be "translated" into secular and national concepts.

---

2. Ahad Ha'am, *Kol Kitvei* (Collected writings) (Tel Aviv, 1947), 408.
3. Ibid., 325.

Thus, the claim to Eretz Israel could be established without invoking God's promise to his children and without tying the concept of a modern redemption to the messianic vision. These religious expressions are but one facet of the Jewish spirit which, after the exile of the Jews from their land, naturally took precedence. This view enabled Zionists to invoke the Bible as the land title to Eretz Israel—as Ben-Gurion often did—without observing religious laws and without accepting its teachings.

At the other end of the spectrum, among religious Zionists, a converse process took place. Peace with the heretic and nonobservant Zionists could be facilitated because of the totality of Jewish religion, which regards the Return to the Holy Land and its settlement as a most exalted religious commandment. Coexisting with secular Zionists was possible because the secular lawbreakers were also the legitimate bearers of these commandments and were carrying out one of Judaism's cherished faiths—the Ingathering of the Exiles. Some religious sages went further: It was even permissible to see in the Return to Zion the beginning of redemption in its traditional, religious meaning as ushering in a Messianic period. In other words, just as the secular view saw in religion a valid expression of the national spirit, so did the religious view recognize Jewish nationalism as valid expression of the religious spirit.

Of all religious personalities, the Yishuv's chief rabbi, Abraham Isaac Kook (1865–1935), symbolizes this compromise between the two parts of the Zionist movement. Rabbi Kook, posthumously destined to be claimed as the guiding light of Gush Emunim, the post-1967 religious settlement movement, invoked the unity of nationality and religion in order to justify this cooperation:

> It is a grave error to be insensitive to the distinctive unity of the Jewish spirit, to imagine that the Divine nature which uniquely characterizes Israel is comparable to the spiritual content of all the other national civilizations. This error is the source of the attempt to sever the national from the religious element of Judaism. Such a division would falsify both our nationalism and our religion, for every element of thought, emotion, and idealism that is present in the Jewish people belongs to an indivisible entity, and all together make up its specific character.[4]

---

4. Abraham Isaac Kook, "The Rebirth of Israel (1910–1930)," in Arthur Hertzberg, ed., *The Zionist Idea* (New York: Harper Torchbooks, 1966), 425.

Against this background of a common link between secular and religious Zionists, based on the versatility of Jewish experience, should be seen the Zionist attempt to wrestle with the issue of traditional Jewish exclusiveness. The issue itself did not trouble the great majority of political Zionists, involved as they were with the practical hardships of turning a dream into reality. The principal goal was to save the Jews from their misery and to establish a base in Palestine. Naturally, the Jews would establish a perfect, exemplary society that would lead the other nations by showing the right way to progressive modernity. But that striving toward a good and just society could not pretend to be a substitute for Jewish chosenness: The declared aim of every national liberation involves such utopian proclamations. To the Zionists, what mattered was that Israel become a nation of healthy, liberated people.

There were rebels against this thesis not only outside the Zionist camp, among the great majority of Orthodox Jews, but also within it. Judah Leon Magnes, American Reform rabbi, founder and first president of the Hebrew University, became famous in the 1930s for his opposition to a national Jewish state in Palestine. In a pamphlet entitled "Like All the Nations?" published in 1929 in the midst of Arab riots against Jews, Magnes dared attack the very premise of Zionist dogma by comparing it with the traditional Jewish vocation:

> The desire for power and conquest seems to be normal to many human beings and groups, and we, being the ruled everywhere, must rule; being the minority everywhere, we must here be in a majority. . . . We are to have a Fatherland, and we are to encourage feelings of pride, honor, glory that are part of the paraphernalia of the ordinary nationalistic patriotism. In the face of such dangers, one thinks of the dignity and originality of that passage of the liturgy which praises the Lord of all things that our portion is not theirs and our lot not like that of the multitude.[5]

And this view was seconded by Martin Buber, who said, in the midst of World War II:

> I am setting up Hebrew humanism in opposition to that Jewish nationalism which regards Israel as a nation like unto

---

5. Judah Leon Magnes, "Like All the Nations? (1930)," in Arthur Hertzberg, ed., *The Zionist Idea* (New York: Harper Torchbooks, 1966), 447.

other nations and recognizes no task for Israel save that of preserving and asserting itself. But no nation in the world has this as its only task, for just as an individual who wishes merely to preserve and assert himself leads an unjustified and meaningless existence, so a nation with no other aim deserves to pass away.

By opposing Hebrew humanism to a nationalism which is nothing but empty self-assertion, I wish to indicate that, at this juncture, the Zionist movement must decide either for national egoism or national humanism. If it decides in favor of national egoism, it too will suffer the fate which will soon befall all shallow nationalism, i.e., nationalism which does not set the nation a true supernational task. If it decides in favor of Hebrew humanism, it will be strong and effective long after shallow nationalism has lost all meaning and justification, for it will have something to say and to bring to mankind.

Israel is not a nation like other nations, no matter how much its representatives have wished it during certain eras.[6]

Magnes and Buber did not succeed in changing the course of Zionism, and the Holocaust and Israel's emergence finally relegated their views of an extranationalist Zionism to oblivion.

To the contrary, Zionist thinking was more influenced by the other end of the spectrum—by those who wanted to eradicate any relic of past Jewish uniqueness. A blunt spokesman for this view was Brenner, whose angry homilies against retaining the past became the hallmark of the radical Labor view. In Brenner's writings, the "negation of galut" is equated with the negation of Jewish history and is coupled with angry warnings against its continuation in the Jewish homeland. Brenner refused to admire Jewish survival per se, because "existence itself does not attest to its importance." He denigrated the cherished values of Judaism. To be the "treasure nation," according to Brenner, is to turn tradition upside down: "We exist. We live. Yes. But what is our life? We have no inheritance, and what we have inherited—the rabbinical literature—we would have been better off without."

6. Martin Buber, "Hebrew Humanism," in Arthur Hertzberg, ed., *The Zionist Idea* (New York: Harper Torchbooks, 1966), 459.

Hence, the only solution was total, unmitigated normalization: "If we do not become now, with the changing circumstances of our environment, the 'treasure nation'—i.e., a nation like all other nations, who are all a treasure unto themselves—we shall be lost as a nation."[7]

With Brenner, a total turnabout was achieved: The distinguishing feature of the Jews was to be the loss of any shred of uniqueness. They would be merely different from others in the same way that other peoples differ from each other. Other Zionist thinkers followed suit. Micha Joseph Berdichevsky, author and journalist, called for a complete break with the past and wanted to give full precedence to Jews over Judaism. The choice was simple: To be the last Jews or the first Hebrews. In order to be the first Hebrews, the Jews were entitled to break the chains and shackles of an outdated Judaism.[8]

Jacob Klatzkin placed every emphasis on uninhibited nationalism:

> In longing for our land, we do not desire to create there a base for the spiritual values of Judaism. To regain our land is for us an end in itself—the attaining of a free national life. The content of our life will be national when its forms become national. Indeed, let it not be said that the land is a precondition for a national life; living on the land is ipso facto the national life.[9]

Between these two extreme groups—retaining chosenness at all costs or denying it completely—moved the Zionist ideological pendulum in search of a balanced, middle road. In his speech opening the First Zionist Congress, Herzl declared that "Zionism means a return to Judaism even before the return to the land of the Jews." Such a declaration was required from a political point of view, if only to quell religious suspicions and to form a united framework in which all Zionists could find a place. But Herzl, like Nordau, Weizmann, and Jabotinsky, did not lend substance to such declarations. None of

---

7. Joseph Chaim Brenner, *Kol Kitvei* (Collected writings) (Tel Aviv, 1927), 259.
8. Micha Joseph Berdichevsky, "Wrecking and Building (1900–1903)," in Arthur Hertzberg, ed., *The Zionist Idea* (New York: Harper Torchbooks, 1966), 293.
9. Jacob Klatzkin, "Boundaries (1914–1921)," in Arthur Hertzberg, ed., *The Zionist Idea* (New York: Harper Torchbooks, 1966), 319.

them indicated how the unique destiny would find expression in the state to come.

The answer was given in many ways. The great majority of Zionists wanted to preserve a certain Jewish quality that would define their future society. Two themes recur: the need for adherence to Jewish heritage and the singularity of the future state as an exemplary model society. The link between these two themes is not clear. The view was utopian and almost always included a reference to the "vision of our prophets," side by side with lofty ideas of social justice. But the specific Jewish content was eroded by the weight of hyperbole. Lofty social ideas and Isaiah's prophecy of universal peace embellished Zionist speeches, but these could have served any highly motivated society.

In fact, what happened in Palestine was a constant process of political compromise that permitted the largely urban population to retain some Jewish customs and tradition. Naturally, these citizens paid little attention to an issue as remote as the future state's position vis-à-vis the nations of the world. In Labor Zionism a different process took place. There, a conscious attempt was made to cast new content into the old mold. The workers' parties adopted a credo that was not content with Jewish sovereignty, with being a mere nation among nations, or even with being an "exemplary society." Zionist socialism regarded itself as the legitimate heir of biblical ideas and prophetic visions. Israel would indeed become a "treasure nation," but in a modern context this meant the new workers' society embodying the highest goals of Zionist socialism.

It is beyond the scope of this book to examine the manifold factions and movements of socialist Zionism that left their indelible mark on the extraordinary and impressive history of the Labor movement. Suffice it say that Mapai, the dominant party, under the leadership of Ben-Gurion, saw Jewish choseness as intertwined with the socialist message. The revolutionary fervor of the pioneers of the Second and Third Aliyot—founders of the Histadrut and Labor's economic and social infrastructure—was the Palestinian successor to Jewish revolutionary tendencies in eastern Europe. Out of this combination of revolution and nationalism, Labor's new tree of life emerged. Within this Labor environment, international links and the posture toward the outside world acquired a special meaning: While political Zionism revolutionized Jewish existence by the adoption of prevailing notions of political self-determination, the Labor movement endeavored to translate the Jewish terms of uniqueness into a contemporary universal language.

Labor philosophy was not satisfied with mere liberation from past shackles and a break with the Jewish tradition that praises the Lord "who has not made us like the peoples of the earth"; it sought to go further and place the new Israel at the helm of international society, pointing the way to a new Jerusalem where equality and brotherhood prevail. The role of traditional Scripture and prayer books was replaced by new writings that spoke with Messianic passion about a new millennium: a classless society, the religion of work, the redemption of man, the communal settlement experience, the kibbutz and the moshav, the Histadrut as a workers' society. The pretense was immense: Israel, said Labor ideologist Nachman Syrkin, "will redeem the world which crucified him; Israel will once again become the chosen of the peoples!"[10] This was a new prophetic statement, transplanting the ancient spirit into a contemporary, secular and social context.

Ben-Gurion, both as Yishuv leader and as Israel's first prime minister, gave this notion a popular expression. He insisted that the "Jewish nation is not a mere national and political entity but embodies a moral will and bears a historical vision since the moment it made its appearance on the stage of history." And he continued:

> Not helpless longings for the tales of an imaginary past but a tense expectation of a perfect future and a vision of the universal rule of justice and peace is the historical philosophy which we inherited and through us, the whole world inherited—from the prophets of Israel. This expectation, this belief in the future, stood us in our days of persecution and adversity, and it is this which brought us here, to the very beginning of our national redemption in which you will also find the first sparks of a universal human redemption.[11]

---

10. Nachman Syrkin, "The Jewish Problem and the Socialist-Jewish State (1898)," in Arthur Hertzberg, ed., *The Zionist Idea* (New York: Harper Torchbooks, 1966), 350.
11. David Ben-Gurion, *Yihud Ve'yiud* (Singularity and destiny), IDF ed. (Tel Aviv: Israel Defense Ministry, n.d.), 13.

Socialist Zionism thus turned a full circle. The Jews who were pushed out of history—into a "historical corner," to use Ahad Ha'am's phrase—return to it as a latter-day guide to the perplexed. The message that the new Jews bore was a new kind of redemption—not divine grace but a social gospel; not a Messiah to come but Messianic action now. If political Zionism sought to return Israel as a normal nation to the international fold and thus establish equality on a national basis, Labor Zionism wanted to turn Israel into a moral leader. A social duty replaced religious devotion; a universal commitment replaced the old Covenant. Labor Zionism retained the tradition of Messianic chosenness, and indeed many referred to its teachings as "secular Missianism."

Religious Zionism, a minority group within the Zionist movement and the Yishuv, certainly could not accept such substitutes to Mosaic law and traditional Jewish thought. Such substitutes, national as well as socialist, ignored the very foundations of Judaism and dismembered, in religious eyes, the one argument through which the Jews could claim Zion as theirs. Religious Zionism was ready to make a compromise with secular Zionists, to belong to their organizations and to coexist with them politically—much to the fury of the big, non-Zionist Orthodox camp. Religious Zionists were not ready to compromise their very credo. Nevertheless, there was no better proof of the intensity of the Zionist craving for normalization than the universalist attitude adopted by the leaders of religious Zionism.

Until the Six-Day War—that watershed event—Israel's status among the nations did not particularly trouble the leaders of Hamizrachi and Hapoel Hamizrachi, the religious and labor-religious Zionist movements. They accepted the political aims of secular Zionism, including the return to the family of nations within the framework of a secular nation-state. Their interest lay inward, and their goals were defined within the Zionist movement and in light of the Yishuv's political, social, and settlement problems. They acted for their own religious interests and way of life without addressing the struggle for international equality. On the contrary, in the period preceding the 1967 war, the religious parties exercised a restraining and moderating influence on Israel's foreign and defense policy. And although Hamizrachi's vote in the 1903 Zionist Congress, which supported the Uganda plan—the "Night Shelter" intended to temporarily replace Zion—was not characteristic of their future policies, there were no signs in their policies and utterances of any isolationist chauvinism. When religious leaders and thinkers expressed themselves on Israel's external dimension— again, before that traumatic war—their words bore the message of humanism and universalism bequeathed by enlightened Zionism. This was also true of the religious precursors of Herzl's Zionism. Rabbi Zvi Hirsch Kalischer, who published his famous pamphlet, *Drishat Zion,* calling for the Return to Zion in 1862, saw in it the beginning of redemption in the traditional sense but simultaneously imbued it with political and practical viability, drawing inspiration from the national independence wrested by the Bulgarians from the Ottoman Empire. Like the political Zionists, Kalischer, too, thought that the restoration of independence and the return to agriculture would improve Israel's image among the Gentiles, a sentiment to be reflected years later by Herzl's *Der Judenstaat.*

Rabbi Moshe A. Amiel, chief rabbi of Tel Aviv in Mandatory Palestine and one of Hamizrachi's ideological leaders, explained religious Zionism in terms that seem incredible in our day of Gush Emunim zealotry:

> Internationalism in Judaism is not only a conclusion but the very concept which gave birth to our ideology, our alpha and our omega. . . . There is no greater historical forgery than that which limits Judaism to vulgar and simplistic nationalism whose only foundation is nothing more than the urge to exist and the egotistical impulse which is part of every creature.[12]

And while the Nazis were trampling over Europe and murdering the Jews, he wrote:

> Judaism's outlook is pure, even extreme, internationalism. After all, our history begins not with the Patriarchs but with Adam. . . . Our Torah is not content with nationalism alone but has regard for the whole world and general humanity

---

12. Moshe A. Amiel, *Hatzedek Hasotzialisti Vehatzedek Hamishpati Vehamussari Shelanu* (Socialist justice and our moral and legal justice) (Tel Aviv, 1936), 110.

precedes our Patriarchs . . . and our holidays, including the Sabbath, have not only a national character but also a universal human nature and are founded not only on historical national events but also on the nature common to all dwellers of this earth.

Rabbi Amiel went on to blame secular Zionism for drawing its "inspiration not from God's image in man but from the Gentiles' hatred of the Jews, while our religious ideology draws on love— Israel's love of God and of every human being created in His image."[13]

Another well-known rabbi, Yehuda Ashlag, wrote in 1940: "The peace of the world precedes the Ingathering of the Exiles. In other words, as long as self-love and egotism reign among nations, the sons of Israel too will not be able to worship the Almighty."[14] He explained that Israel was not able to inherit its ancestors' land without a universal observance of the rights of minorities and the liberties of the individual, a condition precedent for world peace.

What a far cry from the rhetoric of the extremist religious groups that began to dominate the Israeli scene after 1967! Yet these excerpts demonstrate how ready the religious-Zionist segment was to accept the general assumptions of Zionism and how far removed it was from any trace of Jewish xenophobia or chauvinism.

This pre-1867 tradition survived within different moderate groups who, under the leadership of Rabbi Yehuda Amital, formed Meimad. After Rabin's assassination, Shimon Peres invited Rabbi Amital to join his cabinet. But Meimad decided not to put up an independent list in the 1966 elections, because it had no chance of passing the 1.5 percent threshold.

The consequence of these elections was astounding. The National Religious Party, more extreme than ever before, won a dramatic victory: Its representation in the Knesset increased, partially because of the new electoral system, from five to nine seats. And all this happened a short time after the assassination of Rabin by a person who brought the nationalist-religious dogma to its bloody conclusion.

13. Moshe A. Amiel, *Lenivchei Hatkuffah* (On the perplexities of our age) (Jerusalem, 1943), 236.
14. Yehuda Ashlag, *Sefer Matan Torah* (The book of the giving of the Torah) (Jerusalem, 1940), 106.

The turnabout that took place within the religious camp after 1967 had no roots in the prestate period. Gush Emunim and the philosophy it represents are the creation of the postindependence period. Let us, therefore, examine now how the idea of normalization withstood the test of events that led the Yishuv toward the fulfillment of Herzl's dream. Our first examination (discussed in the following chapter) leads us to the Zionist endeavor to establish a foothold in the Middle East.

4

Can Israel Be Part of the Middle East?

Can Israel be an authentic part of the Middle East? Can it be separate but woven into the Oriental tapestry that surrounds it? This question, which has always accompanied the Zionist idea, has acquired special relevance as the peace process has developed and the issue of the cultural integration of the Jewish state, carrying its European founders' tradition into an Arab-Muslim world, has become more acute.

This question—albeit in a different form—arose with the birth of Zionism. Inherent in the Zionist awakening, from its earliest days, was a certain duality. Zionism came into being in Europe and sought to return the Jews to the Middle East. "We are foreigners, outcast foundlings, unwanted guests in Europe," declared Lilienblum, one of the founders of the "Lovers of Zion" in Russia:

> In the heyday of religion, we were strangers in Europe because of our faith, and now with the ascent of nationalism, we are strangers because of our race. Yes, we are Semites within Aryans, the sons of Shem within the sons of Japhet, a Palestinian tribe from Asia within the lands of Europe. . . . Yes, we are strangers and strangers we shall be forever.[1]

---

1. Moshe Lilienblum, *Ktavim Autobiographi'im* (Autobiographical writings), vol. 2 (Jerusalem, 1970), 196.

And Lilienblum ended his exhortation by a call to go East, to the "unforgotten land of our ancestors."

In the East stood the cradle of Jewish civilization. In the East stood Jerusalem and the Wailing Wall; in every synagogue "East" is where the Ark and the Holy Scrolls of the Torah are—the side pointing toward Zion, symbolizing an age-old craving. The Jews in their Western Diaspora could never, despite their long ancestry in Europe, forget their Eastern origin. When they wanted to forget this, there were enough anti-Semites around to remind them of their Semitic, foreign origin. Moreover, Zionism drew inspiration, at least partially, from other national liberation movements that emphasized a return to authentic, historical roots. For the Jews such a direction meant a return to that Eastern civilization that had molded their nation and to the country from which they had been exiled.

In eastern Europe especially, where to Jews Europe meant oppression and abject poverty, Zionism's awakening was tinged with a nostalgia for the East. In one of his early poems, Chaim Nachman Bialik, Zionism's poet laureate, greeted a migrant bird returning from the East with all the pangs of longing for the "warm lands" of the Bible. In his short novel *Whither?* the Hebrew writer M. Z. Feierberg describes the torment of a young Russian Jew who has forsaken the old ways without finding alternative solace. The book ends with this man delivering a sermon to a Zionist meeting in his township. Stunning in its verbal power, this sermon links the Return to Zion to momentous global events and to the ongoing conflict between East and West. The Second Temple and the bondage to the Romans is interconnected with a global change in which the East lost out to the new Western power. With the fall of the East, the people of Israel fell. Now the tables were turned:

> Europe is sick; everybody senses that its foundations are rotten and its society crumbling. Our destiny lies in the East. I do know that a day shall come when the hundreds of millions of people who live in the East, these dry bones, will come to life, will rise to their feet, a mighty host; then the East will reawake and will rule the world, replacing western hegemony. . . . Then new vigorous peoples will emerge and will establish the new society . . . and you, my brethren, when you go now eastward, you must always remember that

you are Oriental by birth . . . that the worst enemy of the
Jews is the West and that, therefore, it is unnatural that we,
the Hebrew, Oriental people should put our lot with the
nations of the West. . . . If it is true that the people of Israel
have a mission, let them bear it and carry it to the Orient,
not merely to Eretz Israel but the whole Orient. . . . My
brethren, inscribe on your flag: Eastward! Eastward![2]

The hymn of the religious Zionist Hamizrachi movement ended
with the same exhortation to go East. For many eastern European
Jews, turning their back on Russia and Europe was accompanied by
an idealization of the Orient. The age-long yearning for Zion, its
sunny landscapes, deserts, and orchards, was part of this vision that
regarded the Jew as a captive of a hostile environment returning to
his natural soil. The theme recurs in Zionist literature, and as late as
1935, after a series of bloody conflicts between Jews and Arabs,
Itamar Ben-Avi, a famous Hebrew journalist—the first Hebrew-
speaking Sabra son to Eliezer Ben Yehuda, reviver of Hebrew—
wrote:

We are Asians, because our land has always been an integral
part of the greatest continent on this planet. . . . We are
Asians because we have not come to a vacant land but to a
populated region, part of whose inhabitants are doubtless
remnants of the old Hebrews who converted to Islam and
Christianity after the destruction of the temple.[3]

Israel Belkind, a First Aliyah early settler, clung to a similar view:

It is certain that among the Palestinian Arabs, we meet a
great number of our own people who had been severed from
us for the last fifteen hundred years. . . . Based upon these
facts, we shall determine our attitude to them, and it is clear
that our relationship can be only that of brothers. Not only
brothers in the political sense—since history decrees that we

---

2. M. Z. Feierberg, *Le'an* (Whither?) (Tel Aviv, n.d.), 62.
3. Itmar Ben-Avi, *Chalomot U'milchamot* (Dreams and wars) (Jerusalem, 1975), 205.

share the same state together—but also brothers to the same race, the sons of the same nation.[4]

And in 1914, Nahum Sokolov, president of the Zionist organization, in an interview with the Egyptian journal *El Muq'atem* expressed his view in favor of a joint Arab-Jewish effort to build "a great Palestinian civilization which will replace the civilization of the earlier era."

In those same years, Yitzchak Ben Zvi, who would become president of Israel, was busy searching for traces of the ancient Hebrews among the Bedouins, and he found evidence of Jewish tribes who had assimilated into the local Muslim inhabitants of Kurdistan and Afghanistan.

All these were expressions of one extreme view. However, there has always been in Zionism an opposite view which regarded Zionism as bringing Western enlightenment to an underdeveloped region. Herzl's *Altneuland* is wholly European. And Nordau, in response to the Orientalist outlook, claimed that Zionist realpolitik dictated an alignment with Great Britain and the West and warned against a patronizing attitude toward the Arabs.

Jabotinsky, a totally committed Westerner, recalled that the culture of the Yishuv was principally Western and expressed his relief that "Ishmael is not our uncle." These attitudes can be seen, in contemporary terms, as an expression of paternalistic colonialism, which was part and parcel of an enlightened, liberal outlook.

The "Arab" habits of the new settlers were not praised by all. Joseph Klausner—the historian—deplored the new way of life, and from the pages of the Odessa-based Hebrew periodical *Hashiloah*, harangued the readers: "Our hope that one day we shall be masters in our land is not based on our fists or swords, but on the collective advantage we have over the Arabs and Turks."[5]

Jabotinsky hears of these explicit and up-to-then unheard of words and draws his brilliant pen in order to settle accounts with all the Orientalists, especially those who lecture about the virtues of the East from their heavens in Prague and Berlin.

---

4. Israel Belkind, *Ha'aravim Be'eretz-Israel* (The Arabs in the Land of Israel) (Tel Aviv, 1969), 23–24.
5. Joseph Klausner, *Hashilo'ah*, vol. 17 (Odessa, 1907), 574.

Jabotinsky is unequivocal: Zionism turns eastward but brings with it the culture of the West, of Europe: "We Jews have nothing in common with what is called 'The East', and thank God for that." His words—nowadays totally inconceivable—are strong: Zionism seeks to "eradicate every trace of the Eastern soul." As to the Arabs, this is their own business, "but if we could do them one favor, it would be to help them extricate themselves from 'The East'."

Jabotinsky is no racist: He yearns for the day when the whole Middle East can advance toward the Western stage of development. Consequently, he is not deterred by the Eastern origin of the Jews: because of their long exile in Western countries, they have succeeded in weaning themselves from the "Asian pace of life" and integrating in the European mold, whose values are nourished by the two testaments of "our Bible." And as to the Oriental Jews, he utters words that today would be anathema:

> I am aware of another, even sadder, fact: within religious Jewry, there are still to be found savage Eastern customs—a hatred of uninhibited inquiry, religious intervention in everyday life, women wearing wigs, who will not shake hands with men. Had we thought that these qualities are part of the imminent essence of Judaism, we would have despaired of perpetuating such an essence. We have been educated for this very purpose: to separate superstition and ancient customs from the Judaic essence.

Jabotinsky's attitude toward religion is that of an enlightened Russian liberal. He analyzes the state of Arab and Islamic society of his time and writes prophetic warnings, which apply to both Arabs and Jews:

> Islam is surely a noble and wise religion. But it is not the issue of Islam which is at stake but the Eastern insistence of introducing religion to every facet of our life. The East wants to see the stamp of God in everything: in the statute book, in the nature of scientific inquiry, in leisure, in the kitchen. The West insists on delineating the role of the religion: the individual attitude to God.

And he finds a major tragic fault in Eastern tradition:

More than anything else, this division manifests itself in the attitude to women. This is apparently the most serious, as well as the most tragic, hindrance to progress in the East. . . . It is not a minor matter that a man grows up knowing that his mother is not a valued human being, that her face and hair should not be visible . . . and that, generally speaking, she is the property of her husband . . . and that she is not alone in this because the same rules apply to his sisters and future wife.[6]

Thus, from the early days of Zionism, two differing conceptions can be discerned as to the cultural-political orientation of the state to come in Eretz Israel. When the pioneers of the early *Aliyot* began to settle the land, the Oriental inclination seemed to be in control.

Palestine was the Orient. Its sights and smells were not alien to the pioneers, because the Bible is replete with them. When in 1912, the painter Reuven Rubin traveled as a young man of eighteen from Jaffa to Jerusalem, breathless excitement filled his heart: "It was truly wondrous in my eyes that everything seemed so familiar, as if I knew every rock, every tree, every desolate hillside. When the train arrived in Jerusalem, I felt that I was coming back home."[7] And he rushed to be photographed, as was the custom of many Zionist immigrants at that time, in Arab dress and headgear.

The new land, not confined to present-day Israel but incorporating Jordan and Sinai, was mostly desolate and forsaken. Only small patches of greenery dotted its wide wastelands, and a few villages pockmarked its marshlands. But in the eyes of the fervent pioneers, as well as in their literature, the country gloried in all its biblical beauty. The wishful heart took over from the objective eye. The first songs written in Palestine by the new pioneers adoringly depicted its Oriental visage: the "ululation of jackals at night," the "shepherd's flute singing to descending herds of sheep," the "flute's melancholy song like a breeze touching a blossoming orchard," the "desert into

---

6. Ze'ev (Vladimir) Jabotinsky, *Reshimot* (Notes) (Tel Aviv, n.d.), 275 at 281–282 (Heb.).
7. Reuven Rubin, *An Autobiography* (Tel Aviv, n.d.), 53.

which one is carried by slow pacing camels, on whose necks great bells will ring." In Palestine the young European settlers met with Oriental Jews, members of the Old Yishuv, and with newcomers from around the world who had come to Eretz Israel upon hearing the call of Zionism. But it was the encounter with the local Arabs that was the most significant and that encouraged the Orientalist tradition among the new pioneers.

Isaac Epstein, a teacher, created a stir in 1907 when he published an article, "An Invisible Question," on the future relations between Jews and Arabs in Palestine.[8] Epstein charged that the Zionists were oblivious to the Arab question and were turning a blind eye to the existence of strong nationalist feelings among the Arab inhabitants of Palestine. Since then, it has become customary to claim that Zionism, in its initial phases, was unaware of another people in the ancestral homeland. But this allegation has been only partially true.

No one within the Zionist camp—or indeed outside it—perceived the force of the impending collision between the two national movements. Perhaps such blindness was Zionism's fortune, as an early realization of forthcoming events would have discouraged those who needed every iota of courage for routine existence. However, even before the Young Turks' revolution against Sultan Abdul Hamid in 1908—a date that usually marks the first signs of Arab nationalism—Zionist leaders had addressed the Arab question in general and the attitude of Palestinian Arabs to Jewish immigrants in particular. Yet the Zionist response was, to say the least, inadequate. It was naive in the sense that it did not estimate correctly the full measure of the Arab-Muslim violent rejection of any foreign presence on a piece of land they regarded as wholly Arab.

Zionist leaders were thinking in western European terms and emphasized the benefits to the Arabs from the Zionist enterprise. This attitude ran through the early phase of Zionist thinking, from the early founding days to the beginning of the British Mandate in Palestine. It retained its hold even in the face of growing Arab resistance. Thus, in Herzl's *Altneuland,* the Arab dignitary Rashid Bey praises the benign influence of the new society on all the inhabitants, Arab and Jew alike. In the same spirit, Herzl wrote to Yousuf Al'Khaldy: "The inhabitants ought to understand that they will gain

---

8. Isaac Epstein, "An Invisible Question," *Hashilo'ah,* vol. 17 (Odessa, 1907), 193–206.

excellent brothers and the Ottoman sultan will gain good and loyal citizens, who will turn the region into flourishing land."[9] In his memoirs, Ben-Gurion stated that before World War I he assumed the Arabs would receive the Zionist enterprise with open hands inasmuch as it harbored prosperity for the country and all its dwellers.

So strong was this belief that it persisted, especially in the Labor movement, even in the face of continual Arab riots and constant evidence of the Arabs' hatred of Zionism. In 1946, Mapam, the United Labor Party, which was to the left of Ben-Gurion's Mapai party, presented to the Anglo-American Inquiry Commission a memorandum advocating a binational state in Palestine. The proposal included a demand to open Transjordan to Jewish immigration and settlement:

> We are convinced that when the Palestine problem is satisfactorily solved and when the Transjordanian Arabs are given a chance to see how their brethren across the river benefit from prosperity and progress, they shall willingly open the gates of Transjordan to Jewish settlement.[10]

Moreover, socialist Zionists had a "scientific" explanation for the frequent clashes with Palestinian Arabs and for their growing resistance to the Jewish presence. The conflict was merely another local product of a global "class struggle."

Ben-Gurion's views were significant. Like many of his colleagues, and like the socialist ideologist Ber (Dov) Borochov, Ben-Gurion believed that the local Arab fellachim were descended from the ancient Jews who, in time of trouble and strife, "preferred to deny their religion, rather than leave their homeland."[11] When these allegedly "Jewish" Arabs refused to make any compromises with the new Jews, Ben-Gurion and his colleagues viewed this as a typical class struggle, in which the landed effendi class exploits the friction with the Jews in order to divert the attention of the masses from their real class interests.

---

9. Theodor Herzl, *Igrot* (Letters) (Jerusalem, 1957), 309–310.
10. A. Karlebach, *Va'adat Ha'chakirah Ha'anglo-Americait Le'inyenei Eretz-Israel* (The Anglo-American Inquiry Commission on Palestine), vol. 2 (Tel Aviv, 1946), 675.
11. David Ben-Gurion, "Leverur Matzav Ha'falachim" (On the state of the fellachim), 1917, republished in *Anu Ushchneinu* (We and our neighbors) (Tel Aviv, 1935), 13–25.

On the other hand, Ben-Gurion believed a common interest—and a future common front—would unite Jewish and Arab workers. Eventually, class consciousness would prevail, and only then would Arabs and Jews coexist in their common land. Only later, after the bloody riots of 1929, in which whole families of Jews were slaughtered by Arab mobs, did Ben-Gurion reluctantly change his mind. He began to fathom the depths of the Arab rejection and to relinquish orthodox Marxist explanations.

This sobering process would take place at a later stage. In the early period, before the true nature of Arab opposition to Zionism became sufficiently clear, the encounter with the Arabs of the land did not produce in the Jews the type of conflict one would have expected. On the contrary, the Arab was the Semitic relative, a freshly rediscovered brother who had kept the family tradition and, in many respects, was regarded as a model for the new Jew.

The Yishuv's early literature is significant. It is devoid of any trace of hostility to, or suspicion of, the Arab; many authors filled their writings with empathy and admiration for the native-born, free-spirited local Arabs. If the Jews sought a release from galut images and searched for their new, authentic identity, the distant relative rediscovered, the uninhibited Arab, was a figure worthy of emulation. This belief was shared by many early settlers, and some went even further and advocated intermarriage with the Arabs as a means of a quick merger. Inevitably, the settlers encountered banditry and violence, but this did not diminish the image of the Arab fellah and Bedouin as an authentic resident of the land of the Bible, a successor to, and perhaps a descendant of, the biblical patriarchs.

Looking back, one is tempted to dismiss these expressions as the fancy of romantic Orientalism, always a characteristic of newcomers to the Middle East. But the emotional intensity that attracted the young Jewish settlers to their future enemies cannot be overlooked. Moshe Smilansky, one of the first pioneer-authors wrote, under an Arab pen name—Hawaja Mussa—a series of books depicting with love and adoration the life of the Palestinian Arabs. He was succeeded by a whole genre of similar literature. The Bedouins aroused a special interest. Their ways and customs, as nomadic shepherds, reminded the settlers of the biblical stories and lit their eager imaginations. "Let us live like the Bedouins!" exclaimed Meir Wilkansky, one of the stalwarts of the Second Aliyah. He saw the nomads as guides to the right way of life upon the land. The Arabs appeared as noble, proud people whose ways should be adopted by the settlers. Thus, for instance, Joseph Luidor, Brenner's author friend who was assassinated with him by Arabs in 1921, described a young Hebrew, a native of the new land: "He was more friendly with the Arab boys and spent more time with them than with the Hebrew boys because among the Arabs he found boys after his own heart. For his Hebrew friends and their ways he had nothing but scorn and contempt."[12]

In fact, such stories are not unlike the biographies of actual individuals. Moshe Dayan, born on the first kibbutz to Second Aliyah parents, spent many of his childhood days with Arab boys, whose resourcefulness, wisdom, and friendship he came to admire. A Bedouin boy, two years his senior, became a constant friend. When Dayon was ten years old, he published a short story in the school paper in which he described an adventurous journey across the desert he and his two Arab friends, Ali and Moustapha, shared: They were attacked, and the young Dayan was saved by his Arab friends and—as he wrote—"with the help of Allah and his Prophet Muhammad."[13]

Pesach Bar Adon, who later became a famous archeologist, assumed in the early twenties the Arab name Azis Effendi and joined a Bedouin tribe in their long trek across Palestine and Transjordan. And when Hashomer, the first Jewish self-defense organization formed prior to World War I, wanted to introduce sheepherding into the new settlements, three of its members lived among the Bedouins, sharing their life, wearing Bedouin dress, learning their ways.

The image of the new Jew in the literature of the early settlers acquires an Oriental-Arab aspect that stands out against the traditional image of the old Jew. He masters riding his Arab horse, wears Arab headgear, and is unafraid of the Arabs. He fights them, when necessary, and, therefore, they respect him and accept him as one of their own. The old Arab name for Jews, "Sons of Death," is not applicable to the new manly Jew. One of the first stories written in Hebrew in the new land set the tone. In "New Year for the Trees," a short story written in 1892, Ze'ev Yavetz described a boy who came from galut to Petach Tikvah when he was six years old and

---

12. Joseph Luidor, *Sipurim* (Stories) (Ramat Gan, 1976), 65.
13. Shabtai Teveth, *Moshe Dayan* (London and Jerusalem: Weidenfeld and Nicholson, Steimatzky, 1973), 46.

whose physical prowess contrasted, as expected, with that of his brethren across the sea. The boy "learns from the Arabs to accustom his body to heat and frost, to flood and drought." In Jabotinsky's short story "A Little Jew," he told how a native-born, Arab-speaking young boy leads him to an Arab village and through his astuteness wins the respect of the dignitaries of the village. Asked about his education, the young boy says that in his Russian village he heard from Gentile children that the Jews are not a nation. Why? Because they cannot curse in their own language and they cannot fight back when attacked. These two deficiencies were, as we shall see, going to be set right.[14]

The Arab in these and similar stories was the non-Jewish goy whom the new Jew sought to resemble. The Arab represented the answer to a twofold need: to be released from the grip of galut and to become a goy. An extreme manifestation of this tendency is found in one of the earliest Hebrew plays written in Palestine. The play *Allah Karim* (an Arabic title), written by Levy-Ariyeh Orloff-Arieli, was published in 1912 in *Hashilo'ah,* the main Zionist organ in Russia. It depicts a group of young pioneers from the Second Aliyah who live, as was the custom of those days, in a commune under the photographs of an unlikely, but then common, pair—Herzl and Marx.

Naomi, the heroine, rebuffs the love of two members of the commune, all of whom are depicted as soul-searching, helpless creatures. She prefers Ali, an Arab boy vendor. When one of the pioneers kills an Arab, Ali avenges his slain friend by killing the pioneer. But even this deed does not change Naomi's love for Ali, and the play ends with an amazing, tempestuous monologue in which she renounces the commune: "My soul despises you, civilized worms! From the wild Arab I have learned something. He taught me the words 'Allah Karim.'. . . I have chosen the way of life and war! 'Allah Karim,' God is merciful!"[15] Such sentiments naturally expressed an extremist mentality, but they embodied an authentic nucleus. Israel returned to the Orient, and the Arab was the true son of the East, the authentic representative of healthy rootedness, the native-born who stood in total contrast to "civilized worms."

14. Ze'ev (Vladimir) Jabotinsky, *Sipurim* (Stories) (Tel Aviv, 1980), 7.
15. Levy-Ariyeh Orloff-Arieli, "Allah Karim," *Hashilo'ah,* vol. 27 (Odessa, 1912), 508. See also Gideon Ofrat, "The Arab in Israeli Drama," *Jerusalem Quarterly* 11 (spring 1979), 70.

But in spite of these literary expressions, reality took its own independent course. Clashes with the Arab farmers and workers, whose livelihoods were often endangered by the same pioneers who insisted on "Hebrew self-work," became more menacing. The Hebrew literature of the time contains many admonitions against any exploitation, any step that might adversely affect the local Arabs. In 1907, Rabbi Binyamin (the pen name of Joshua Feldman-Reddler) published in a London-based Hebrew periodical edited by Brenner, a sermon in biblical style addressed to the Jews of Palestine, which ended with an explicit commandment: "Thou shalt love the Arab dweller of the land for he is your brother, a flesh of your flesh, and thou shalt not close your eyes to him."[16]

This book does not deal with the history of the Arab-Jewish conflict but, in this chapter, only with the role played by the Arabs within Zionist consciousness and their impact on the new Jews' quest for a new "normalized" identity. From this point of view, this quest cannot be regarded as merely denoting a fashionable romanticism. It had acquired a new dimension, a true search for a substitute to the European-Jewish roots that, ostensibly at least, were cut by the revolutionary act of leaving Europe and creating a new Jew.

The First World War marked the beginning of the end of this hankering eastward. The Yishuv was divided between the pro-British Nili underground and those who, like Ben-Gurion and future president Ben Zvi, had cast their lot with the Ottoman Empire. But with the British conquest of Palestine during World War I, a new era began. The postwar Aliyot brought not only pioneer settlers but also thousands of Jews who preferred urban life. The Balfour Declaration and the terms of the British Mandate, commanding Britain to allow free immigration of Jews to their destined national home, accelerated and exacerbated Arab resistance to the growing Jewish presence. Pro-Arab ideology was gradually eroded by the harsh facts of strife. To the Arabs, the Mandate policy was a perennial object of opposition. Consequently, the Jews had to be ever alert to prevent Britain's betrayal, and the Arabs began to lose their heroic-biblical aura. They became a hostile and unrepentant enemy, whose leaders attacked Zionism in vitriolic language and

---

16. Rabbi Binyamin, "Massa Arav," in Joseph Chaim Brenner, ed., *Hameorer* (London, 1907), 278.

pressured Britain to revoke its policy toward the Jewish settlement of Palestine.

And yet, notwithstanding these harsh facts, the former outlooks managed to survive, especially within Labor Zionism. When the Histadrut—that unique combination of trade unions, worker-owned enterprises, and a social-educational network—was established in 1921, one of its first decisions was to establish an Arab workers union and to cooperate with the Arab working classes. Thus, class interests would cut across the national barriers put up by the scheming effendis. The workers' cooperation would build bridges linking the two Semitic relatives. In 1927, the Histadrut decided upon a "joint organization" in which Arab workers were to participate with Hebrew workers. All these efforts bore meager fruit, but at one point the Histadrut managed to crown its endeavors with a strike of both Arab and Jewish railway employees.

The literature of the period between the two world wars lacks the Oriental enthusiasm of the Ottoman days but occasionally retains its strong East-Arab orientation and, despite the increasing bloodshed, rarely includes a word of hate or animosity toward the Arab. Thus, in a story by Yacov Rabinovitch, a Hebrew *shomer*, a guard defending a settlement against Arab marauders, thinks aloud about his wish to live like a Bedouin. Intertwined with this wish is the question, "Have we come here to create a life of our own spirit or to return to Ishmael and Lot?"[17]

The yearning toward the Arab, Oriental, and Mediterranean ambience expressed also itself in the art and music of the Yishuv. The painter Abel Pan (né Fefferman), who came to the Bezalel Academy of Jerusalem a short time after World War I, is representative of the school that sought to create an indigenous art form, unlinked to Western fashions. His paintings, depicting biblical figures in the guise of local Arabs, embody this tendency, as do the early paintings of other artists—Nahum Gutman, Moshe Kastel, and Reuven Rubin.

Among the composers, who arrived in Palestine laden with a European musical education, a conscious effort was made to listen and give voice to the sounds of the new Oriental reality and to its singular melodies and tempos. Thus, Paul Ben Haim arrived in

---

17. Yacov Rabinovitch, *Nedudei Amshi Hashomer* (Jerusalem and Tel Aviv, 1929).

Palestine in the 1930s, having established a reputation in his native Germany. But the new land left its mark on his Palestinian works in their Oriental melodies and orchestration. In the works of Uriah Alexander Boskovitch, the Oriental influence reached new heights in such works as the concerto for violin, which includes an original theme based on a Bedouin melody, and the "Semitic Suite," the very name of which attests to its musical connotations. This is also true of other works, such as Menachem Avidom's "Mediterranean Symphony" and Abel Ehrlich's "Bashrav," which ignored Western tonality and was entirely written in the Oriental-Arab scale.

Yet, once again, reality gradually manifested itself. The riots of 1929, in which Jews were massacred in Hebron and its ancient Jewish community ceased to exist, stunned the Yishuv. In their own country, Jews were subject to the very affliction from which Zionism was supposed to deliver them. The quarrel had been transformed into a bloody battle, which could not coexist with the former Oriental romanticism. Within a few years, the Haganah, the Yishuv's self-defense organization, would split and two new militant offshoots were to emerge: the Irgun, that is, the Irgun Zvai Leumi, later headed by Menachem Begin, and the "Stern Gang," that is, Lohamei Herut Israel. The Arabs were now the enemy, and although the old romanticism did not die out, a new voice was heard in right-wing poetry. Itzhak Lamdan praised the matriarch Sara for discerning that behind Ishmael's laughter lay a dagger.[18]

The Yishuv's leaders began to comprehend the depth of the Arabs' incorrigible resistance to Jewish attempts to control any part of Palestine. Reluctantly, and much to its chagrin, the Hebrew Yishuv began to recognize the rising tide of Arab nationalism and its uncompromising determination to see the whole of Palestine as part of an Arab-Muslim domain. Beyond the Zionists' own internal disputes on the Arab issue loomed a wall of unmitigated rejection in which the Jews were looking vainly for a crack. Even the most moderate elements in the Yishuv, such as Judah Magnes's Brit Shalom movement for Arab-Jewish understanding, which was ready to relinquish Jewish sovereignty, could not reach an understanding with the Arabs. Thus, a local Palestinian Arab leader responded to the advances of one of Brit Shalom's spokesmen:

18. A. Aharon Amir, *Eretz Meriva* (Contentious land) (Tel Aviv, 1992), 37.

I shall tell you quite frankly that I would rather deal with somebody like Jabotinsky than with you. I know that Jabotinsky is our unremitted enemy and that we have to fight him, while you seem to be our friend. But truly I do not discern a difference between your goal and that of Jabotinsky. You also stick to the Balfour Declaration, to the National Home, to unlimited immigration, to Jewish purchase of Arab land—everything which for me is an issue of life and death.[19]

Similarly, one of the leaders of the Arab Istiqlal (independence) Party wrote in response to Dr. Magnes's proposals, which renounced the idea of a Jewish state and sought to establish a limited autonomy for the Jewish community in Palestine:

In your opinions and proposals I can see nothing but a blatant provocation against the Arabs, who will allow nobody to share with them their natural rights . . . as to the Jews, they have no rights whatsoever except spiritual memories replete with catastrophes and woeful tales. . . . It is, therefore, impossible to have a meeting between the leaders of the two peoples—the Arab and the Jewish.[20]

All attempts at cooperation or cultural dialogue were swept aside by such Arab stances. The efforts of the Histadrut to have a binational workers cooperative crashed against the wall of Arab rejection. Within Labor there were a few holdouts: In 1931, Chaim Arlozoroff, head of the Jewish Agency political department—whose murder a few years later would ignite a near civil war between Left and Right within the Yishuv—still declared that coexistence and true self-interest would bring about a cooperation between Arab and Jewish workers. He still believed that Arab leaders would see the light and appreciate the benefits accruing to them from cooperation with the Yishuv. After the outbreak of the Arab riots in 1936, even such pious hopes disappeared in gunfire and smoke.

19. Y. Porath, *The Emergence of the Palestinian-Arab National Movement, 1918–1928* (London: F. Cass, 1974), 68.
20. M. Assaf, *Hayechassim bein Aravim Veyehudim Be'eretz Israel* (The relations between Arabs and Jews in the Land of Israel) (Tel Aviv, 1970), 180.

Worse still was the fate of the Jews' attempt to return to their Eastern origins, to establish a bridge with Oriental tradition, and to merge their culture with that of their Semitic cousins. The Arabs never accepted this idea of Orientalism. When the Second Aliyah settlers arrived, the Arabs nicknamed them "Muscob" (Muscovites), a label defining their inferior strangeness. In the beginning of the British occupation, the Arabs often alleged that the Jews were German spies, only to change to a persistent charge that the Zionists were communist agents and Bolshevik spies.

In 1937, Jamal Husseini, secretary of the Higher Arab Committee, appearing before the British Royal Commission on Palestine, described the Palestinian Jews as foreign agents who carried with them into the Muslim Middle East the dangerous virus of communism:

> As to the communistic principles and ideas of Jewish immigrants, most repugnant to the religion, customs, and ethical principles of this country, which are imported and disseminated, I need not dwell upon them as these ideas are well known to have been imported by the Jewish community.[21]

Ironically, at that time the Yishuv was virtually ostracizing the small communist party, which was in sympathy with the Arab cause!

In the eyes of the Palestinian Arab leaders the Jews were not merely strangers. From the beginning of the British Mandate these leaders invoked the language of Christian anti-Semitism as a weapon against the Yishuv. To the traditional anti-Jewish elements in the Qur'an and Islamic tradition, they now added a modern ingredient borrowed from Europe: The Jews were the microbes of death and doom and carried with them the destruction of their host states. In his testimony before the British Royal Commission on Palestine in 1936, Ouni Abdul Hadi, leader of the Istiqlal Party, charged that the Jews were a nation of usurers and added that if sixty million Germans could not bear the presence of six hundred thousand German Jews, how could the Palestinian Arabs be expected to accept the presence of four hundred thousand Jews in a much smaller country? To the Jews of the Yishuv, such expressions, deriving their inspiration from Nazi Germany, bore the only-too-familiar seed of

---

21. Minutes of the Palestine Royal Commission (London, 1936), 236.

an ancient hatred that they never dreamed would take root in the new soil.

In vain did the Zionists try to prove to the Arabs that they were not dealing with the old Jews but with the new Hebrews, who saw in the Arabs long-separated members of the same family. At first, the Arab leaders were still trying, for tactical purposes, to draw a distinction between Western foreign Jews and their "own" Oriental Jews with whom, so the legend goes, they lived in peace and harmony. But soon even that claim was dropped, and it remained as a relic in the Palestine Liberation Organization's (PLO) notorious covenant that allowed the Jews who resided in Palestine before 1917 to remain behind, and all the other Jews to be expelled from Arab Palestine. In their verbal and actual war against the Yishuv and the state, the Arabs no longer made any distinction between Oriental and Western Jews.

In the history of the Yishuv, at least since the 1929 riots, a total Arab rejection drenched all Zionist hopes of turning eastward. The very idea of a Jewish presence in Palestine, any Jewish presence, was now an anathema that could not even be contemplated by the Arabs. Single episodes, such as the short-lived Weizmann-Feisal accord and Ben-Gurion's futile dialogues with Palestinian Arab leaders, lost their significance in the face of this rejection. In 1938, when His Majesty's Government covened the St. James Conference on Palestine as a prelude to its capitulation to Arab demands, the lines were clearly drawn. The Arab delegation, which included the representative of Arab states, refused to sit at the same table, even at the opening ceremony, with the Jewish delegation which was composed of delegates from the Yishuv and from the Diaspora.

When Israel gained its national independence after a bitter war, a most brutal and paradoxical situation occurred. The newly created Israel absorbed hundreds of thousands of Jewish refugees from Arab-Muslim countries. Its demographic nature altered radically, and it became more Mediterranean, more Oriental than ever before. It was then that the Arabs, with the aid of their newly acquired power and wealth, unleashed a propaganda war of unprecedented magnitude against Israel in which the Jewish state was presented as the paradigm of white, European presence in the Middle East. The Arab anti-Semitic diatribe acquired a new Nazi-inspired ferocity. The notorious *Protocols of the Elders of Zion*, the czarist police's forged document, has been used throughout the Arab states against the descendants of those very Jews at whom it was originally aimed. A full circle was completed.

With the growth of the fundamentalist Islamic movements, this old-new anti-Semitism acquired a menacing dimension. To the nationalist conflict was added a fanatic religious dimension that waged a jihad, a holy war, against the infidels who had invaded a sacred, Islamic land.

Zionism, which began with an attempt to redeem the Jews from Gentile-Christian hatred, crashed into the same reaction from the Arab-Muslim world. At the roots of these two rejections lay two different reasons, but the similarity was too striking for Jews—both old and new—to disregard. The analogy between the two rejections was obvious. Zionism, like Jewish emancipation and assimilation in nineteenth-century Europe, sought to retain only part of the Jewish tradition and was ready to discard that part that expressed Jewish exclusiveness and separated Judaism from the surrounding world. The assimilationists attempted to achieve this on an individual level, the Zionists on a national level. In both cases, the attempt failed. The world they wanted to enter—Christian Europe or Arab Middle East—was not ready to accept them as equal partners, either individually or as a nation-state. In both cases, rejection was tainted with bigotry and racist prejudice. In both cases, the Jews tried to extend a friendly hand and were ready to make far-reaching compromises in order to achieve integration. In both cases, there was no response. The enlightened assimilationists were ready to relinquish any facet of national allegiance, to renounce the Jewish "tribal" existence, to introduce extensive reforms into their religion to gain entrance to the civilized salons of Europe. Secular Zionism was ready to give up the traditional Messianic element in Judaism, to exchange the traditional blessing "thou hast chosen us from the nations of the earth" with "to be a goy like all the goyim" to gain acceptance to the Middle East. But these concessions, as well as the Jewish readiness for territorial compromise, served no purpose: Jewish identification was forced on Zionism, just as it was, a hundred years before, forced on Jews seeking emancipation.

On examination this analogy is found wanting and flawed in many respects. Yet the Arab rejection of Israel—of any Jewish state—was bound to have a traumatic effect on Israel's national psyche. The two rejections could not be seen in isolation, and a tendency grew to regard them both as part of some invisible scheme that frustrated any attempt by Jews to shake off their singular fate.

The words of Israeli author and journalist Aharon Megged are illuminating in this respect. In his essay "Bitter Thoughts," Megged somberly reflected on the failure of the Israeli attempt to win the hearts of the Arabs and on the obtuseness of the Arab mind toward the feelings and views of its Jewish adversary. Megged drew a comparison between the failure of German-Jewish assimilation and Israel's failure to win Arab acceptance. He quoted Professor Gershom Scholem, who described the one-way dialogue between German and Jew in the heyday of the German Enlightenment:

> The Jews' pleas and begging met with no response. When the Germans finally saw fit to hold some kind of dialogue, in a humanitarian spirit, it was based on the premise, explicit or implicit, of Jewish self-abnegation, of the advanced atomization of the Jews as a society in the process of disintegration.
>
> With whom, then, did the Jews converse in this dialogue! They spoke to themselves. Many acted as if the echo of their own plea would suddenly become the voice of other people, so intensely desirous of hearing it were they. When they thought they were talking to the Germans, they were only talking to themselves.[22]

Megged compared this doomed attempt to the Jewish-Arab experience:

> How depressing it is to consider that exactly the same, almost word for word, could be said of the so-called dialogue we have been holding with the Arabs for the past sixty to seventy years. We kowtow with all the might of our sense of honor, and lack thereof, out of the hope that the echo of our cry will suddenly become the voice of someone else; and when we believe we are talking to the Arabs, we are only talking to ourselves . . . that is indeed a pathetic sight. It

---

22. Aharon Megged, "Bitter Thoughts," *Dvarim Bego* (Explications and implications; Writings on Jewish heritage and renaissance) (Tel Aviv, 1975), 115–116.

arouses sadness and compassion in equal measure, both in its German-Jewish revelation and in its Arab-Jewish context.[23]

What began as a march eastward, away from the Jewish predicament, ended in the recesses of the Jewish psyche as a new awareness of Jewish helplessness in the face of an imposed isolation. The dreams of integration into an Arab Middle East lay in ruins, until they were to be partially resuscitated by the peace process. Against this dark background, the hopes for peace shimmer through: indeed, the paradox is that Islamic fundamentalism and the total rejection of Israel take place alongside a growing realization on the part of Arab states and the PLO that some sort of accommodation is inescapable. The acceptance and the painful rapprochement are intertwined, in the Arab world, with an escalating religious hatred of Israel. Indeed, the future of the Middle East depends on which process will have the upper hand, pragmatic politics or deluded fanaticism, and whether peace and its fruits will mellow a bitter, vengeful Islam.

The peace process with the Arabs is not only protracted and arduous, it is accompanied by something that is very difficult for the Israeli intelligentsia to swallow: Peace does not seem to be leading to a cultural rapprochement between the Jewish and Arab intellectual strata. In diametrical opposition to the situation in Israel, the Egyptian intelligentsia have for the most part, with the exception of a handful of isolated prominent figures, joined with the rejectionists who oppose peace with Israel and refuse all contact with Israelis.

In Egypt, and to an as yet unclear extent in Jordan as well, the intelligentsia and professional classes oppose conciliation with Israel and the Israelis. The Israeli Academic Center in Cairo, originally intended to serve as a bridgehead in the rapprochement between the two nations, is the constant target of routine venomous, slanderous, and false attacks by the Egyptian press. Despite the warmth emanating from the king's palace in Amman, the process in Jordan is also similar, even if more complex. The members of the liberal professions and the academe were the first to come out in opposition to establishing ties and contact with their Israeli colleagues and have

---

23. *Ma'ariv* (Hebrew daily) (Tel Aviv), 9 September 1976.

been conspicuous in their refusal to condemn even as heinous an act as the cold-blooded murder of seven schoolgirls by a Jordanian soldier on "Peace Island," along the border between Israel and Jordan.

Israel has made peace with the governmental establishments, with officers, and sometimes with prominent businesspeople, but those who should be the natural allies of the Israeli peace camp have turned their backs on it, refusing to take heed.

One always hopes that with the final settlement and the establishment of full peace between Israel and the overwhelming majority of the Arab world, this malady will also be remedied. But the true difficulty must also be seen for what it is: The romantic East that the Zionist founding fathers desired has changed, and Israel has also changed—in the opposite direction. The Arab Middle East has become more extreme and is now threatened by Islamic fundamentalists, who sanctify both Arab nationalism and the war against that island of infidels on sacred Islamic soil.

Arab society is driven by various forces, ranging from attraction to Islamic purity—xenophobic toward anything Western, materialistic, or capitalistic—to ordinary nationalism. Although this nationalism is Muslim, in its rules, customs, and conventions, it also seeks to isolate Islamic fundamentalist leaders, grant increasing power to the secular government (whether it be monarchial, military or political), maintain trade ties with the industrial world, and improve its economic situation. Israel lies between these opposing forces as a particularly thorny challenge to contend with, an entity alien both to Islam and to Arab nationalism. Even more than Israel itself, "Israeliness" arouses suspicion a priori, because it has introduced a secular, pluralistic, and permissive model into the heart of the Arab world. This model violates conventions shared by almost all streams and factions of the Arab world. Where there are common interests, such as trade or the prevention of war, the dividing wall can be breached. But the Egyptian intelligentsia, along with their counterparts in other Arab countries, feel that they have no need of Israeli inspiration. The cultural and literary world of the Israeli seems to them—even if unjustifiably so—too alien and distant to be considered a partner in dialogue or debate with its Arab counterparts.

It should be noted that here and there, there are encouraging signs of contact and mutual influence with Palestinian leaders. A complete and permanent peace may eventually undermine the instinctive opposition to what seems to Arab intellectuals to be a cultural invasion. Indeed, this is the source of a great paradox: The greater the strength of the Israeli Left and the more Israel progresses and becomes a more open and diverse society, the greater the cultural alienation between the two cultures. It might have been easier for intellectual Arabs to deal with a conservative Israel. Present-day Israel and its current way of life and practices are far more difficult to accept. Indeed, how can even the most enlightened Arab society make the quantum leap from his patriarchal, religious, family-centered world to the norms accepted by the enlightened sectors of Israeli society? Even the majority of Israeli Arabs find it difficult to make that leap!

The reality is even more troubling. Those very values that are axiomatic to the Israeli peace camp are alien to, and arouse suspicion in, the Arab world with which the Left wants to make peace. Recognition of the sexual freedom of every individual and equal rights for homosexuals are a literal abomination, total anathema to a Muslim-Arab society (regardless of how widespread the phenomenon is in all societies, including in Middle Eastern ones). The same is true for a number of other conventions: the feminist movement and real equal rights for women; protection of the rights of the one-parent family; opposition to any form of corporal punishment, whether in an educational setting or within the family; acceptance of erotica and pornography in the press, literature, and art; and all the other emblems and trappings of any open Western society.

Indeed, there is a basic clash between the two worlds over the status of the individual in society. The Israeli Left staunchly champions the inalienable natural right of the autonomous individual. But this idea is unacceptable even to progressive elements in Arab society. A case in point: An Egyptian court of appeals in Cairo ordered a Muslim husband to divorce his wife against his will because he had behaved like an "infidel." He had read the Qur'an from a historic perspective and determined that certain verses could not literally be implemented. Although some Egyptian intellectuals also protested the verdict and the government itself did not support it, this very issue illustrates the gap between the two societies.

In this respect, at least, it would have been easier for the religious and traditional populations on both sides to communicate, as in the meeting between Sadat's "Bissam Allah" and Begin's "with God's help," than for Israeli and Egyptian writers, journalists, and artists. The problem, of course, is that those who might be able to bridge the abyss between the two cultures have no interest in doing so. This rift also casts light—or, rather, its shadow—on another issue that has begun to emerge in recent years.

The partial peace process, the visits to Arab countries, the contact between Palestinians and Israel's multicultural milieu have led to an aspiration to see the Middle Eastern experience as a bridge, a liaison, common to all the nations lying on the eastern and southern banks of the Mediterranean Sea. This trend correlates with the European concept of integrating all Mediterranean countries, primarily those in North Africa, under the influence of the European Union (EU). The Barcelona Conference, which met on November 27, 1995, with the participation of fifteen countries of the European Union and twelve Mediterranean countries, was the first declarative step in this direction. The conference culminated with a joint declaration that included a commitment to "strengthen cooperation in the war against terror and enhance regional security through the support for the nonproliferation of nuclear, chemical or biological weapons, while honoring the territorial integrity and unity of all the participants." The economic and trade section of the declaration included "commitment to the gradual establishment of a Mediterranean free trade area by means of various trade agreements."

The desire to find in the Mediterranean reality a common experience is not only self-evident but can also serve a beneficial aim: to support the peace process by creating a cultural and folkloristic common denominator. Moreover, if real peace is to exist one day, it can be assumed—and hoped—that real politics and Western influence will contribute their share to bolstering the process of rapprochement. Indeed, today we can already find islands of support among a courageous minority: an article by Hazem Sariya, editor of the op-ed pages in the Arab newspaper, *Al Hayyat,* published in London, which discusses the need of the Arab countries to become familiar with the Jewish Holocaust; the Egyptian delegation to the Copenhagen conference, headed by the late Lutfi El-Khouly, a member of the Egyptian left-wing A-Tejmoua Party and one of the mainstays of the Egyptian intelligentsia, who came out publicly in favor of making peace with the Jewish state. These are the harbingers of a potential process of reconciliation between Arabs and Jews.

In 1996, the Israeli Forum for Mediterranean Cultures was formed, headed by Professor Nehemiah Lev-Zion. The first conference of the forum was dedicated to the memory of Jacqueline Kahanov, an eminent Egyptian-Jewish writer and essayist who, upon her emigration from Egypt, brought with her, the echo of a different culture to the closed, self-contained society of Israel in the 1960s. It was she who spoke bluntly to the Israeli establishment of the time, hurling her challenge, "I am a Levantine!" Since the day of that provocative cry, something has changed in Israeli society. What had seemed an aberration in the 1960s is now an almost routine phenomenon.

But the conference debates revealed the inherent difficulties involved in this positive trend. At the time she spoke, Jacqueline Kahanov recalled her childhood in a heterogeneous, multiethnic Egypt, an Egypt that no longer exists, whose upper classes were influenced by European culture and the Francophone hegemony. She spoke of that Levantine culture in its classic sense:

> As a child, I believed that it was only natural for people to understand each other even though they spoke different languages, for them to have different names—Greek, Muslim, Syrian, Jewish, Christian, Arab, Italian, Tunisian, Armenian—and at the same time be similar to each other.

That Egypt has gone with the wind. It disappeared with the arrival of Gamal Abdul Nasser, the awakening of Islam, and with their coming disappeared the Egypt of Kahanov's youth, when she went to church with her "Italian maid" and adored the smell of St. John's Cathedral.

At that same conference of the forum, one of the participants made this point very clear:

> When Jacqueline Kahanov introduced herself as the representative of the generation of the Levantines, it became evident that she was talking about a very thin stratum of minorities in Egypt and other Mediterranean countries: Jews, Copts, Greeks, Italians. . . . The important works we associate with this experience are, for example, the work of the Greek, Cavafy, who knew hardly a word of Arabic, . . .

and the work of Jacqueline herself, who was the product of a French educational system, an offshoot of French culture that took hold in Egypt following the Napoleonic conquest.

Indeed, the past has gone. Alexandria, once the symbol of nostalgic Mediterraneanism, has metamorphosed. In 1947 almost 60,000 "foreigners" resided there, British, French, Turks, and Jews as well as two important European communities—Greeks (30,753) and Italians (12,370). The Egyptian-Islamic reality and Nasser's actions—the expulsion in 1956 of the Jewish and Greek communities that still lived there—created a new Alexandria, one that is homogeneous: Arab, Muslim, devout, and devoid of any nostalgia.

Konstantin Cavafy, Alexandria's Greek poet, who was born and died there, who lived between the light of its sun and the darkness of its pleasure catacombs, who met with his Greek comrades in the salty sunshine on the seashore and at night made love to his boys "in hidden rooms, shameful to even call by name," felt that he was living on borrowed time: "Thus pass the days and we have not tired / of our stay here. For it is clear / that it will not last forever." Cavafy died in 1933, before darkness fell and before Nasser expelled the Greeks from Alexandria. Where would he want to live now, were he to return to life? Certainly not in the city he had loved so much.

All the Alexandrian memories remain frozen in time, in the Alexandria Quartet by Lawrence Durell, the Levant Trilogy by Olivia Manning, and the many books written by Israeli writers who reminisce about their youth in Egypt. Yosef Algazi, a writer for Ha'aretz, returns to Alexandria, the city of his birth and education, and mournfully relates how he is torn between his longing for the city of his memories and the squalid and neglected ruins of foreign communities that once existed there: "foreigners" who were expelled from Alexandria return to visit, staying at the Hotel Cecil that Durell made famous; the Christian cemetery robbed of its gravestones; eleven worshipers crossing themselves surreptitiously in the Greek Orthodox church; four elderly worshipers praying in the Elijah the Prophet synagogue—a pitiful remnant of a once glorious ancient Jewish community; and even the Copts gathering only under heavy guard, as if they were Jews needing protection. Extreme fundamental Islam has inherited old Alexandria: masses of worshipers in the city square; streetcars in which men and women travelers are separated; and that same segregation—so alien to the Alexandria of old—maintained even in the library next to the Museum of Fine Arts.

There is also another flame burning: intellectuals who supported, and eventually won, the struggle against the decision of an Egyptian court banning the screening of a film by Yousouf Shahin, because of "offenses to religion." But the general feeling is one of pain over a world that has disappeared. Algazi's Italian friend arrives to execute the will of his father, who died abroad, to disperse his ashes in the sea of the city he loved.

Indeed, the eastern Mediterranean is filled with longing for the past, devoid of a present, but attended by a hope for the future. Israeli scholar David Ohannah writes:

> What we really need is a new, refreshing ethos, one which does not estrange itself from our region, or turn its back on universal values, which cuts itself off from the umbilical cord of the ethnic strife of the past and lays out before us a vision of an older, more worthy and broader cultural framework. The Mediterranean option which includes Israelis (oriental, Sepharadi and Ashkenazi), Palestinians, Europeans and North Africans, offers a dialogue, rather than a Kulturkampf in which there are only losers. The Mediterranean option is not an appeal for ethnic separatism, smugness or a return to one's roots. It is rather a common cultural setting, clarifying separate identities.[24]

If only such an option indeed existed!

At the same founding convention of the Forum for Mediterranean Cultures, Israeli writer Shulamit Hareven repeats Jacqueline Kahanov's appeal, "I am a Levantine," but her Levant has clear folkloristic symbols, with no hold on present reality: "The Levant is the epitome of colorblind pluralism in all matters of race, ethnic origins or religion. The Levant goes almost nowhere—everyone comes to it, and its hot sun molds everything." If only we had such a Levant! And when Professor Lev-Zion seeks current-day relief, he

---

24. David Ohannah, "Toogat Hamizrahi'im" (The melancholy of Oriental Jews), *Panim*, vol. 1 (January 1997).

looks to monarchial and Francophone Morocco, because it is "an Arab country blended with Europe," and one with which Israelis of Moroccan extraction can establish intellectual and cultural ties.

But if we move from wishful thinking to present-day realities, we are in for a rude awakening. Anyone searching for a surrogate for the Alexandria of old, of the blend of cultures and styles, the color-blindness under a hot sun, will not find it now among Israel's neighbors. As paradoxical as it may seem, this surrogate may be found in Israel, on the seashore—from Ashdod and Ashkelon, to Acre and Nahariya—with Tel Aviv in the center. The Tel Aviv promenade of today is the substitute for the famous Alexandrian Corniche of yesteryear, filled with many different cultures, styles, skin colors, tolerant of all and assimilating everything.

Indeed, Israeli society has taken a few significant leaps forward: from a European-Ashkenazi hegemony to a multicultural and multiethnic society, recognizing the uniqueness of each of its various elements; from a society that sought to assimilate all those who entered it and mold them by means of the melting pot into the model of the classic "Sabra" to a society that recognizes the ideological and educational value of retaining the traditions of the parental home; from the pain of severed roots to a search for roots. When the large waves of immigration from the Soviet Union and from Ethiopia arrived in Israel in the eighties and nineties, the educational system did not repeat the mistakes of the fifties and sixties, when the Francophone North African culture of tens of thousands of immigrants was forcibly eradicated. From its aspiration to be a melting pot, Israel has moved on to being a multicultural salad in which there is real and true creativity in all forms of folklore: music, poetry, cuisine—a unique blend, spiced with a Mediterranean seasoning.

But it is not only folklore that is valued; there are other more important areas of creativity, ranging from the establishment of a department for Mediterranean music in Bar Ilan University to the great success of Oriental writers: Sammy Michael, Eli Amir, Ronit Matalon, Dorit Rabinian, Dan Benaya Seri, Haim Sabbato, and others.

The problems of disparity and lack of equal opportunity have yet to be solved. Although the direction of progress is clearly apparent, the desire to create an exclusively European model has retreated in the face of Israel's diversified reality. It is this relaxed, let-live atmosphere that gave life to a varied and flourishing literacy and art scene, accompanied by economic and technological prosperity.

If the heart can allow the intellect to rule, the Israeli model may become a model worthy of emulation for the Arab countries of the Mediterranean: not to sever roots, but rather to preserve the traditions of the past, based on openness and tolerance. This democratic framework, rather than nostalgia for a colonial Levant, should be the identity of the new Mediterranean community, combining a mosaic of the past with a prosperity that will banish ignorance and poverty. For the time being, however, this Mediterraneanism is still but a dream.

5

The Holocaust and the Struggle for Israel's Independence

The increasing friction with the Arab world in the late 1930s did not seem to the leadership of the Yishuv and the Zionist movement to endanger the Zionist concept of a twofold Jewish return—to their land and to the world. Even when Britain betrayed the Mandate and the Balfour Declaration and in Europe the Nazi beast was slouching toward Auschwitz, the Zionist credo remained unshaken. In those days of torment—of impotent debates at the Evian conference on Jewish refugees—when the world was closing its gates to Jewish refugees of Nazi terror as if they were the carriers of some dangerous plague, Zionists remained constant in their devotion to Herzlian thought. There was much anger, clenched fists were waved at perfidious Albion, but there was no attempt to reexamine Zionism's basic assumptions.

The exacerbating conflict with the Arabs had put an end to the yearning eastward, but Zionist leaders still thought that the conflict could be localized and limited. In this context, Britain's betrayal was seen as the unjust, cynical machinations of a government and its politicians. When Chaim Weizmann realized the magnitude of Britain's treason, he could not contain himself. At the Twenty-first Zionist Congress in 1937, as the lights were going out in Europe, he could not continue his speech and, overcome with emotion, burst out crying publicly. But Weizmann, lifelong friend of Britain that he was, assured the congress that the English people, unlike their government, still supported the Zionist cause. The dissidents, headed by Jabotinsky, protested Weizmann's timid response and wanted a total evacuation of European Jews, but they too sought Zionist integration into the world community and proposed that the future Jewish state become a dominion in the British Commonwealth.

In retrospect, one wonders at the absence of any signs of despair. Zionism's basic assumption, that it would miraculously put an end to anti-Semitism, was totally destroyed by the Nazis; its hope of saving the Jews before the imminent catastrophe was frustrated by a combination of evil and indifference. After years of Zionist activity and after the establishment of a truly model society, hatred of Jews reached unimaginable heights and the plight of Jews fell to an even more unimaginable nadir. Every English or American archive that is opened to public scrutiny, every new research, divulges how widely prevalent blatant anti-Semitism was and how it penetrated the highest echelons of policymakers. This anti-Semitism had two facets: The first was a hidden indifference to the Jews' fate, the second was the probably justified fear that giving them shelter would fan the ever-present embers of the old hatred.

What must be understood, however, is that the full horror of the Nazi nightmare was not, and could not have been, realized at the time. The Zionists were preoccupied with political work: how to save the menaced Jews; how to fight Britain's policy and, at the same time, participate in her war effort; how to survive. Moreover, in her capitulation to Arab demands, Britain resorted to realpolitik, citing the need to placate the Muslim world on the eve of a world war. The Zionist movement refuted this argument but refused to see in such betrayal a deeper significance.

Indeed, during the time when Europe's Jewry was being systematically slaughtered, Zionist ideology of normalization remained unchanged. The news from Europe caused heartbreak, fury, and a renewed attempt to open Palestine's doors to those who sought escape. Toward the end of 1942, when news from Europe about the mass murders reached Palestine, a delegation of Polish Jews turned, panic-stricken, to Yitzchak Greenbaum, head of the Yishuv's Salvation Committee. They wanted desperately to draw attention to the danger of extermination and tried to make Greenbaum swear to act so that there "[would] not be one moment of peace and quiet

until the slaughter [was] stopped and the remnants saved."
Greenbaum's reaction was so stunning as to be unbelievable:

> I told them: No, I shall not swear to it! The fate of the Jews
> in Europe may be the main issue but it is not the only issue
> which troubles us. And once again I spoke to them about our
> need to extract ourselves from the position of extraordinary
> people and be a nation like all other nations. Two thousand
> years of galut were enough. Let us be equal members in this
> world.[1]

These words are not really indicative of Zionist ideology. A normal nation and an "equal member in this world" would certainly not react—toward the other nations, toward its own people—in the way Greenbaum reacted. The normal and instinctive behavior would have been to give total precedence and attention to saving helpless Jews from the Nazi slaughter. But this irrelevant reaction by a dedicated and devoted Zionist demonstrates how deeply rooted was the Zionist concept of normalization: It remained unmoved, in its grotesque version, even in the face of the Holocaust. We shall return to the radical and revisionist claim that the Zionist leaders, by their insistence on immigration to Palestine as the sole solution, relinquished the Jews who could be saved elsewhere, and will refute it as too facile and doctrinaire. But that Zionist beliefs distorted some of the leaders' judgment, cannot be disputed. This distortion did not stem from a indifference to the fate of kith and kin, but from a perhaps understandable failure to come to grips with a reality that exceeded any Jewish experience.

By the end of the war, when the full horror became known, Zionist leaders doubled their efforts to open the closed gates of Palestine and save those who had escaped extermination. The heroic days of Exodus and illegal immigration, the anti-British underground and political action finally culminated in the United Nations' partition plan. But even then, instinctive pre-Holocaust reactions survived and asserted their irrelevancies. The old Jews, the galut Jews, so ran the insane legend, went like sheep to the slaughterhouse. They did not behave as the new Hebrews would have

---

1. Reported in *Haboker* (Hebrew Daily) (Tel Aviv), 7 December 1942.

behaved, by fighting back, resisting the Nazis and saving their Jewish honor. The Yishuv's instinctive reaction to the Holocaust was to emphasize the few desperate Jewish uprisings against the Nazis. Not everybody betrayed the gospel. The partisans, the fighters of the Warsaw Ghetto, the Jewish resistance, saved the Jews from total humiliation. Hence, the day of remembrance of the six million dead is named the Day of Holocaust and Heroism, and the monuments and museums put special emphasis on the courage of the Jewish resistance. How the helpless, unarmed Jews could have resisted remained unexplained. Why it was dishonorable to die in Auschwitz, without fighting back, was not elucidated. The old Zionist credo denouncing the galut passivity was instinctively applied to a situation that lies beyond human experience, to which there is no moral guide and in which standard criteria of honor and courage are not applicable.

This ambivalent attitude to the survivors continues when the first representatives of the Yishuv meet them in the DP (displaced persons) camps. Horror mixed with disappointment characterizes their reports. But one should not attribute too much importance to the utterings of these young ideologically motivated men and women. Facts are stronger than their reports. Most Jews in Palestine had relatives who perished in Europe and were fanatically looking for the few survivors in order to bring them to Palestine. Their despair and hope are, at least partially, unrecorded history. One central fact looms above all: The Yishuv, a community of six hundred thousand, absorbed, within a few years, those survivors as well as the penniless immigrants from Arab countries, in what must be regarded as a unique national effort. Such an absorption, despite the difficulties of the newly arrived and the mistakes of Yishuv's leaders, could not have taken place without a total sense of dedication and commitment to the survivors.

And yet today's reader cannot but wonder at the insensivity caused by Zionist doctrinaire beliefs. With their arrival in Palestine, the first refugees to filter through Britain's infamous armada often encountered an oddly anachronistic reaction. When Ruzhka Korczak, one of the legendary figures of the Warsaw Ghetto revolt, told the Histadrut council, in her native Yiddish tongue, about the horrors of her experiences, Ben-Gurion said that they were shocked and moved by the tale of woes, "although it was told in a foreign and jarring language."[2] The suggestion that Ruzhka Korczak be sent to America to alert public opinion to the plight of the Jewish refugees in Europe was rejected because she had not had enough of an Yishuv experience for such a mission. When Yacov Chazan, leader of the left-wing Mapam, goes to London for the first Zionist meeting after the war, he meets the legendary Chaika Grossmann, heroine of the Jewish revolt against the Nazis. He scolds her for wanting to unite all Zionist youth movements and writes to his wife that the survivors have brought with them many good traits but also "some dangerous things." "They ought to recuperate" within their own ideological movements.[3] When the first films of Nazi atrocities were shown to a private group and a stunned silence descended on the audience, Ben-Gurion, mustering every iota of strength, broke the silence by telling about similar tragedies—of Armenians, of Russians, of gypsies. The Jews are not alone, he said; man's inhumanity to man has had other victims too.

But these awkward manifestations of an ill-applied concept did not alter the one crucial lesson: Zionist insistence that the Jews are safe only in their own land had received a most wrenching testimony. Although none could have foreseen the full scale of the horror, the Zionists' urgent insistence on a home and shelter for a menaced people was prophetic. After the Holocaust the long dispute between Zionists and non-Zionists disappeared. Zionism became the leader of all Jews. The formerly powerful Jewish anti-Zionists groups vanished, and the few relics, such as the American Council for Judaism, shriveled into insignificance and eventually ceased to exist. The substitutes to political Zionism—Ahad Ha'am's idea of a spiritual center, Magnes's concept of a binational state, anything short of full sovereignty—were rejected and disappeared into the limbo of vaguely remembered history.

On the other hand, the Holocaust raised some doubts about primary Zionist premises. After Auschwitz it was impossible to deal with the specter of anti-Semitism according to the concepts laid down by Herzl in nineteenth-century Vienna. There was to be no more understanding of, or neutrality to, anti-Jewish bigotry. There was no longer a reason for blaming the sufferings on the galut Jews,

---

2. *Ha'aretz* 2 (Hebrew Daily) (Tel Aviv), 2 February 1945. Ben-Gurion's words created a storm of protest both at the Council and in the Yiddish press in America.
3. Zeev Tsachor, *Chazan* (Tel Aviv, 1997), 173–174 (Heb.).

no more escaping from Jewish history into the cozy shell of normalization at all costs. The spoiled Hebrew son, the Sabra, would have
to grapple with the reality of the Holocaust and with the meaning of
Jewish history. The lessons of the world's indifference to Jewish suffering and its refusal to save their lives from the German genocidal
machine could not be disregarded and had to be explained. A reexamination of the old truisms had to be undertaken.

That reexamination did not occur overnight. The impact was not
immediate, but slow and cumulative. The soul-searching turnabout
was bound to come, because the initial reaction against "Jewish passivity" was perverted from its inception. It turned a blind eye to the
very vitality of the Jewish communities—the wellspring of so many
intellectual and revolutionary movements. The image of the weak
Jew was also misconceived. Where they were given equal rights,
Jews fought bravely for king and country, and their graves in military cemeteries throughout Europe attest their devotion to imperial
Germany, to the Allies, to the country of their citizenship. And
where did the heroes of the Yishuv come from if not from this very
Jewish civilization that was looked down upon? And was there ever
such courage, such defiant bravery as that demonstrated by the Jews
who rebelled, in the ghettos and in the partisan movement, against
the might of Nazi Germany with but a few rifles in their hands?

To this one may add that the morally insane argument, which
blamed Yishuv passivity during the Holocaust, ignores that millions
of Russian and Slavs, including prisoners of war, were brutally
butchered and massacred without any attempt at resistance. But the
doubts run even deeper. What would have happened to the proud
Hebrew Yishuv had Rommel's troops not been stopped at the gates
of Alexandria? Had Palestine been overtaken by the Wehrmacht,
how would the new Jews have fared? The Yishuv underground had
its plans for resistance, but given the overwhelming might of the
Nazis and their experience in crushing opposition, it is safe to
assume that the Jewish resistance in Palestine would have come to
naught. Within a short period of time the Nazi death machine, with
the gleeful assistance of many Palestinian Arabs, whose Grand
Mufti, Haj Amin al Husseini, sat in Berlin spreading his own brand
of Jew-hatred, would have begun its process of total annihilation of
the Palestinian Jews. Because of their relatively small number—six
hundred thousand Jews—their concentration in small areas, and the

active enmity of the Arab majority, liquidation of the Yishuv would have been a relatively simple affair. As a matter of fact, the Germans planned such an extermination, aided and abetted by Nazi Arabs and Palestinian Germans, sons of the Templar settlers, who joined the Nazi Party in Palestine in the 1930s.

The ramifications of such a possible turn of events could not escape the newly awakened consciousness of young Israelis, and their effect on the traditional image of the new Jew can be surmised. Seen in this light, the Holocaust, far from reaffirming the dichotomy between old inferior Jews and new superior Hebrews, erased prior Zionist distinctions between the two branches of a menaced Jewry.

Years would pass before the attitude to the Holocaust and its victims would be transformed: from shame at the helplessness of the slaughtered the pride in their courageous survival. Finally, in 1995, the rabbinate, at the insistence of Dov Shilansky, former chairman of the Knesset and himself a survivor, deleted from the Holocaust prayers the now offending words "who went like sheep to the slaughterhouse."

All this was still to come: in 1948 the State of Israel was born, clinging to the original Zionist vision. Independence was granted according to international law and with the assistance of the great majority of nations, including the superpowers, all in accordance with Herzl's foresight. The drafters of Israel's Declaration of Independence in 1948 saw Israel in the image of the early Zionist congresses: a secular state based on Jewish national history; a model society embracing equality regardless of religion or race; a people inspired by the prophets' vision of justice to all; a dutiful member in the family of nations.

David Ben-Gurion led the state in accordance with this political gospel: Unbearably hard indeed is the lot of the Jews, but the State of Israel will bring remedy to a two-thousand-year-old malady. Jewish national revival will put an end to the perverted relations between Jews and Gentiles. The Jewish people are indeed different in their history and culture, but their fate will be that of a normal nation. The roots of Jewish malaise lie in the dispersion of the Jews among other nations, but the Ingathering of the Exiles will cure this malaise. The Nazis devoured other people too. Israel must reconcile not only with the world but, first and foremost, with Germany itself. Yet all that is not enough. Israel itself, in its social order and spiritual content, must become "a light unto the nations." The Jews in their land will again be a "treasure nation" in the secular sense of the world.

Israel's dawn was characterized by a unique situation—military weakness and strong international support (later to reverse completely). The new Jewish state acquired international fame and drew general admiration. And, indeed, in many respects its achievements were truly unparalleled. With this in mind, Ben-Gurion outlined the philosophy underlying his policy:

> In defining a new road toward a world of liberty, freedom, peace, justice and equality, there is no monopoly to big powers. . . . Small states can nowadays guide humanity in scientific, social, and spiritual progress. . . . With the establishment of our state we have become more than ever citizens of the world. Our national independence has placed our world citizenship on a solid base. Not because of unrootedness do we espouse these issues of humanity and are aware of its needs and problems but because we are equal partners in these needs and problems.[4]

There is no trace of despair here: neither at the failure of the do-nothing Bermuda conference—convened in 1943, on the eve of victory over Nazi Germany while the efficiency of the Nazi death machine was at its murderous height—nor at the pogrom of the few surviving Jews, taking place in a Polish town called Kielce in summer 1946, after the war has ended. There is no sense here of the unmitigated anger mixed with a sense of disbelief that seizes a contemporary reader.

The first foreign minister, Moshe Sharett, lay down the rule governing the young state's orientation:

> We have not come into our home from the four corners of the world in order to isolate ourselves and to be alone within it or in order to cut or weaken our links with other nations and with the great world of culture and progress. We

---

4. David Ben-Gurion, *Yihud Ve'yiud* (Singularity and destiny): IDF ed. (Tel Aviv: Israel Defense Ministry, n.d.), 40–42.

do not see ourselves as merely another state in the Middle East. . . . If we have acquired during our sojourns and dispersion a world vision and perspective, we do not intend to give them up now. . . . This world perspective, regarding things through a global vision, is not only our heritage from the days of sojourns and dispersion. We believe it is from earlier times than that, because in this vision will be found the quintessence of our ancient tradition, before the sojourns and dispersion, which always emphasized the universal in our spiritual world and all which is supranational in our road to morality and progress.[5]

These shades of Altneuland indicate clearly that in the first years of independence there was no soul-searching reexamination of traditional Herzlian concepts. Current political need and the effort to bring in and absorb hundreds of thousands of people from East and West exhausted both physical and intellectual resources. Moreover, a world shocked by what the Nazis had perpetrated lent Israel unprecedented support and assistance. Both the Soviet Union and the United States supported the fledgling state. Nazism was seen as a passing dark cloud of crazed inhumanity. Even in those early years there was talk about cooperation with Adenauer's Germany. So all-encompassing was the basic idea of Zionism, so total was the desire to have a normal state, that it refused to be veered from its steady course even by Apocalypse.

Many years passed before Israeli writers and politicians would speak about the need to revise this Zionist theory. Eliezer Livneh wrote twenty years after independence that in a post-Holocaust world there was no return to Herzlian Zionism:

As of now, the attitude of the Jewish people to the outside world (and perhaps also to itself) will not be as of yore. Zionist thinking before 1939–45 and Zionist thinking after that, are not one and the same thing. . . . Is the civilized humanity which was seen by Moses Hess, [Leo] Pinsker, Ahad Ha'am and Herzl the same humanity which was seen

---

5. A. Ben Asher, *Yechassei Chutz, 1948–1953* (Foreign relations, 1948–1953) (Tel Aviv, 1956), 9.

by our generation? And can our self-understanding and the understanding of the tension between us and the Gentiles remain without change? Indeed, we may endanger our survival if we shall act according to criteria and practical conclusions drawn in a former era, before the monstrous light of the gas chambers went up.[6]

These words were written after the Six-Day War, that historical turning point in Israel's attitude, not in the period following the Holocaust and the War of Independence. In those years, Israel established strong links with the European Right and her emissaries were treated with respect and admiration in circles not noted for their philo-Semitism. Those were the heydays of "Israeli first, Jewish later," of the Sabra cult, of the Canaanite movement. In those days, Israel established links with most countries and her very name was synonymous with Democracy, Liberty, Socialism. More than a million refugees found shelter and home in their new country. For Zionism it was a singular moment. Herzl's dream had become a reality.

After the 1967 war the postponed soul-searching burst out. Would it have taken place without the Arab menace? Perhaps. But the Six-Day War did bring about a new attitude that emphasized a common Jewish fate, and this perspective was accompanied by far-reaching social and political changes within Israeli society.

True, as the friction between Israel and her friends overseas increased during the 1950s, a new, militant attitude engulfed the leadership of the young state. When it was realized that the Arab world regarded the armistice agreements not as a prologue to peace but as a mere respite, Ben-Gurion gave vent to a growing disregard toward international opinion. It was he who coined the phrase—destined to become emblematic after the 1967 war—"It is not important what the Goyim are saying; it is important what the Jews are doing." It was he who spoke with growing contempt of the United Nations, whose decisions condemned Israeli acts of retaliation against Arab infiltrators and murderers. But it was the same Ben-Gurion, who, standing by these dicta, navigated the ship of

---

6. Eliezer Livneh, *Israel Umashber Hatzivilizatziah Hama'arivit* (Israel and the crisis of western civilization) (Tel Aviv, 1972), 11.

state so as to avoid collision with the superpowers and without leaving the threatened ship alone at sea.

There was another duality in Ben-Gurion's policy. In his statements he kept clinging to the universalist message, but this did not prevent his government from adopting a harsh policy toward Israel's Arab population, which included massive confiscation of land without proper compensation, imposition of martial law, and discrimination in the allocation of public funds. Indeed, the case of Israeli Arabs was seen as an exceptional security issue to which the universalist message was not applicable.

After 1967 a new, nationalist wind of change blew away Ben-Gurion's concepts. It is not mere coincidence that the old man's views—against going to war without foreign support and for almost total withdrawal after the lightning victory—were regarded as marginal and almost dotty. The Israelis were drunk with their newly discovered power. In the following chapter, we shall deal with this turnabout.

6

From the Six-Day War to Oslo

The ideological and practical ramifications of the Six-Day War were so all-encompassing in Israeli thinking and politics that there is justification for regarding it as a turning point in Zionist and Israeli history.

To understand the nature of this turnabout, a reconstruction of its background is necessary. The June war was preceded by a period of national anxiety such as Israel had not known since the days of the War of Independence. The Arab forces seemed, on the eve of the war, to menace the very existence of the state and the lives of its inhabitants. Moreover, this threat descended upon Israel unexpectedly, after years of believing that the status quo with the Arabs would be long-lasting. This anxiety was compounded by shock at the impotent apathy of the international community in the face of Nasser's aggression. Within hours, international guarantees of Israeli free navigation sank into the waters of the blocked Tiran Straits and the United Nations observers' force vanished into thin Sinai air. Anxious Israelis followed, with a mixture of contempt and fury, the Security Council's perfidy and its cynical refusal to say one word that could be interpreted as a condemnation of the Arabs' blatant and openly declared attempt to strangle Israel.

Abba Eban described the sensations of Israelis on those fateful days: "As we looked around us we saw the world divided between those who were seeking our destruction and those who would do nothing to prevent it."[1]

Remembering a time in which Europe's Jews encountered a similarly divided world, Israelis would not soon forget these days of "clenching fists and pounding hearts." Today, with the help of a hindsighted knowledge of the real balance of power between Israel and its neighbors and of the absence of offensive preparations in the Egyptian army, these words sound highly exaggerated; nevertheless, they testify both to the prewar anxiety and to the bursting emotions following the victory.

As a result of the war, the land that until then had lain beyond the impenetrable armistice line was reunited with Israel: Old Jerusalem, the Jewish Quarter lying in ruins, the Wailing Wall, Rachel's Tomb, Samaria and Judea—the sites and places whose very names evoked biblical connotations and past memories. The press reported that when the paratroopers reached the Wailing Wall, they—the symbol of Sabra toughness—wept on the ancient stones, the relics of past Jewish greatness and the destination of age-old longings.

In the religious sector, this encounter with holy places gave the war a new Messianic meaning. Within a short time, a strong movement seeking to settle Judea and Samaria began to take root within the religious camp, thus signaling a radical change in the traditionally moderate National Religious Party. The June war, by bringing Israel in touch with these cradles of Judaism, was for many religious Israelis the commencement of a new era. Religious thinkers and rabbis did not hesitate to see in Israel's victory a divine miracle. A profusion of religious writings argued the case for regarding the crushing of Israel's enemy, the liberation of the Wailing Wall and the Temple Mount, as God's hand in action.

For the nonreligious sector, too, these were great days. Anxiety gave way to exhilaration, peril to euphoria. The siege was lifted, and beyond the barbed wire lay the enchanted lands to which no Israeli could be indifferent. Within Israel the war unleashed a national debate as to the aims and goals of Zionism and its relationship with Judaism. A new sense of history began to permeate the public debate, and the words "Jewish fate" became almost ubiquitous. The need to go back to the original Jewish sources, to return to the roots,

---

1. Abba Eban, *An Autobiography* (New York: Random House, 1977), 392.

was constantly expressed. The Sabra paratroopers' weeping at the Wailing Wall—true or alleged, nobody knew—became an enduring legend.

To Meir Roston, professor at Bar Ilan University, these tears proved that "after generations of intellectual rational education, after years of consistent secularism, Israeli youth seeks faith and the soul of its culture. The intellect becomes banal—the spiritual link renews its attraction."[2] Since the war, a new movement of repentants, or born-again Jews, became widely publicized, and the mass media celebrated the conversion to Orthodox religious life of famous Israelis-ex-kibbutzniks, air force pilots, and show business people. The transmutation of pop stars from hashish and sex to yeshiva and synagogue became a regular feature of the popular press. This movement included many authentic and moving stories of men and women who found peace of mind and a true vocation by turning to religion; often they were presented as indicative of a new repentant mood that had allegedly descended on secular Israelis and of their wish to return to the religious sources of Judaism. But the war had not brought about a renaissance of religious observance among the majority of secular Israelis. For a fleeting moment, the emotion laden encounter with the biblical cradles of Jewish civilization was clothed with religious sentiments. But aside from the natural reaction of any Jew coming face-to-face with the relics of the Jerusalem built by King David and King Solomon, the excitement subsided, leaving behind it, in addition to the repentants and the born-again Orthodox Jews, a nationalist awakening within the Zionist religious camp. The seeds of a polarized society were thus sown during the days of the war.

The stunning victory, sharp and quick as a surgeon's scalpel, that came in the wake of menace and fear, created a mood of exuberance. The adjective *invincible* was prefixed, as a matter of routine, to the name Israel. The country became, in the eyes of its beholders, a mighty military power that the Arabs could not conquer. "No one can budge us from staying forever on the Suez," said General Ariel Sharon a short time before the Yom Kippur War, "and our hold on the canal disintegrates Egypt from within."[3] Yitzchak Rabin

---

2. *Hatsofeh* (Hebrew religious daily) (Tel Aviv), 19 October 1971.
3. *Ma'ariv* (Hebrew Daily) (Tel Aviv), 13 July 1973.

explained that the defense lines along the canal radically altered Israel's strategic posture, "because its military might will be sufficient to prevent the other side from undertaking any military initiative."[4] Military experts reinforced the view that the postwar status quo was preferable to all other alternatives and that no one could upset it. Five months before the outbreak of the Yom Kippur War, Yigael Yadin, former chief of staff, said: "I do not believe that in our generation there will be another war like those of 1948 and 1967. This is one of the successes of the Six-Day War."[5]

These statements nourished a new mood of self-confidence. "The world," which had betrayed Israel in its dark days, was not entitled to tell her what to do and how to behave. Self-reliance was Israel's only weapon.

The consequence of this new attitude was a gradually growing friction with the outside world and with Western public opinion. Immediately after the war, Israel enjoyed wide international support, which enabled her in September 1967 to repel an Arab-Soviet motion at the United Nations calling for a total Israeli withdrawal to the prewar lines. In November 1967, the Security Council accepted the famous Resolution 242 (the exchange of land for peace without demanding that Israel return all territories occupied by Israel in the war), which many Israelis rightly regarded as an Israeli achievement and which Jerusalem endorsed. In Khartoum, the Arabs issued their three no's—no to peace, no to negotiations, no to recognition—vis-à-vis Israel. The African nations, except for one, maintained their strong links with Israel. But with Israel consolidating control of the territories conquered in the war, with the proliferation of settlements there, and with increasing Arab economic strength, the conflict with her Western and Third World friends was constantly exacerbated. As the years passed, and within the country the ideas of "Greater Eretz Israel"—which contend that Judea, Samaria, and Gaza are part of Israel—acquired more political support, the Jewish state met harsher reactions from outside. The Security Council, never a friend, exhibited an almost Pavlovian reaction to anything concerning Israel and habitually issued one-sided condemnations. Public criticism in the Western press grew. Third World

---

4. *Ma'ariv*, 13 September 1973.
5. *Ma'ariv*, 6 May 1973.

countries became restless. The politics of this new situation called for the same cool assessment that had guided Ben-Gurion in the difficult 1950s.

But for postwar Israel, just awakened from nightmarish fears into euphoric reality, the confrontation with the world heralded a new significance: Israel inherited the mantle of the rejected Jew, differing only in her ability to be defiant. This ideology started in hubris—Israel the invincible—and terminated in despair—Israel the pariah state. This dominant attitude found expression in a popular song of the period that topped the hit parade at the time. Titled "The Whole World Is Against Us," the song begins:

> *The whole world is against us.*
> *This is an ancient tale*
> *Taught by our forefathers*
> *To sing and dance to.*

Having thus established the link between the persecution of the Jews and Israel's isolation, the song goes on to establish the difference between the forefathers and the Sabra sons:

> *If the whole world is against us,*
> *We don't give a damn.*
> *If the whole world is against us,*
> *Let the whole world go to hell.*[6]

The same mood invaded even the usually detached atmosphere of the Supreme Court. In a 1970 cause célèbre concerning the question "Who is a Jew?" Justice Moshe Silberg wrote in a minority opinion, "We are a people dwelling alone and fighting alone. When our youthful fighters stood by themselves in battle facing a hostile world—at the best, indifferent—they saw clearly that *Israel has no friend but herself*"[7]—all this despite the growing assistance given very generously by the United States to the victorious Jewish state.

"The nations of Europe who did not help us during the Holocaust," said Golda Meir in response to the growing criticism of

---

6. *La'ohavim et ha'aviv* (Collection of Hebrew lyrics) (Tel Aviv, 1981), 32.
7. H. C. 58/68 *Shalit v. Minister of Interior*, Selected Judgements of the Supreme Court of Israel, special vol. (Jerusalem, 1971), 35 (English).

her policies, "are not entitled to preach to us."[8] Later, this view was reiterated and amplified by former prime minister Begin. Europe's anti-Israeli stand was directly linked by him to its long and bloody history of anti-Jewish persecution.

The movement for Greater Israel, comprising public figures from both Right and Left, religious and secular, harangued the public with its constant demand to annex the territories—the term *occupied,* or *administered,* was gradually deleted—and to form one entity, without bothering to specify what would happen to the Palestinian inhabitants.

With the Yom Kippur War, this period of self-righteousness and intoxication with imaginary power suffered a defeat. The vision of a solitary Israel defying the world could no longer be as attractive as it was during the days before October 1973. Israel's dependence on foreign aid grew to frightening proportions. Thus, when Sadat's plane touched down at Ben-Gurion Airport that Saturday night in November 1977, he found a country ready to trade Sinai, the very symbol of its conquests, for peace.

Yet the suspicion of the outside world implanted during that period affected the national psyche. Its detrimental impact on the traditional, liberal, and humanitarian concepts of historical Zionism, andthat it was led and encouraged by Golda Meir's Labor government, surely constitute one of the paradoxes of that strange period. During that time only a few iconoclastic politicians and journalists asked where this way of thinking might lead Israel and how it jibed with Zionism's aim to bring Israel into the community of nations.

Indeed, the Yom Kippur War and the dramatic demonstration of Arab oil power that followed worsened Israel's isolation. Third World countries, which had begun to sever their links with Israel before the war, completed the process after the war. Condemnation in the West grew to deafening dimensions. To Israelis, this was an unjust attitude, a cynical capitulation to Arab blackmail. Be that as it may, the country found itself a small Jewish island, menaced, misunderstood, and maligned by all, a successor to the Jewish community of older times. Like the old Jews, Israel now began to conceive of herself as fighting for survival in a foreign and alienated world that denied her rights accorded as a matter of routine to others.

---

8. *Ha'aretz* (Hebrew daily) (Tel Aviv), 30 April 1973.

Many Israelis began to adopt a traditionally Jewish stance: There are the righteous few friends, such as Holland and much of the United States, just as there were such exceptional, righteous Gentiles in Jewish history, but the world is inherently a stranger—at best alienated, usually belligerent. Jewish fate, which Zionism sought to flee, had overtaken it. Of the song "The Whole World Is Against Us" only the refrain linking the grandsons "to our forefathers" remained relevant. The Yom Kippur War obliterated the part that told the world "to go to hell."

This post–Yom Kippur mood had a conflicting impact on the country. On one hand, it induced Israel's gradual withdrawal from Sinai, which had actually begun in 1975 as a unilateral act with hardly a quid pro quo from the other side; on the other hand, Israel was asked to give up assets that almost all her citizens regarded as vital to their very lives. Hence, the despondency and the seeming paranoia. In this new ambience it was only natural that the small determined minority of religious nationalist zealots, devoid of doubt, innocent of misgivings, would increase their hold over Israeli society. With the decline of traditional Zionist thought, with the fading ideas of normalization, the irrational, Messianic element grew stronger and manifested itself everywhere: in mass demonstrations, in the creation of illegal settlements, in a rash of bumper stickers quoting Genesis, "Do not have fear, O my servant Jacob."

Indeed, Israelis swayed between two contradicting poles: the Zionist urge for normalization and the older Jewish instincts. The changing mood of the country reflected the relative strength of these two competing forces. When Israel's isolation grew, the influence of classic Jewish elements and their traditional reflexes surged to the surface, with the notion of a society encompassed by a hostile world taking root in a soil fed by generations-old subconscious fears. When "the world" sided with Israel in its few moments of glory, such as during the Six-Day War or the Entebbe rescue operation, the Zionist credo took over.

As Arab power grew, Israel's position became more precarious. Arab propaganda, which even before 1967 had emphasized anti-Semitic sentiments, gained self-confidence and sophistication after the Six-Day War. Prompted by Arab propaganda and Third World rhetoric, a rabid stream of denunciation, culminating in the United Nations' "Zionism is racism" resolution, was aimed at Israel. Israel herself—not her policies—was now being denounced from international pulpits as a "crime against humanity." Helped by their economic prowess, the Arabs unleashed against the Jewish state a campaign seeking to strip the country of its right to exist. The lyrics may have been new, but the tune was old and familiar to Jewish ears. Side by side with legitimate criticism of Israel—and Israel's settlement policy was certainly not immune from legitimate and understandable attacks—there arose a new phenomenon, under which anti-Zionism concealed something else, much older. In the West, a new generation that never knew the Holocaust was willing to listen to these seemingly progressive views without detecting the oil-rich reactionary forces manipulating them.

Thus, the post–Six-Day War period ushered in not only a stronger affinity between Israel and the Diaspora—now perceived as the only true and constant ally—but also a new alliance between old and new foes of the Jews: the Arab states and the traditional Jew-baiters of the Russian East and the Western Right. In the past, the Jews were told by the anti-Semites "to get out and go to Jerusalem"; now they were vilified having done so. The traditional European Right—eager to appease the new Arab power—could, on this one issue, join hands with the new Left. For Soviet *agitprop,* before it vanished with the disappearance of the Soviet Empire, nothing was more natural, more instinctive, than the combination of traditional, folk-anti-Semitism with a routine attack on Israel's "imperialistic, land-grabbing" policies. To their horror, the new Jews found themselves pilloried for the very same alleged faults as their forefathers'.

De Gaulle's lashing out against Israel after the Six-Day War, perhaps a politically insignificant event, exemplified this new situation. Before 1967, Charles de Gaulle personified, more than any other ruler Israel's new status. Israel was, according to his own phrase, "France's friend and ally." His friendship with Israel, demonstrated the sharp distinction the French made, and the Israelis enjoyed, between Jews and Israelis. But after the war, when France's policy switched to a pro-Arab stand, the French president shocked Israel by his reversal. He criticized Israel for the war, for refusing to withdraw, and on November 27, 1967, denounced it as embodying all the negative, traditional traits of the Jews, whom he defined as "an elitist, arrogant and domineering people."

Israelis saw in this outburst a dramatic confirmation of a doubt that had always lingered in their hearts, that despite the provisional camouflage, the world, the goyim—including transient allies—remained anti-Jewish. De Gaulle's words proved that Israel's existence did not cure this malady.

With the growth of the anti-Semitic slant in anti-Israeli propaganda, with the United Nations becoming the platform for a new brand of racism, Israelis reluctantly found themselves more and more playing the traditionally Jewish role of scapegoat for humanity's ills. In the United Nations–inspired Conference on Women, which took place in Copenhagen in 1980, Israel—not hunger, not backwardness, not war—was blamed throughout the proceedings for every affliction, conceivable and inconceivable. Eliahu Salpeter, a columnist for *Ha'azetz* daily, wrote: "Israel now is blamed, as the Jews of yesteryear, for Nature's disasters, as well as for the sufferings caused in underdeveloped societies through the greed and incompetence of their leaders."[9] The anti-Israeli offensive inspired in Israel a typically Jewish response.

Aharon Megged, author and essayist, published in *Davar*, the former Histadrut daily, a series of articles linking the predicament facing the Jewish state with traditional Jewish suffering. The libelous attacks against Israel were compared to the infamous blood libels against Jews for allegedly using Christian victims' blood for baking Passover matzoth. After the notorious Damascus blood libel of 1852, Ahad Ha'am wrote an article in which the libel was seen as a semiconsolation. Without such a preposterous accusation, Jews could have fallen into the trap of believing what the whole world had been saying about them, of thinking, it inconceivable that what so many different people had consistently been saying for so many years was utterly without foundation, a complete travesty, a bundle of lies, that there must be at least some foundation for it. The blood libels enabled them to dismiss such doubts and apprehensions and to reassure themselves that the allegations were indeed all false. They could tell the world: You are all wrong and have been wrong all these generations. If you believe the blood libel, anything you may be saying against us is equally baseless.

---

9. *Ha'aretz*, 8 August 1980.

Megged used the same reasoning for the United Nations' vehe-
ment diatribe against the Jewish state: When Zionism is decried as
racism—by nations whose whole structure is founded on racial
exclusiveness—then Israelis, in the wake of their ancestors, can say,
Everything you ever said about us is equally false. Israelis began saying to themselves that they were witnessing an irrational, but tragically consistent, phenomenon: The refusal of the Christian West to
accept assimilation and the refusal of the Arab-Muslim world to
accept a Jewish national presence in the Middle East was followed
by the world's refusal to accept Israel—an Israel that seeks to be a
normal member of the world community.

More significant was the failure of the Israelis, at least the secular
Israelis, to understand the reason for this new eruption of the old
volcano. In this respect, too, Israelis shared their lot with nineteenth-
century emancipated Jews and were unlike their religious ancestors
who could endure traditional anti-Semitism.

Medieval anti-Semitism was intolerable and unrelenting in its
oppression of the defenseless Jewish minority. But it contained some
guarantees for Jews and had a theological raison d'être. Although
the Jews could not accept their image as the killers of Christ, the reasoning did contain a logic of its own. The Jews were the keepers of
the Covenant, and their sufferings were part of a collision between
two faiths. The purpose of Christian anti-Semitism was twofold: the
censure and punishment of the Jews and the constant striving to lead
them into the Mother Church, thereby demonstrating her rightness.
Thus, it was necessary for theological reasons to keep the Jews alive.
The intention was to oppress and persecute them, but not to destroy
them. The Jews were to be witnesses to the truth of the New
Testament and to survive as a living exemplar, as a people dispersed
among the nations, in punishment for their sins.

The assimilation and emancipation of the nineteenth century were
supposed to put an end to such superstition and prejudice. But the
utterly bewildered modern Jews discovered that these had been sup-
planted by a new monster; for the first time they encountered a secular and racial anti-Semitism, lacking any religious inhibitions or,
indeed, any rationale, theological or otherwise. Religious Judaism
could cope, albeit with dreadful suffering, with the Inquisition, persecution, and pogroms, overcoming through martyrdom their tor-
turers. Their deaths had a religious significance; it was the

Sanctification of God's Name, *Kiddush Hashem*. Belief clashed with belief, religion with religion, Messiah with Messiah. The historical combinations of Jew pitted against Christian could somehow coexist: Nachmanides and Pablo Cristiani, Pope Benedictus XIII and Rabbi Joseph Albo, Nicholas Donin and Rabbi Yehiel of Paris. Each side found a meaning and justification in this confrontation—if one may use such an expression for the persecution of the weak by the strong.

The new twins—secular Judaism and modern anti-Semitism—which arose like a phoenix from the ashes of the Dark Ages, could not coexist. Zionism was, therefore, the only solution. Yet a hundred years later, Israelis found themselves in the same perplexed position. Irrational reality clashed with their very philosophy.

The secular Israelis could not cope with the new animosity, just as Dr. Herzl could not cope with the anti-Dreyfus mob in Paris. In the wake of the Yom Kippur War, Harvard professor Nathan Glazer wrote:

> Jews for the most part have wanted to be like everybody else. Indeed ironically, the establishment of Israel was an attempt to make Jews like everybody else. They would now have a state. It has not worked out that way. Israel has made Jews more, not less, exceptional. The pariah people, it seems, have simply succeeded in creating a pariah state.[10]

This awareness has radically altered Israel's outlook. The interrelationship with the outside world was not a side issue but the one subject on which different Zionist factions agreed. It is this factor that helps to explain the meteoric rise and disproportionate power exercised by the religious-nationalist zealots: They had all the answers to Israel's problems. By relating all her difficulties to the old conflict between Jews and Gentiles, they could furnish a consistent, historical answer to the mystifying riddle. It is no accident, therefore, that the post-1967 period saw a double shift of power. In 1977 the right-of-center Likud unseated the Labor Party which, in the face of the growing hostility to Israel, lost much that distinguished it in the past from the Right; within the Right, the new religious leaders

---

10. Nathan Glazer, "The Exposed American Jew," *Commentary* 59 (June 1975): 25, 27–28.

inherited the place occupied in the past by Jabotinsky's Revisionist Party. Gush Emunim, the settlement lobby, leading this new nationalist wave, forced its will on successive wavering cabinets. In a period of confusion and bewilderment, it represented conviction and commitment.

By the time the peace treaty with Sadat's Egypt was signed, this reality had already set in, part and parcel of a new political map. What was worse, a deeper process was now under way. The two central events that brought about Israel's birth were the Holocaust and the War of Independence. The experience of newly won sovereignty was so overwhelming that it pushed from national awareness the full meaning of the Holocaust. But as time passed and the veil of secrecy was lifted from classified documents, the West's betrayal of Europe's Jews and a new recognition of Jewish aloneness became painfully apparent. In 1961, Eichmann stood trial in Jerusalem, and young Israelis heard for the first time the whole tale of the horror that had occurred just a few years before statehood. That transition between the most tragic demonstration of Jewish helplessness and the rebirth of Jewish power—between doom and dawn—was so sharp, so traumatic that its impact filtered only gradually into the consciousness of the nation. Just a few years separated the total subjugation of Jews to the Nazi murder machine from their heroic victories in Palestine. Within a short span of time, those orphans of Auschwitz, the relics of Europe's Jewry, became fighter pilots and tank commanders. Within the very same generation, the Jew was transformed from victim to victor. In Amos Oz's unforgettable story, "A Late Love," the elderly hero daydreams about an Israeli armored column marching through Europe avenging the blood of the innocents:

> And with lightning speed my tanks turn and thunder eastward. It's coming, it's coming, it's here. With furious wrath they hound all the bands of the butchers of the Jews: Poles, Lithuanians, Ukrainians. . . . And I see Moshe Dayan, in his dusty battle dress, standing awesome and gaunt, as he receives in a grim silence the surrender of the governor general of Kishinev.[11]

11. Amoz Oz, "A Late Love," *Unto Death* (New York: Harcourt Brace, 1975), 156–158.

But the reflections on this contrast between the stooped march to the gas chambers and the march of Israel's armed heroes raised anew the question of the alleged inherent difference between the galut Jews and the new Hebrews. Was this metamorphosis solely a product of the new reality, of the Zionist rebirth? Is the galut Jew's inferiority truly inherent? And can anti-Semitism be remedied by the Zionist cure-all?

Chief of Staff General David "Dado" Elazar addressed this question a short time before the outbreak of the Yom Kippur War, in a ceremony commemorating the thirtieth anniversary of the Warsaw Ghetto uprising:

> Only five years separate 1943 from 1948, between the revolt of the ghettoes, and the battles of liberation in our land. Only five years separate the most horrific tragedy that our people have ever known from their most glorious victory. When we, fighters of the Palmach, first heard on the sandy beaches of Caesaria the tale told us by the survivors of the Warsaw Ghetto, we felt that we belonged to the same fighting corps, sons of the same nation, fighting the same war. We do not know why and for what reason those millions were massacred in the days of that total eclipse. We do know that they died a thousand cruel and unusual deaths because they were the exiles, the different, the weak, and because we did not have the State of Israel in those cruel days. This is why we are convinced that power is vital. This is why we have sworn to be strong and well armed. This is why we have decided not to live by the sufferance of others.[12]

Such expressions began to raise doubts about truisms previously taken for granted. The Sabra fighter was not inherently different from his allegedly inferior stepbrothers. Their betrayal by the outside world, during World War II, aroused new doubts as to the authenticity of the acceptance of the Jewish state after the war. Did the United Nations General Assembly vote for the partition of Palestine, on that historic night of November 29, 1947, really signify

---

12. Chanoch Bartov, *Dado*, vol. 1 (Tel Aviv, 1978), 261. The English version (Tel Aviv, 1981) does not include this passage.

the opening of a new chapter in the relationship between Jews and Gentiles? Was the recognition of Israel truly a revolutionary occurrence that would have long-range effects, or was it merely a passing event, a nervous and short-lived reaction to European and Christian guilt? Are not the lessons of the Holocaust doomed to be forgotten as the unbearable sights fade into oblivion?

Saul Friedlander, himself a survivor from Nazi Europe, attempted to grapple with these lingering doubts. He dealt with the analogy made by Hannah Arendt between the pariah Jew and the hero of Franz Kafka's *The Castle,* who cannot gain admittance to the castle because he is the foreigner, the nonbelonger. Friedlander saw the analogy particularly pertinent in regard to the end of the novel. When the outsider, the pariah Jew, believes that he is invited to enter the establishment represented by the castle, he discovers that no one is really ready to accept him. He then becomes a halfhearted revolutionary, rebelling against this palpable injustice, siding with the other outcasts of the social system. But the real end of *The Castle,* which Kafka never wrote but which he related to his friend Max Brod—is the most poignant. The hero, the pariah, sinks lower and lower into an abject state, when suddenly a message arrives from the castle: He is accepted. But the message comes too late, the hero is dying or is already dead. Comments Friedlander:

> When, at the end of the war, western society opened its arms to the Jews; when, in reaction to the discovery of the whole magnitude of the Nazi massacres, the western anti-Semitic tradition was—temporarily at least—discarded, most of the Jews of Europe could no longer enter into that new society. But the most terrible question remains to be answered, the one question that will probably never find its answer, although for us it is the most crucial one to understand the past or foresee events to come: Did the castle send the messenger because the injustice, the evil done, was recognized? Or was the messenger sent because the hero was dead?[13]

These were not easily said words, and they were voiced by a spokesman for reason and moderation within Israel. But if such

---

13. Saul Friedlander, "The Historical Significance of the Holocaust," *The Jerusalem Quarterly* 1 (fall 1976): 36, 59–60.

doubts could be cast about the reconciliation between Jews and non-Jews in the wake of Israel's independence, how can one support the basic tenets of Zionist ideology! Had not Herzl been oblivious to the irrational and, therefore, ineradicable element in the rejection of the Jews by the outside world? Is not Herzlian Zionism guilty of a naive belief that turns a blind eye to an ancient and even pre-Christian phenomenon?

Had Israel lived in peace with its Middle Eastern neighbors, it would have been possible to discuss these probing questions dispassionately and frame them within the appropriate global and historical perspectives. But Israel was fated, from its inception, to experience war and Arab rejection, which forged a link between Israelis and their galut parents. In the years preceding the 1967 war, such questions did not pervade the mainstream of Israeli thinking, but their latent rumblings could be heard by the trained ear. Still heading the state in those years were the founding fathers for whom Israel continued to be a miracle, to be anxiously guarded by incorporating her into the fabric of international society. These leaders still clung to the Herzlian credo and staunchly believed in Israel's socialist message.

By the time the Six-Day War broke out, that message had already been eroded by the constant abrasion of harsh facts. From the days of fervor, of pioneering communes and utopian visions, Labor Zionism had to move to a position of political and economic leadership in a country beset by increasingly painful problems. Originally Labor had seen itself as a future leader of the world, as a potential redeemer of the Arab working classes. Through the communal settlements, the Histadrut and the cooperative movement, Labor sought to provide a universal example to both the advanced industrial societies and the underdeveloped countries. Many of Labor's unique achievements have survived the transition from Yishuv to state. Its system of productive cooperation, from the urban cooperative through the partially private moshav to the total collectivity of a kibbutz, remained almost intact in the 1960s, but the cracks in the walls—cracks that would bring the whole structure down after the Likud's victory in 1971—began to appear. But despite all these truly magnificent achievements, Labor has not succeeded in carrying out Ben-Gurion's much-touted vision of Israel's becoming *am segula,* a "chosen" or model nation. Its own socialist tenets have been frustrated by a new poststate reality. Independence has brought to Israel's teeming shores the tired and poor refugees from Arab and Muslim countries. They have come from underprivileged and undereducated societies, and for them the transition from religious-patriarchal patterns to the secular-socialist values of the old-time European settlers has been too radical a step. Most of the new immigrants bypassed the kibbutz movement and gradually formed a new proletariat, whose special problems did not fit into Labor's traditional organization and program. On the international front, Labor managed to establish good relations with her sister parties abroad, had a good standing in the Socialist International, and became a focal point of interest and education for African and Asian students, politicians, and labor leaders. But the voice of its universal message was lost in the sound and fury of the Arab-Jewish wars. In the fifties, the Soviet-led bloc, the "world of the future," for which Labor Zionism had some affinity, and with which leftist factions had fleeting love affairs, turned from friend to foe. In the sixties, the New Left picked Israel as an appropriate target for hate and derision and, together with South Africa, the Jewish state was branded an outcast. Israel, which had set out to lead the world into a new epoch of justice and equality, found itself, even before 1967, gradually edged out of the new Third World entente in which the Muslim and Arab states have played a leading role. The potential leader of enslaved workers was now being castigated as the alleged last stronghold of white imperialism in Asia.

After the Herzlian disappointment with European liberalism at the turn of the century, after the treachery of Europe's extreme Right during World War II, came growing disenchantment with the Left. In the post–World War I era, Zionism was fashionable in progressive circles because it fell within the accepted matrix of self-determination. But after World War II, this concept was conceived as applicable only to the nonwhite, non-European world. Israel was perceived as falling outside this category despite its non-European majority, and its socialist message was often rejected because of this alleged blemish.

On the domestic front, too, Labor lost much of its former appeal after statehood. The utopian message was gradually crushed by the necessity to accommodate Israel's conflicting needs. Industrialization required a new capitalist approach, which was hardly compatible with the Tolstoyan ideals of a return to the soil. Agriculture could not absorb the massive waves of new Jewish refugees; nor was it capable, because of the scarcity of water and land, to solve the country's economic problems. In the communal settlements the traditional commandment of self-work was tainted by the increased employment of hired labor, usually Arab daily workers. A prolonged and unchallenged labor rule proved the universality of Lord Acton's famous dictum about power that corrupts.

In 1977, the Likud government put an end to Labor's monopoly. Since then, in all general elections, the right wing, aided and abetted by a growing and growingly militant religious front, won a majority—a decisive majority among Jews, a small majority among Israelis, as most of the Arab vote went to the Left. The interval of Rabin's government, elected in 1992, was facilitated by a split in the Right that resulted in small right-wing parties not passing the threshold of 1.5 percent. But in 1992, as well as in 1996, the Right could attract more votes than the Left. It was a tragic mistake that the Arabs—Sadat first, Arafat and King Hussein later—decided finally to seek peace with Israel only after this process, and this post–Six-Day War environment became entrenched.

Nevertheless, and despite the escalating verbal war and growing violence of the religious Right, the peace-seeking majority prevailed. It was this majority that supported, despite the alarums and the exhortations, Begin's deal with Sadat, and it was this majority that, more surprisingly, supported the astounding deal made in Oslo: a mutual recognition between Israel and the up-till-then vilified PLO. The religious Right, augmented by an increasingly nationalist ultra-orthodoxy, demonstrated, warned, threatened, and cajoled, but the Oslo accords were given, despite the initial shock, a clear backing in public opinion polls. The Likud leadership could not even impose party discipline on three dissenting deputies who decided to abstain in the Knesset vote approving the Oslo accords by a sixty-one to fifty majority. The old craving, to put an end to bloodshed and partition the land between the two opponents, was still alive.

Why, then, did Labor lose in 1996—narrowly among Israelis, decisively among Israeli Jews? Aside from organizational and propaganda failures, the main reason was plain and simple: Acts of terrorism by the Islamists, and, more important, the failure of the

Palestinian authority to wage war against them, as well as the almost instinctive Arab venom leveled against Israel and Israelis, were Netanyahu's best campaign tools. Not only did Netanyahu use Islamist terror as his main propaganda tool, he also managed to appeal to the deeply rooted anxiety that had accumulated, layer upon layer, since that crucial watershed—the Six-Day War.

7

Toward Rabin's Assassination

Rabin's assassination was not a single shot, nor was it a single unforeseen incident perpetrated by a single deranged person. It was predestined, foreseen, forewarned. A chain of events, starting with the victory in the 1967 war led up to it, almost inevitably, almost by a random sequence of events. Yet not all the players in this tragedy foresaw its bloody ending. Most of the actors and participants certainly did not desire it. But looking back, we know now that it all started thirty years before the three shots were fired in the Tel Aviv square.

We have seen, in the previous chapter, the political transmutations that have changed the face of Israel since the Six-Day War. This process had an easily recognizable opening scene.

On April 4, 1968, the eve of Passover, a group of sixty Israeli Jews arrived at Hebron. With their children, the ten families went to a small Arab hotel that they had rented for the holidays. The members of the group had told the Israeli military authorities that they were going to stay in the hotel for only two days; to the owner of the hotel, they presented themselves as tourists from Switzerland. Ostensibly, no fault could be found with this pilgrimage of observant Jews seeking to spend the holidays in a town whose very name arouses biblical memories.

Yet this innocuous Passover in Hebron marked the rise of a new religious movement destined to change the course of Israel's fortunes.

The ten families were headed by Rabbi Moshe Levinger, up to then a marginal figure known in religious circles for his total devotion, as well as for his quarrelsome nature. Under his leadership, the mission to Hebron was well organized: The families were all hand picked; the financing was done by the Movement for Greater Israel, which originated after 1967; the whole operation was kept secret from the mass media and came as a total surprise to most cabinet members.

The visitors took over the two-story Park Hotel, turned its kitchen kosher, celebrated the Seder in high spirits, and went on to announce that they were not going to let anyone eject them from the town of the Patriarchs.

The cabinet was caught unaware by this unilateral act. Levinger's men were openly defying the government's authority, blatantly trying to force its hand and compel it to include Hebron in its settlement plans. The military authorities and the defense establishment were patently resentful. Hebron, a devout Muslim town, had not been giving the Israelis any trouble at the time and its mayor, Sheikh Ali Ja'abri, cooperated with the military authorities in ensuring a peaceful coexistence between the Hebronites and the new regime. It was no accident that no representative of the military governor came to visit the Jewish guests exposed to danger in midst of an Arab town. But others did come: rabbis, settlers from nearby kibbutzim, leaders of the Movement for Greater Israel, and hundreds of enthusiastic supporters from all over the country. The news that the Jews were returning to Hebron ignited a dormant spark of half-forgotten memories. Hebron was the town where the patriarch Abraham, the Father of the Nation, bought for four hundred shekels of silver his first piece of land in Canaan, the field of Ephron the Hittite. In the Cave of Machpelah he buried his wife Sarah, thus gaining the first foothold in a land promised to his seed.

For hundreds of years after the Jews went into Exile, Hebron remained with Jerusalem, Safed, and Tiberias, one of the "holy cities," in which the scattered Jewish communities in Palestine huddled, waiting for redemption. In 1929 its thriving Jewish community was virtually wiped out by an Arab massacre, and the tales of the atrocities committed then became imprinted in the national memory of the Yishuv. After the 1929 riots, Jews were not permitted to live in Hebron. And ever since the Muslim conquest of Palestine,

Jews were not allowed to enter the Tomb of the Patriarchs, a mosque that the Muslims regarded as exclusively theirs. It was time to right this humiliating wrong. Labor Minister Yigal Allon, who had also come to visit Rabbi Levinger's group in order to lend support, said: "There have always been Jews in Hebron, the cradle of the nation, until they were violently uprooted. . . . It is inconceivable that Jews be prohibited from settling in this ancient town of the Patriarchs."[1]

Thus began a protracted cat-and-mouse game between a hesitant and divided government and a determined, widely supported group. The religious settlers not only had faith on their side; they also spoke ostensibly in the name of the very right upon which the Zionist claim to Eretz Israel has always been founded. The political debate, the rights of the Palestinians, were shunned.

The settlers' announcement that they were not going to leave Hebron prompted a nationwide debate. Emotion clashed with reason. Thinking Israelis foresaw the dangers inherent in the resettlement of Hebron, and *Ha'aretz,* the Tel Aviv daily, warned against succumbing to this fait accompli. Theirs was a reasoned appeal to accept the partition of Palestine between Jews and Arabs and to refrain from actions that would both disrupt peaceful relations with the Hebronites and weaken Israel's international posture. But these arguments seemed ineffective in the face of such highly charged symbols as the settlers' wish to celebrate the return to Hebron of a Torah scroll saved from the 1929 pogrom. The Torah had been saved from the blazing synagogue by a rabbi who later died from burns suffered in the rescue, the scroll at his head. Before he died, the rabbi bequeathed the scroll to a friend, stipulating that when the Jews returned to Hebron, he should bring the Torah back to its ancient abode. Now the grandson of that venerable rabbi was seeking to fulfill his last wish. Could this wish be denied by the Jewish authorities? Could reasons of expedience countervail such an act of faith? Indeed, the military authorities eventually had to rescind their prohibition against the public installation of the scroll at the settlers' newly established synagogue, even though such action lent an air of permanence to what had started as a pilgrimage.

---

1. *Ha'aretz* (Hebrew daily) (Tel Aviv), 16 April 1968.

Eventually, this was to become a precedent-setting case. The government capitulated and Qiryat-Arba, the Jewish town bordering Hebron, was established. Gush Emunim—as this movement was later named—won a decisive victory.

Rabbi Levinger's enterprise demonstrated the new orientation of religious Jewry, as well as its newly discovered power. Leaders of Kiryat Arba, a Jewish settlement bordering Hebron, indicated that the religious-nationalist movement now had the determination, the stamina, and the men to impose its will upon a wavering political establishment.

The new self-confidence gave birth to Gush Emunim. The Gush officially came into being in 1974, shortly after the Yom Kippur War. But Gush members had been active as a pro-settlement movement from the time of the successful enterprise of Kiryat Arba. The group consisted of idealistic young men and women within National Religious Party circles and was naturally embraced by the Movement for Greater Israel. They were educated in state religious schools and in Bnai Akiva, a religious youth movement whose graduates set up some of the country's most successful communal settlements. Many of the Gush leaders went to a yeshiva headed by Rabbi Zvi Yehuda Kook, son of Chief Rabbi Kook, who in an earlier generation had established the doctrinal bridge linking religious and secular Zionists. Before the war, their voices had never been heard in political controversies. They were, up to then, the "knitted skullcap good boys,"a reference to the one article of clothing and their unassuming manners that distinguished them from their secular Sabra contemporaries. But after the "liberation of [their] forefathers' estate" in Hebron, they were to become the religious spearhead of a national demand to retain the whole of Eretz Israel under Jewish sovereignty and to implement this claim by settlement.

In dealing with the phenomenon of Gush Emunim and the other groups of religious-nationalist zealotry that sprang into action after 1967, it is important to realize that their significance is not confined to the political arena and does not lie merely in their ability to force their will upon the country. Gush Emunim—the name is used here collectively to denote all the religious militant groups—provides a vociferous, and occasionally, theatrical voice to a wider tendency within Israeli society. Just as the Hebrew "Canaanites" were in effect an expression of the Yishuv education that saw in the negation of galut the essence of the new society, so the dedicated members of the Gush are a product of poststate society and the state religious education network. In the Yishuv there were also religious personalities who saw in the Return to Eretz Israel and its settlement the beginning of redemption in the religious sense, but never before were the deeds and actions themselves clothed with a Messianic meaning. In addition, religious Zionists shared with their secular colleagues a philosophy that saw Jewish nationalism in a universal and humanistic context. The two main religious parties, Hamizrachi and Ha'poel Hamizrachi, never resorted to mystical terms and never cast any doubt on the underlying Herzlian premises of Zionist thought. On the contrary, in the period preceding the Six-Day War, the religious parties, who sat in a Labor-led government coalition, were the traditional spokesmen for moderation and restraint in the country's foreign and defense policy and often spoke out and voted against the retaliatory border raids that Ben-Gurion initiated in the 1950s. When the Six-Day War broke out, their two ministers voiced their view against taking East Jerusalem—a stunning and unbelievable fact in today's atmosphere.

The new religious tenor of the post-1967 mood was radically different and viewed the whole Zionist endeavor in a new light. Rabbi Yehuda Amital, now a leader of the moderate Meimad movement, defined this Zionism of Redemption:

> This Zionism does not seek to solve the problem of the Jews by setting up a Jewish state but is an instrument in the hands of the Almighty which prepares the people of Israel for their Redemption. The settlement of Eretz Israel through the ingathering of her sons, the greening of her deserts, and the establishment of Jewish independence within it are merely stages in this process of Redemption. The purpose of this process is not the normalization of the people of Israel—to be a nation like all other nations—but to be a holy people, a people of a living God.[2]

This open defiance of Herzlian Zionism, and of everything the Labor movement stood for, was repeated wherever and whenever

---

2. Yehuda Amital, *Ha'ma'alot Mima'makim* (Up from the depths) (Jerusalem, 1974), 42–43.

the Gush spokesmen defined their philosophy. Their views were characterized by a self-confidence untarnished by any doubt or uncertainty. The Six-Day War and the Yom Kippur War brought in their wake typical, soul-searching dialogues among secular Sabra soldiers. Some of these dialogues were published and were acclaimed for their inherent humanity, hatred of war, and yearning for peace. But a similar dialogue at a Gush yeshiva yielded no self-doubt. The specter of constant war and bloodshed did not deter the participants. Rabbi Meir Yehiel rejected the very ideas that had become synonymous with Zionism: "We have not settled here to look for peace and quiet; we have come here despite the sound and the fury, in order to fulfill the Lord's command; consequently, no obstacle shall obstruct or hinder us."[3]

This was the state of mind of the Gush and its many supporters. Their credo was enchantingly simple: The Land of Israel to the People of Israel according to the Torah of Israel. The existence of a prosperous Diaspora did not weaken their resolve, because a true fulfillment of religious commandments—principally, the commandment to settle the Land of Israel—was possible only in Israel. Chosenness needs no substitute because it relates directly to the idea of the Covenant between God and his people as manifested in the new reality of Israel. Israel is the embodiment of that Covenant.

Israel's difficulties could thus be explained in light of its ancient history and special mission. Biblical quotes acquired a direct relevance, and its wars and armed struggles were an integral part of a truly Messianic process leading to true redemption.

The Lord's words to Abraham acquire, in the eyes of the Gush followers, a direct, political meaning. The land is bestowed by divine will, whose authority cannot be gainsaid by secular institutions and considerations of political expedience. The recruits of the Gush are Israelis, molded in the state religious school network (which is financed by public funds but has its own independent supervisory boards and curricula). Unlike the Zionist religious founders, who were educated in Europe and were constantly aware of the precarious situation of the Jews, these young militants grew up in an atmosphere emphasizing Israel's might and the world's hostility. More important is the Gush readiness to apply the traditional

---

3. Meir Yehiel, *Machshavot* (Thoughts) (Benei Brak, 1975), 7–8.

pioneering spirit to the new reality: They call on their faithful to leave towns, abandon their comfortable urban abodes, and settle the barren land—in the tradition of the old days of unadulterated idealism. The Bible lives in the ancient names they give their settlements, in the constant reference to the sights and sounds linking the new Jewish presence to evidence of its past glory: the Tomb of the Patriarchs in Hebron, the wall built by King Herod around Solomon's Temple, the very hills—Shiloh and Beth-El—where Jewish kings and priests uttered their immortal words.

After the victory in Hebron the Gush succeeded not only within the religious segment, transforming it from a moderate force to the vanguard of extremism, but also within large parts of the secular sector. Many nonobservant Israelis, including major political and literary figures, began to regard the Gush as the true executors of a national will, as the authentic successors to the pioneering tradition and a valuable barrier against compromise with, and surrender to, external pressures. Within Labor itself a circle was formed that pledged allegiance to the Gush, and its policy found favor in Labor's settlement lobby. The influence of the Gush, always numerically a small fractional minority—on Labor cannot be overestimated. They imposed their will on successive Labor cabinets and forced the government's hand on critical issues. They openly defied Rabin's first cabinet by establishing in 1973 an illegal settlement in Sebastia, threatened to clash with the army, and managed, despite this challenge to the government's authority, to have their way. In reality they did not have to force their will; the Labor cabinets themselves were split on the proper attitude to the Gush, and many of their tacit supporters occupied important positions in Labor's hierarchy.

When the Likud came into power in 1977, the hold of the Gush on the government was complete. Prime Minister Begin had been an avid Gush supporter before his ascent to power; he participated in their marches and attended the ceremonies establishing their settlements. Under his leadership, the government elevated the Gush to a leading settlement movement; showered money on its projects, creating in effect a Gush militia in their settlements; and surrendered to its wishes whenever there was a clash of wills. The Camp David accords and the peace treaty with Egypt hindered this romance with the government, but on the Gush's major point, the settlement of Judea and Samaria, the two agreed. Any government attempts to resist the growing demands of the Gush gave way to its "moral pressure."

In Begin's second term, starting in 1981—as well as under Shamir's cabinet—there was no need to resort to such tactics. Settlement on a wide scale on expropriated land acquired new dimensions with the establishment of "dormitory suburbs" in the West Bank, thus luring many Israelis to purchase an apartment or a house, attractively priced, within an easy ride from their work. Gush Emunim can be seen as the ideological trailblazers in whose steps followed thousands of ordinary Israelis.

Thus, after the 1967 watershed, the Gush became the spearhead, the guiding light, of the new Israeli Right. This new Right had three components: the Labor supporters of the Movement for Greater Israel; the new religious zealots; and the old nationalist Right, formerly the Jabotinsky-led Revisionists, now transformed into the Begin-led Herut Party. The Gush transformed the old Revisionist Right. The new Right was hardly recognizable as the heir of the old nationalists.

Young Israelis find it hard to believe that Begin's forerunners were wholly irreligious and objected to any form of religious tampering with politics. Jabotinsky, Begin's leader and mentor, was so detached from ways Judaic that he advocated the adoption of Latin script for modern Hebrew and willed his body to be cremated—an act that is contrary to Jewish law and every Jewish instinct. Today, it is difficult to believe that the atheist Nordau, the total European who was ready to forgo the Jewish Sabbath, was acclaimed by the old Revisionists as their very own prophet, that his writings were published by them and edited by Benjamin Netanyahu's father. The leadership of the new religious nationalists obliterated all this. It brought to the Israeli Right a combination inherently hostile to its traditional tenets. In place of a secular, pro-Western orientation, the Gush returned to Jewish singularity, shining in its loneliness against the dark backdrop of an alleged universal rejection. Instead of the political action and international recognition regarded by both Herzl and Jabotinsky as primary tools, the Gush created "facts" by settling the land. Yet, under the new, post-1967 circumstances, the secular Right readily accepted this mantle and gave total support to a political ideology that was, in many respects, foreign to everything it had preached in the past.

The Gush's emphasis on settling the land naturally appealed to the more activist elements in the Labor movement and its various settlement organizations. Settling the land had always been more than a means toward accomplishing the Return to the Homeland. It had always been the cornerstone of the Labor Zionist ethic. Settling the land fulfilled two functions. The actual, physical act of populating the land extended the Jewish holdings in Palestine and created new sources of livelihood. The nonmaterial aspect of settling the land provided a symbol for the Zionist revolution. It represented an act of defiance against everything that was negative—galut, parasitism, capitalism—and an affirmation of all things positive—earthiness, independence, socialism.

All Zionist youth movements have consecrated attachment to the soil as a hallowed commandment. Their whole educational system, until very recently, was aimed at bringing Jewish youth to self-fulfillment through one channel: joining a settlement. Few among the Labor leadership, past and present, have not had their days in a kibbutz. In fact, the Hebrew terms depicting settlement and settlers have acquired such a unique meaning that they are hardly translatable. English equivalents are somewhat misleading, as they are sometimes charged with negative connotations. The Hebrew connotations are all positive and synonymous with "pioneering," "new frontiers," "rural innocence." The very name of the Jewish community in Palestine, the Yishuv, means "settlement."

When the Gush applied this Zionist ethos to the sites of biblical Eretz Israel, when it enlisted thousands of enthusiastic idealists to carry out the traditional Zionist task of "self-fulfillment," it naturally aroused acclaim and support from many Labor circles, particularly from its powerful kibbutz and moshav movements. Some, like Moshe Shamir, former leftist author, became the secular spokesmen for the Gush, seeing in traditional Jewish elements, as distinct from Herzlian Zionism, the true force governing Jewish and Israeli history. They turned their backs on the old much-shaken Labor dogma and found new solace in the renascent forces of religious-inspired nationalism.

In the early 1980s, Yacov Chazan, veteran leader of the left-wing Mapam, stunned his followers by his admiration for the pioneers of the Gush. They reminded him of his movement's early days: they shared "the readiness to take upon them the toughest national

challenges, the stubborn holding-on to the soil in the most dangerous places, the mutual assistance, the readiness to the self-fulfilment
of their ambitions."[4]

The ideological foundation of the Gush has all the features of a
panacea, and their Zionism is part of a fundamentalist religious outlook. From this viewpoint, the wheel of history has gone a full turn.
The Jewish people are returning to pre-Herzlian, Messianic yearnings; but unlike their helplessness in the past, their present might can
be used to implement their right. The demand for a Greater Israel is
not dictated by security needs; it is a manifestation of a right, a duty
that Jews have no authority to relinquish. The perception of Israel
in the world must also undergo radical transformation. The
Herzlian vision of a normalized relationship between Israel—the
state and the people—and the outside world is replaced with the
new interpretation given to biblical maxims. Balaam's blessing, in
Numbers, of the people who "shall dwell alone and among the
nations shall not be reckoned" is seen as a prophecy with a direct
and political relevance to the Jewish state. The Return to Zion is not
to be a return to the family of nations but its diametric opposite—a
new polarization between the Jews and the Gentiles of the earth.
Harold Fish, former rector of the religious Bar Ilan University,
emphasizes this in his book *The Zionist Revolution*. According to
Fish, Zionism was not a result of the emancipation of the Jews but
had its foundation in Jewish liturgy and myth. In today's post-
Enlightenment world, he asks, does not the Zionism of Herzl and
Weizmann "begin to look a trifle old-fashioned"?[5]

Fish, like other new religious nationalists, sees Zionism as a
movement dominated by pre-Herzlian religious sentiments and
spearheaded by the Orthodox immigration to Palestine. The
Zionism with which he identifies preceded political Zionism and
had no relation to the rational, secular, and liberal trends defecting
Herzlian thought.

This new perception involves more than the question of origins.
In this formulation, the very status of the land Eretz Israel takes on
a new mystical meaning, radically different from that attributed to
it in classic Zionist thought. Even those Zionists who vehemently

---

4. Zeev Tsachor, *Chazan* (Jerusalem, 1977), 264–265.
5. Harold Fish, *The Zionist Revolution* (London, Weidenfeld and Nicholson, 1978), 7.

rejected any alternative to Zion, such as Uganda—the "Palestinian Zionists," as they were called—saw the Return to Zion as the only national solution to the problems of postemancipation Jewry. The redemption was that of the people and their values, not a redemption of the land per se. Eretz Israel was the only framework within which such a solution could take place, but it was never seen as having an eschatological meaning, or as a metaphysical entity, standing above reality and beyond the needs of the people.

Israel's Declaration of Independence adopted this inherently secular view characteristic of political Zionism:

> The Land of Israel was the birthplace of the Jewish people. Here their spiritual, religious, and national identity was formed. Here they achieved independence and created a culture of national and universal significance. Here they wrote and gave the Bible to the world.

But is not such a perception somewhat outdated, according to the new post-1967 religious thinking? Is not the land itself sacred? Joel Florsheim, a religious thinker, explains how utterly mistaken was the approach of the declaration. This paragraph (quoted earlier), he claims, is not peculiar to the Jewish people, and its contents could be applicable to all other nations: "We need only replace the terms 'Israel' and 'the Jewish people' with the parallel terms and instead of 'the Bible' insert the appropriate cultural contribution; in other words, this view expresses the Zionist yearning for normalization."[6] Florsheim shatters one by one the factual statements of the declaration. The people of Israel were not born in Eretz Israel but in Egypt and the desert, in God's words to Moses; their spiritual, religious, and national identity—from the Babylonian Talmud to Zionism itself—was formed mainly in exile, outside the land of Israeli, its cultural and universal contribution was certainly the fruit of long periods of exile and dispersal when the Jews lived far from the Promised Land.

What, then, is the real status of the Land of Israel? It is based on an idea that "there is an ideological chasm between the people of

---

6. Joel Florsheim, "Mahi Eretz Israel? Le'am Israel?" *Petahim* (Quarterly of Jewish thought) 47–48 (September 1979): 66.

Israel and the nations of the earth until this very day." Eretz Israel is
a constituent part of a universal message: God Almighty is not only
the creator of the world but also king of the universe, and his kingdom takes body in the obligation undertaken by the Jewish people
in the Covenant with Abraham the patriarch, which preordained
that the Land of Canaan shall be granted as an estate in perpetuity
to the seed of Abraham. This is divine will and justice, and without
it there is no way of explaining the Jewish claim to the Holy Land
and the priority of this claim over Arab right. Without this divine
justification, the restitution of the land to the Jews is an irrational
act spelling injustice to the Arab inhabitants of Palestine. According
to this view, Zionism has committed a basic error: "It failed, because
of the attempt to turn the Jewish people into something which they
are not—a normal nation—and thus turn Eretz Israel into something which it is not, what every homeland is to the people living
in it."

In other words, Israel's solitary position is a necessary and
unavoidable outcome of the uniqueness of the Jews, a fate Zionism
sought in vain to escape, and not an affliction that descended upon
the state.

Another religious thinker, Chaim Peles, expresses the same fundamentalist idea in a different vein: Zionist history is divided into
three parts that are constituents of a dialectical development. The
thesis is represented by the religious precursors of Zionism who preceded Herzl and spoke of the Return in exclusively observant terms;
the antithesis is secular Herzlian Zionism, which succeeded in creating a state but failed to infuse it with Jewish content and consequently reached, after the Yom Kippur War, a point of spiritual
bankruptcy; the synthesis is the post–Yom Kippur War, which is
characterized by a new religious-national renaissance. This new
form of religious Zionism extends the ancient concept of commandments, which are not to be contravened whatever the cost, to the
injunction prohibiting the relinquishing of any part of Eretz Israel.
Hence it does not share, according to Peles, "the traditional anxieties of Zionism and the secular camp, who are horrified by the
prospect of Israel's isolation." On the contrary, it is precisely this
solitude that the Gush relishes. Balaam's blessing comes to life: Israel
shall indeed dwell alone and not be reckoned by the nations and not
reckon with them. This "splendid isolation" is necessary; otherwise

the state might lose its right to, and sole justification for, its independent existence. Moreover, Balaam's curse-turned-into-blessing is necessary in order to retain that very Jewish uniqueness "which we refused to sell for a mess of pottage."[7]

Accordingly, Israel's isolation, and even its wars, are seen as acts of divine grace. Peles says:

> The reason for the prohibition to make a pact of friendship and love with the goyim is that we should not fraternize with them too much, so as not to learn from their ways. The people of Israel are presently in such a state that a formal peace with the Arabs will bring about assimilation of large parts of our people in the Semitic region. Consequently, we may see in the state of war between us and the Arabs the hand of Providence which sees to it that the integrity of the people is maintained.[8]

Rabbi Yaacov Ariel adds that the religious Jew, despite his higher moral stature, objects to peace because he retains "a more developed historical consciousness, which does not let him forget the events of his past and induces in him a more cautious attitude toward the outside world." Moreover, the opposition to peace is draped in an ideological cloak: Peace, like the concept of Redemption, cannot be a secular, earthly matter. Peace, like Redemption, can have only a religious, Messianic meaning. "Believing Jews who hold the idea of peace as a sacred prophetic and sublime ideal are not prepared to convert it into a phoney 'peace' of trips to the pyramids."[9]

Thus, true peace becomes a metaphysical concept involving a millennial recognition of the absolute monotheism of the Lord who is One, and a recognition by non-Jews of Jewish Jerusalem as their "spiritual capital." Peace—the goal toward which every Zionist stream and faction has always striven—is not included in the political platform of the Gush and is relegated to a distant millennial future.

---

7. Chaim Peles, "The Dialectical Development of the Zionist Idea," *Deot* (A journal of religious academics) 45 (1976): 333.
8. Ibid.
9. Israel Sadan, "Talks with No'am Student," *Niv Ha'midrashiyah* (Religious periodical) 11 (1974): 159.

Some are not content to stop there: Aloneness is not sufficient. In order to complete the return to pre-Herzlian concepts, the relationship between Israel and the world must be grounded on that very "eternal hatred" between Jews and Gentiles that Zionism sought to cure. Thus, Rabbi Ephraim Zemmel describes the conflict between Israel and the outside world as part of a "satanic heritage" that puts every "descendent of Esau in a consistent and perpetual ambush against the sons of Israel, so as to hurt and destroy them when the opportunity arises." The origins of this conflict are not to be found in mere human factors but in the "confrontation between Good and Evil in the world of eternity and in Satan's ambition to uproot our Holy Scriptures." Furthermore, nothing can be done to relieve this bitter and eternal hatred. In fact, this hatred is "growing by leaps and bounds from generation to generation." For this reason, there is no point is seeking any political solution, as the "forces of Satan will not abide the existence of the people of Israel" and "[they] would be better off isolated from the nations of the earth."[10] Moreover, the present conflicts of Israel are a direct continuation of biblical sagas: Israel's condemnation by the Security Council is part of the conflict between Esau and Jacob, and the ongoing war with the Arabs is directly related to the struggle between Isaac and Ishmael.

In Gush parlance, the Arabs are the Ishmaelites, Jesuits, Amalekites, and the seven Canaanite peoples against which the Pentateuch rails. Rabbi Israel Sadan claims: "The people of Israel are not like the other nations. All our efforts to integrate into the Middle East are doomed. The whole world is on the one side and we are on the other. If we forget this uniqueness, Esau and Ishmael will remind us of this fact by whips and scorpions."[11] Biblical and halachic dicta are cited as directly applicable to Israel's security dilemmas. The Deuteronomy injunction to smite Amalek and "blot out his memory" is taken, despite all religious evidence to the contrary, as referring to the Arabs. Consequently, and because Israel's wars are described as a "war of religious obligation," ordinary rules of humanity should not be applicable to these new "Amalekites." Rabbi Menachem M. Kasher, in his post-1967 essay entitled "The Great Era," maintains that this astounding analogy should be made

---

10. Yehiel, *Machshavot*, 6, 8.
11. Sadan, "Talks with No'am Student," 159.

and that the biblical verse ". . . I will drive them out before you little by little, until you have increased and possess the land," applies to Israel's relationship with the Arabs. Military rabbinical chaplains have scandalized the public by asserting that under Halachic law, Arab civilians may be killed in these wars of religious obligation. Rabbi Israel Hess, of Bar Ilan University, went even further and unwittingly mocked his own views by resorting to Muslim terminology and declaring that "God personally intervenes in this war of religious obligation against the Amalekites and declares a counter-*Jihad* against them." Lest anyone miss the innuendo, the article, published by the Bar Ilan Students Union, is entitled "The Torah's Commandment of Genocide."[12]

In this semimystical world, where ancient quotations are taken out of their historical context and Judaism's great humanistic tradition is thrown to the wind, Messianism acquires a strange interpretation, unprecedented in Jewish thought. The millennial vision of peace to all nations and divine justice reigning throughout the universe is left in its traditional place—a distant era of Revealed End, a target of age-old yearnings and aspirations. On the other hand, the political reality of Israel's existence and wars is seen as a present manifestation of this otherwise remote vision. In the blunt language of the late Rabbi Zvi Yehuda Kook, this Messianic quality manifests itself in every aspect of Israel's political and military might: "The Israel Defense Army is total sanctity, it represents the rule of the people of the Lord over his Land."[13] The territories conquered by Israel are thus also clothed in sanctity and rabbinical pronouncements are issued with monotonous regularity proclaiming that the relinquishing of these lands bequeathed by the Patriarchs is an act of sacrilege. One faction claimed that according to its interpretation of biblical sources, there is hardly room for non-Jews in Israel. Rabbi Eliezer Waldenberg, holder of the prestigious 1976 Israel Prize for Halachic Studies, argues that a non-Jew should be forbidden to live in Jerusalem and that "we should have driven all the goyim away from Jerusalem and purified it completely."[14] Similarly, non-Jews should not be allowed to form a majority in any Israeli city.

---

12. *Bat Kol,* (Bar Ilan University students' journal), 26 February 1980.
13. Zvi Yehuda Kook, *Lentivot Israel* (Jerusalem, 1967), 118–119.
14. *Ha'aretz,* 9 May 1976.

Thus, a growing identity was established between chauvinistic and xenophobic extremism and the religious community in Israel.

The total identification of religious Zionism with this dogma is not universal, and it certainly does not extend to the Sephardic Shas Party and its spiritual leader, Rabbi Ovadia Yosef. Within the National Religious Party there are islands of dissent; Meimad under the leadership of Rabbi Yehudah Amital wages a courageous and laudable campaign for a return to the humanistic Jewish tradition.

But there is no doubt as to who has the upper hand and leads the national religious camp. An appeal launched by religious academics and published in the Israeli press in 1977 calling the faithful to prayer was typical of the new mood engulfing the country. It did not come from an obscure group of fanatics but from highly respectable religious professors at various Israeli universities, who stated:

> When we ponder the root causes of Israel's difficulties, we find ourselves of necessity entertaining a sense of loneliness, in keeping with the biblical saying, "People that shall dwell alone and among the nations it shall not be reckoned," beginning with Abraham the Hebrew, "All the world on one side and Abraham on the other side" until our very days, this period of Holocaust and Revival. Our situation resembles that of the Children of Israel standing on the shore of the Red Sea, surrounded on all sides by enemies, both near and far, desirous of destroying us.[15]

The religious-nationalist message of the Gush gave an ostensibly complete answer to the question of Israel's place in history. As distinct from the soul-searching questions of Israelis who saw old foundations giving way to new doubts and ancient instincts, the Gush statement is based on an alleged unshaken continuity of Jewish history. The power of the Gush lies, therefore, not only in its capacity to establish settlements but also in its capacity to place an ideological exclamation mark where questions still linger.

Before we discuss the issue of how the religious Right succeeded in forcing its own agenda on the nonreligious population—still the overwhelming majority in the country—we must first examine two

---

15. A paid advertisement in several journals.

developments that took place in the 1980s and 1990s. One bears upon the haredi public—and the second, upon the radical direction taken by the national-religious camp.

From the outset, both sections of the haredi camp, the Ashkenazi and Sepharadi, had doubts and reservations about the Messianic and nationalistic fervor of Gush Emunim and their like. There were good reasons for these reservations. From the theological aspect, the haredi, non-Zionist camp could not accept the concept of the Zionist redemption or the vision of Messianism, which has its source in military and physical strength. Ultimately, this was the essence of the haredi opposition to the Zionist attempt "to hasten the Redemption," to defy the nations of world, and to commit a profanation of God's name, a sin so terrible that some haredi rabbis see it as the reason for the Holocaust. But beyond this halachic reservation, there were fears as well. The haredim were frightened lest this nationalism lead to a clash with the nations of the world and to catastrophe, which should be avoided at all costs because of the prohibition against endangering human life.

Moreover, because the members of the haredi community do not serve in the army, and because the toll in human lives was constantly increasing, the haredi rabbis and leadership did not want to contribute to the inflammation of passions and to a policy that could lead to an additional military confrontation, in which they do not participate. But this position was also gradually worn down. After the Knesset elections of 1977 a new situation was created. Not only did the elections lead to a political upheaval with the election of Menachem Begin as prime minister, but for the first time since the establishment of the state, the haredim—first Agudat Yisrael and later Shas—had become an increasingly powerful balance pivot that could tip the scales of power either way. In the 1977 elections, Agudat Yisrael decided in favor of joining a coalition headed by the Likud, thereby setting a precedent for the future. Since that time, the haredim have preferred to support the Right, and the participation of Shas in Yitzhak Rabin's government was made possible because of two singular factors: Rabbi Ovadiah Yosef's personal support for the peace process, and the formation of a "blocking majority" made up of the left-wing and Arab parties, which prevented a Likud-led government from being formed. In 1990, Shimon Peres initiated a maneuver, known bluntly as the "dirty trick," that sought to unseat

Prime Minister Shamir with the help of the Haredim. But the maneuver failed with the decision of Rabbi Schach to continue to support a Likud-led government.

This political preference was, in fact, supported by the general atmosphere prevalent in the haredi community, drawn more and more to the commandment of settling the Land of Israel and other symbols generally characteristic of the national-religious camp. The Left, in any case, was hated because of its being identified with secularism—"eaters of rabbits," as Rabbi Schach put it at a gathering in 1990, when he announced his support for the Likud. The Right was perceived as more amenable from a religious aspect, even though its very leaders may have been guilty of transgressing the severest of biblical prohibitions. Thus, support for the more extreme ideas put forth by Gush Emunim and the rabbis of the settlements grew among the haredi community. The Chabad movement headed by the Lubavitcher Rebbe came out in full support of the Movement for Greater Israel camp and became one of its political engines. Gradually, caution evaporated, along with fear of the goyim, and the fear of endangering life was now replaced by a new haredi-nationalistic coalition, unheard of in the past. This coalition led to an almost total identification of the most extreme elements in the religious Right with the large and increasingly stronger masses of non-Zionist haredim. This was a paradox: Those who refused to recognize Israeli national symbols—the flag, anthem, and memorial days—whose representatives in the government publicly announced their refusal to send their sons to the army, now identified with the nationalistic policies of the Right. In the period that preceded the Rabin assassination, the haredi press outdid itself in its invective and abuse aimed at him and his government. Haredi groups were active in violent demonstrations and incitement against Rabin, and in the 1996 Knesset elections all the haredi groups joined forces, spearheaded by Chabad and the followers of Rabbi Schach, in a massive propaganda campaign under the slogan "Only Netanyahu is good for the Jews." In their all-out effort to help Netanyahu to be elected, rabbis directed yeshivot to suspend Torah studies and to send yeshiva students out to the streets. Election fever reached such a pitch that even mourners were ordered to interrupt their "Shiva" mourning period and vote for Netanyahu. When two youths were caught spitting and urinating on Rabin's tomb, it did not come as any great surprise to the Israeli public to hear that they were haredi yeshiva students. Even the refusal of some haredi journals to attach the words "of blessed memory" to the late prime minister's name— common Jewish practice—did not have any serious reverberations. In fact, three elements, both in and beyond the settlements, began to grow closer: the extremists among the settlers, Kahane followers, and the haredi-nationals joined together under one umbrella, inflamed by the common denominator of their extreme nationalist-religious anti-Arab, anti-Gentile, antisecular sentiments. Yigal Amir, Yitzhak Rabin's assassin, and his large group of supporters are all products of this amalgam, and it is difficult to attribute them to just one component of it.

Indeed, there has been an entente between the various elements of religious and haredi Jews, both Ashkenazi and Sepharadi, with the unifying element being national and halachic extremism.

> Religious Zionism moved from political expressions of extra-halachic nationalism and Messianic historic philosophy to the halachic dialogue, and it is now seeking within Jewish law a grounding for its nationalistic outlook. The haredi public is now going in the opposite direction: from an isolated parochial halachic world, content to leave the political game and decisions to others, committed to ghettolike "dovish" positions ("don't provoke the goyim"), it has moved in the direction of the militant nationalistic discourse.[16]

Thus, a surprising and unexpected alliance has been formed between two camps that not long ago had been clearly and unequivocally distinct from each other: They differed on matters of national symbols, army service, integration in general society. A large and powerful political bloc came into being that opposed the "hedonist secular Israelis" from within, and the enemy—Ishmael, Amalek, Esau—from without. In fact, this large political camp had adopted many of the concepts propagated by Meir Kahane. He was the source of the appellation "Hellenists," originally referring to Jews

---

16. S. Fischer, "Haredim min Hashalom" (Frightened of peace), *Theory and Critique* 9 (1996): 233, 235. The author is a member of Meimad.

who adopted Hellenist culture during the Second Temple period, for the secular population.

What was the source of this extremism before the 1996 elections? Where did the animosity against Yitzhak Rabin come from? How can we explain that, according to statistical samples, in the haredi camp there was not even a tiny element who voted for Shimon Peres, with all the votes going en bloc to Netanyahu? There can be no doubt that the principal reason is none other than the peace process—the success of the Rabin government in extricating Israel from the cycle of hostility dividing Israel from the world surrounding it. All at once it seemed as if traditional barriers were being broken down, those that seemed to protect the Jewishness of Israel and its religious population. The spectacles of the various ceremonies held in Oslo, Washington, Cairo, the Aravah desert, and Amman, which warmed the hearts of the Israeli public, dismayed and appalled those who considered themselves the protectors of Jewish tradition and law. The handshake with Arafat and other Arab leaders set off alarm bells: the border, along with the clear delineation between "us" and "them," was about to shatter, allowing a clear and present danger to the very distinction between Jews and Arabs to seep in. At the same time, the religious-Zionist sector saw the peace initiatives gain immense public support—until the Hammas terror attacks—and how the Rabin-Arafat handshake was enthusiastically supported by a great majority of secular Israelis.

The leaders of the religious nationalists began increasingly to find solace in the world of halacha. The alliance with the secular public was crumbling before their very eyes, while the haredi world was beginning to seek harmony with them in their common war against the culture represented by hedonist Tel Aviv, against "nowism" and so-called Hellenism. It is certainly no coincidence that in all the many violent demonstrations against Yitzhak Rabin, which actually paved the way for his assassination, virtually no nonreligious nor nonharedi demonstrators were present among the demonstrators. These were, in fact, Kahanist demonstrations, in which Chabad activists, yeshiva students, and settlers played a pivotal role. While the secular camp was represented on the podium, by Likud leaders, its followers could not be found down in the street, among the seething crowds.

Thus, the religious right enhanced its strength until, in the fourteenth Knesset, following the 1996 elections of the prime minister—both because of the new elections system, which allowed voters to split their vote between the prime minister and Knesset members, and because of their growing demographic advantage—the religious and haredi parties in the Knesset numbered 23 out of 120 members.

But that was not all. The religious Right itself became more sharply radical. In the eighties and nineties, incidents unprecedented in severity occurred in the extreme circles of the nationalist-religious Right. The antihumanistic ideology, all of whose elements had come into being long before, was now being translated time and time again into the language of violence. In retrospect, it seems that that road led directly to November 4, 1995—Yitzhak Rabin's assassination. The process began with the "Jewish underground" affair. That was the first time that undisguised ideological and pseudo-halachic legitimization was granted to indiscriminate murder. The sixth commandment—Thou shalt not kill—was erased from the Decalogue by radical nationalist religious leaders, albeit at that stage only in relation to non-Jews.

In May 1984, twenty-seven people from the core of the settlement establishment were arrested, among them important Gush Emunim activists, charged with a series of terrorist acts and murders perpetrated against West Bank Arabs. The height of this terrorism was an attempt, thwarted at the last moment by the Shin Bet, to booby-trap five Arab buses in East Jerusalem and kill all occupants. The members of the group were eventually convicted of participation in this plot, of the murder of students of the Islamic College in Hebron, of plotting to blow up the mosques on the Temple Mount, of attempting to assassinate mayors of West Bank cities, and of setting two hand grenades to go off in a mosque and a soccer field in Hebron. Although the assassination attempts on the lives of the mayors, supporters of the PLO, could be construed as political attacks, others involved indiscriminate mass bloodshed. The potentially disastrous consequences of blowing up the Temple Mount mosques are self-evident and need no elaboration.

One of the members of the group, Haggai Segal, described the events surrounding the inception of the Jewish underground in his book *Dear Brothers*. The book makes it painfully and unequivocally

clear that the acts of the underground had received rabbinic author-
ization, at least after the fact. The author quotes Rabbi Moshe
Levinger at a meeting of the Jewish residents of Hebron after the
murders at the Islamic College: "Whoever did this sanctified God's
name in public." But the group was not content with public declarations of support. To convince the others, the member who came
up with the idea of blowing up the buses said that "rabbis in Kiryat
Arba and Jerusalem had sanctioned the idea in principle." The book
also quotes Menahem Livni, the leader of the group, who explained
that following a murderous terror attack on settlers in Hebron, a
meeting was held in the yeshiva of Kiryat Arba with the participation of the leading local rabbis. "The rabbis stated unequivocally
that the local population had to be deterred in view of the government's weakness . . . and those assembled resolved unanimously that
a mass attack claiming many lives would be carried out. After the
meeting, Rabbi Eliezer Waldman approached me and asked to participate in the attack." Some of these rabbis claimed that Livni had
perhaps misunderstood them. Rabbi Waldman admitted taking part
in a meeting similar to the one Livni described. He also acknowl-
edged asking Menahem Livni to let him know when a plan of action
had been selected ("When you decide—let me know"), not in order
to participate in it—on the contrary, to prevent any reckless acts.
Several months later, Livni conceded that he may have erred in
assessing the determination of some of the rabbis, although "not all
of them." Segal states that Rabbi Levinger, who was summoned for
questioning following the arrests, considered confessing and turning
the underground trial into a political trial against the government (a
Likud government headed by Yitzhak Shamir!), which had "irre-
sponsibly abandoned security." But after consultation with the other
prisoners, it was decided that his presence "outside" was doubly
important in view of the wave of independent condemnations and
denunciations that had swept the settlers' elite.

And, indeed, despite the manifest or latent rabbinic backing of the
acts of murder perpetrated by the underground, the initial response
of Gush Emunim leadership, at least outwardly, was shock and condemnation. A manifesto published by the settlement leadership condemned "any indiscriminate attacks on people, whether for the
purpose of revenge or deterrence. . . . The lives of all people—Jews

and Arabs—are sacred, as are their dignity, property and rights."[17] But even at this early stage, voices could be heard from within the camp that did not shirk at explicitly justifying the acts of the underground, while criticizing those who condemned or disassociated themselves from it. These individuals were accused of demonstrating weakness of will in the face of the "attacks from the media and the left." As time passed, and with the development of the outspoken campaign in favor of the release of the underground members, the voices that justified and "understood" their motives became much more prominent and dominant. The former condemnations and reservations began to sound like halfhearted and hesitant mutterings, almost totally fading into the shadows. Ultimately, instead of the murderers being denounced, they were represented as "excellent fellows," who at worst had erred in "taking the law into their own hands," having only the best of intentions, with all their actions taken in the name of God. Rabbi Yoel Bin Nun, one of the founders of Gush Emunim, who courageously spoke out in opposition to this trend and who insisted on unequivocally and resolutely condemning the murderous acts of the underground, was attacked for taking this position and became increasingly isolated as a result. He was pushed to the margins of his camp.

The vociferous, and eventually successful, public campaign for the release of the underground prisoners had its source in the extremist fringes of the religious Right, but ultimately swept up the majority of the religious establishment, both religious and haredi, as well as large sections of the Israeli Right. The underground's murderous acts were attributed to "security irresponsibility" of the Likud-led government; their patriotic motives were extolled; the appalling moral significance of the murder of innocents was not considered sufficiently relevant in the eyes of the advocates of those "excellent fellows"; their guilt was summed up as no more than "taking the law into their own hands." Eventually, a proposal was drafted in the Knesset by a group of right-wing and religious members to pass a law granting legal pardon to the members of the underground who had been convicted and other Jews who had com-

---

17. H. Segal, *Dear Brothers: The West Bank Jewish Underground* (Woodmere, N.Y.: Beit Shammai Publications, 1988), 176; see also pp. 186, 238–240, 245–246.

mitted murder with nationalist motives. Minister of Justice Dan
Meridor objected to the draft proposal, and it was defeated, mostly
thanks to votes from the opposition. But the majority of right-wing
parties supported it, and even Prime Minister Yitzhak Shamir voted
in favor of the proposal. Haim Herzog, then president of Israel,
related some time later in a television interview that after that vote,
the minister of justice told him that he feared that the bill would
gain a majority the next time it was put up for a vote, and that this
was the reason he considered it preferable for the president to grant
amnesty to the members of the underground, therefore preventing
serious damage to the rule of law generated by the passage of a special amnesty law. Herzog explained that this was one of the most
important considerations guiding his decision to grant the request of
the underground prisoners. The upshot was that a few years later,
the last of the underground members, sentenced to life imprisonment for murder, were released from prison. The walls of an Israeli
prison were not strong enough to keep such privileged convicts,
enjoying such broad political and public backing, behind bars for
long.

Among those who unqualifiedly supported the actions of the
Jewish underground from the outset, giving them halachic backing,
was Rabbi Yisrael Ariel, one of the most extreme rabbis of the religious-nationalist camp and the head of the Temple Institute in
Jerusalem. In a series of articles published in the monthly journal of
the Jewish settlers in Judea, Samaria, and Gaza, *Nekuda,* and the
journal *Temple Institute,* the rabbi rebutted all arguments raised
against the underground's acts within the national-religious camp.
His claims represent a clearly laid out philosophy with halachic-
ideological foundations—a combination of violent racism and justification for murder—arguing that the commandment "Thou shalt
not kill" does not apply to the killing of a Gentile. His line of reasoning is an explicit appeal to expelling the Arabs from Israel, as
well as total denial of the authority of the secular government as
long as it flies in the face of "the law of the Torah." In the public
consciousness, this philosophy is identified with the name and
movement of Meir Kahane, but it is in fact far more pervasive. In its
original form, it included no more than a small minority within the
Right, where it also aroused intense opposition. But it has considerable influence beyond as well.

In discussing the acts of the underground, Rabbi Ariel whole-heartedly justifies the acts of the underground in the name of senior rabbis, in an imaginary dialogue with an opponent:

> What did the government do in the affair of the underground that was in opposition to the law of the Torah? . . . I am amazed that you wonder. Some thirty people are being held in prison, all God-fearing Jews, who meticulously observe the commandments, some of whom are Torah scholars, and for what? Did they rob a bank? Were their actions not motivated by Torah commandments? Did they not act because the security forces were derelict and indulgent in the face of Arab terror? Was it not the commandment of "Thou shalt not stand aside when thy brother's blood is spilled," which applies equally to the government and to each and every individual Jew, that they had in mind? . . . Does the granting of "autonomy" and proprietorship to Arabs of Judea and Samaria no longer oppose the commandments of the Torah? Has the Biblical commandment to utterly destroy the enemy, and the ban against allowing them to dwell in our land no longer apply? And what of the prohibition against allowing non-Jews to dwell in Jerusalem? Or to approach the Temple Mount? Are we no longer commanded to control the Temple Mount? Are we now permitted to stand by and do nothing while Jewish blood is spilled?"[18]

The rabbinical establishment did not protest these observations by Rabbi Ariel. Nor did it demand that he retract them. They did not consider these comments, which attribute support for murder to rabbis and rabbinical judges, a blot on their good name. Rabbi Ariel's explicit remarks could be considered a violation of criminal bans against sedition, and praise and encouragement for acts of violence. But it goes without saying that the authorities never even considered enforcing these laws where Rabbi Ariel and other rabbis were concerned. Gradually, comments of this type increased, becoming almost routine. In some cases, theoretical "halachic" discussions

---

18. Yisrael Ariel, "Ahavah Mekalkelet et Hashurah," *Nekuda* 79 (October 1984).

were involved; in others, the remarks were made in response to acts of murder actually committed. When three Arab workmen were murdered in December 1993 near the village of Tarkumiah, no one made any particular fuss over comments by Rabbi Melamed, secretary of the Council of Rabbis for Judea and Samaria, as published in Ha'aretz (December 12, 1993). The rabbi himself condemned the act, but pointed out that "he knew of at least two rabbis, whose names he refused to specify, one national-religious and the other haredi, both eminent and highly respected rabbis, from outside Judea and Samaria, who praised actions of this sort at that period." In the same news report, Baruch Marzel, a leading Kach-Kahane activist, is quoted as saying that he hoped that the perpetrators of the murders are Jews. . . . "In any case, the action caused me very great pleasure." Law enforcement agencies took no particular interest in these utterances.

When Baruch Goldstein carried out the massacre in the Cave of the Patriarchs on Purim 1994, it was generally claimed that it had been completely unforeseeable that a Jew would commit such an act. The massacre was said to be "like a thunderbolt out of the blue," and other such unfounded statements were uttered as well.

The indiscriminate butchery of the Muslim worshipers perpetrated by Goldstein—a well-liked and respected figure in his community of Kiryat Arba, a regular fellow, by no means an eccentric or a madman—caused enormous shock. The settlement elite, the heads of the National Religious Party, and the chief rabbis condemned the massacre. But immediately following the slaughter, the voices of extremist rabbis who praised the murderer and justified the murder, either explicitly or implicitly, could be heard. Although the heads of the religious establishment denounced Goldstein's actions, they did not express any reservations about their colleagues who justified them. Rabbi Dov Lior, rabbi of Hebron and Kiryat Arba, one of the most notoriously extremist among the settlement rabbis, said immediately following the massacre that Goldstein was a saint and a martyr; later he elaborated, going as far as to describe Goldstein as a martyr akin to the those of the Holocaust. Rabbi Yisrael Ariel eulogized Goldstein, designating him a national martyr, recounting the virtues of other national martyrs. In both cases, such praise was justified by the fact that Goldstein was "killed by the goyim because of his being Jewish" and was therefore worthy of these appellations.

One can only imagine a situation in which an Arab terrorist carries out a massacre at the Western Wall and is ultimately killed by the worshipers who survive the attack.

In any case, within a short while, Goldstein's supporters would no longer be content with subtleties. Rabbi Yitzchak Ginzburgh of Chabad and the head of the yeshiva in Nablus came out with an article entitled "Baruch Hagever," later publishing a book by the same name.[19] The article and the book that followed, which contains articles by activist and other extremist rabbis, legitimize the massacre, with no attempt to disguise or present it as an expression of personal affinity for the murderer or understanding of his motives. "The actions of Baruch Goldstein (may the Lord avenge his blood)," writes Rabbi Ginzburgh, "aroused immense emotion, but it is very important that we not be content with this, but rather that we explain the acts from their various aspects, within the context of the Torah." The rabbi enumerates five positive commandments embodied in Goldstein's actions: "sanctification of God's name; saving of lives; revenge; purging of evil; and the war over the Land of Israel . . . the crown of them all is of course is the sanctification of God's name embodied in the act."[20]

Rabbi Ginzburgh's contributions to the development and foundation of a racist hate theory are numerous. Shlomo Shamir, *Ha'aretz* correspondent in New York, for example, reports such an incident on April 26, 1996, under the headline "Rabbi Ginzburg, head of Shchem (Nablus) Yeshiva: a Jew that murders a non-Jew is not a murderer." Relying on an article that appeared in *Jewish Week* concerning the rabbi's appearance before an enthusiastic crowd of Chabad hassidim in New York, he reports that Rabbi Ginzburgh reasoned that the commandment of "Thou shalt not kill!" did not apply to a Jew killing a Gentile. "The life of a Jew has a value," he said, "that cannot be measured. There is something in the life of a Jew that is unique and infinite, unlike that of a Gentile."

But among the heads of Israel's Orthodox establishment, no one became upset at the dispensation, just as no one thought it necessary

---

19. *Baruch Hagever,* subtitled *Dedicated to the memory of martyr Dr. Baruch Goldstein, containing the story of the greatness and heroism of the martyr, and the miracle and salvation of the community of Hebron, on Purim of the year 5754.* (The name *Baruch Hagever*— Blessed is the man—is a play on Goldstein's first name.)
20. Ibid., 19–21.

to publicly disassociate himself from Ginzburgh's justification of the massacre in the Cave of the Patriarchs in Hebron, "within the context of the Torah." Designation of the carnage as "a sanctification of God's name," did not cause any of the rabbinic leaders in Israel to lose any sleep either, because after all, this had nothing to do with eating leavened bread on Passover or seafood on weekdays or traveling on the Sabbath.

The manifestations of support among some Orthodox rabbis for Goldstein and his actions became routine, no longer surprising anyone. The murderer's grave in Kiryat Arba was turned into a semishrine, the site of pilgrimages. In December 1996, the bar mitzvah of Baruch Goldstein's son was celebrated there. Rabbi Dov Lior, the rabbi of Kiryat Arba and Hebron, a municipal rabbi holding an official position and formerly a candidate for the supreme rabbinical court, blessed the child with the following words: "Go in the footsteps of your father, who was a martyr and a hero!" No one—in the rabbinical establishment or in the law enforcement establishment—was particularly perturbed by these remarks. Rabbinical dispensation for murder had become something to be overlooked or ignored out of passive support, indifference, or despair. The familiar process repeated itself: Rabbis who openly justified acts of murder were apparently a minority, albeit an influential minority, even among the Right and the settlers, surrounded by much broader circles of support and understanding. This was not an isolated, ostracized minority within its own camp. The heads of the religious establishment, though they condemned murder, were not prepared to disassociate themselves from those rabbis who openly supported it and did not disqualify them or their approach in the name of halacha. Thus, to a potential killer, drawing inspiration for his actions from the "rulings" of extremist rabbis such as Ginzburgh and Lior, the vapid censures of Goldstein's deed by rabbinical leaders would seem like no more than lip service for the benefit of the secular establishment and the hostile media. In this context, Rabbi Yoel Bin Nun's call to the Council of Jewish Settlements of Judea and Samaria sounded like no more than a cry in the wilderness. Bin Nun, a settler himself, appealed to the council to have Rabbi Yitzchak Ginzburgh removed from his position as the head of the yeshiva in Nablus, accusing the yeshiva of encouraging an atmosphere conducive to additional acts of murder. The members of the council met this appeal with disparagement or hostility.

One of the most disturbing and serious examples of the trend involving the legitimization of murder in the name of halacha is the "Halachic Clarification into the Matter of Killing a Goy"[21] by Rabbi Ido Elba of Kiryat Arba. Two of this rabbi's students, the Kahalani brothers, were arrested after a failed attempt to murder an Arab at random. The Shin Bet, who conducted surveillance of the two brothers, rendered their firearms inoperable ahead of time, thus preventing the perpetration of the crime. The brothers were sentenced to long prison terms for attempted murder, and their rabbi was arrested and convicted of aiding a murder (attempting to manufacture a silencer and to obtain ammunition) and of disruption of proceedings (by sending messages to the brothers, asking them to renounce the confessions they had previously made to the police). But the most acute public concern was aroused by the accusation and conviction of the rabbi for encouraging of violence and incitement to racism by means of an article he wrote and disseminated in April 1994. The article contained halachic dispensation and even encouraged the murder of Gentiles. At the heading of the article, the following appears: "Written after clarification of the laws with one of the greatest rabbinical authorities of this generation, to justify the halachic conclusions. This is not to be construed as a halachic ruling, but rather only an academic discussion of the issues for study and deeper analysis for Torah scholars." It seems, however, that at least part of the contents of the manifest was entirely operative. Both the Jerusalem district court, which believed that the paper was sufficient to convict Elba, and the Supreme Court, which upheld the conviction by a majority vote, were convinced that these writings were not a mere academic and theoretical analysis intended for scholars, as the defense claimed, but rather a practical incitation to racism and violence.

Rabbi Elba's reflections go far beyond the conclusion itself—in which there is nothing new—that the killing of a goy does not violate the commandment of "Thou shalt not kill!" They are characterized by an attempt to systematically negate all the possible

---

21. Ido Elba, *Nekuda* 79 (October 1984).

halachic arguments that might be raised against the murder of non-Jews. The entire argument leads to the inevitable conclusion that the murder of a non-Jew in the State of Israel today is permitted and legitimate from the point of view of halacha. Moreover, if the victim is an Arab, and if he can be killed without endangering the life of the murderer, the murder is a *mitzvah*—a praiseworthy deed—and an obligation, regardless of the position taken by the government in the matter.

Elba writes, "The prohibitions of 'Thou shalt not kill' and 'he who spills human blood' do not apply to a Jew who kills an ordinary gentile, and such an act does not involve a prohibition from the Bible [as opposed to a rabbinical prohibition] at all." And although it is true that the Bible forbids the killing of a *ger toshav*—a non-Jew living in the Land of Israel who accepts Jewish authority—"the status of *ger toshav* exists only when the laws of the Jubilee still apply. Therefore, this status no longer exists either." From here, Elba draws his conclusion: There no longer exists today any Gentile whom the Torah forbids killing. According to commentaries such as the Tosfot and Maimonides, there is a rabbinical injunction against killing a Gentile who fulfills the seven laws of Noah that bind all mankind, but "gentiles nowadays, according to the Tosfot and Maimonides are clearly considered as those who do not fulfill the seven laws of Noah. And there are those who hold that ordinary gentiles in our time are considered to be fulfilling the seven laws." But the Gentiles and their left-wing devotees should not leap for joy at this narrow dispensation they have seemingly been granted—that perhaps their murder may be considered a forbidden act, for lack of evidence to the contrary.

Elba goes on to say, "For it is a mitzvah to kill gentiles devout in a faith which denies the fundamentals of the Jewish faith and the eternity of the Torah, and who believe that they are obliged to convince others of the truth of their faith, such as missionaries and Muslims who believe in Jihad." But the main operative claim embodied in his arguments is that "during a war, until the final outcome of the war has been decided, it is a mitzvah to kill any member of the gentile nation that is fighting against us, even women and children, who although they do not pose a direct threat to the killers, it is to be supposed that they will provide succor to the enemy during the continued fighting."

The upshot of his comments is not "Love your neighbor as your-self," but rather a blanket dispensation to kill anyone who is not Jewish. Lest we allow ourselves to believe that this is no more that a theoretical-halachic debate, we must be completely aware that these comments are represented as being relevant and germane to our current state and situation. Rabbi Elba vitiates any possible excuse, invalidating any obstacle barring the way to drawing the practical and necessary conclusions from his analysis: "A war of conquest of the country or to defend the lives of Jews," including "attacks on gentiles about whom it is known that they will to harm Jews, or even only their property," even "if what is involved is mere-ly a remote fear that this will happen, it is clearly a holy war," for fear of damage to property is certainly a harbinger of bodily attacks and attempts to conquer portions of the country. In such a holy war,

> anyone who comes across one of them [the enemy], and does not kill him, is violating a negative precept—of "Thou shalt not stand aside when thy brother's blood is spilled."
>
> And the rabbinical authorities did not condition this war on our military capabilities . . . and even if there are military experts who believe that waging war is more dangerous than not waging war, their conclusions are not halachically bind-ing, because the pronouncements of our sages stem from their recognition of the nature of the gentiles—which has not changed since their time . . . and this is all the more true in a situation where there are military experts who uphold our sages' conviction. Therefore, there is no reason to consider the opinion of those who think otherwise. Moreover, their considerations do not arise only from military information, but rather from their faith in the promises of the goyim.

Rabbi Elba's central claim is that the positive precept of waging war is incumbent on each and every individual, and not only on the entire community and its leadership, and that the observance of this commandment—killing Gentiles (i.e., Arabs) who belong to a hos-tile nation—may involve the willingness to risk one's life, even con-trary to the opinion of the country's leadership:

> And the decisions of those leaders who decide to collaborate with the enemy certainly do not nullify the obligation to

wage war. And in such a case, it seems that one must consult a Torah sage who is aware of the situation as one requiring us to wage war, and he will give instructions how to act in order for the war to succeed. And a situation is possible in which the action that may lead to success must be performed precisely by an individual so that it will not look to the nations of the world as if the action was performed by the entire community. It is incumbent upon all those who have the ability to fight, to do so, and he who sacrifices his life for this aim, is worthy of praise.

And in his concluding remarks, the rabbi sums up:

And in any case, this community [which refuses to adopt the laws of war according to the Torah] loses the duty of war by default to the individual, but he should make sure to act in consultation with sages so that his actions cause no harm, and are efficacious.

These observations were written and disseminated among the yeshiva students of the Cave of Patriarchs some two months following the massacre perpetrated by Baruch Goldstein—at the height of the bitter public debate over the Oslo agreements, whose very validity was repudiated by the Right. It is eminently clear that the only purpose of these writings was to lead the reader to the operative conclusion that not only is the murder of an Arab no transgression at all—neither from the point of view of the commandment of "Thou shalt not kill!" nor from the aspect of the injunction against taking the law into one's own hands—but that, on the contrary, it is a worthy and even obligatory act. Nevertheless, there were rabbis of eminent standing who did not hesitate to defend these loathsome statements.

In his testimony at Rabbi Elba's trial, Rabbi Shlomo Aviner, the rabbi of the Beit-El settlement, claimed that "the author of the article does not write that it is permitted to kill gentiles, but he only says that it is a transgression of lesser severity than the murder of a Jew. But he most certainly considers himself bound not to do so under any circumstance whatsoever." Amazingly enough, in the Supreme Court, Justice Tal, in a minority position, accepted these circuitous comments and suggested acquitting Rabbi Elba of inciting to racism and encouraging violence:

> [The article] does not contain any dispensation to kill gentiles . . . a halachic article which points out the difference and distinction between the attitude of halacha to someone who is not Jewish and to his killing, contains only this difference and distinction. There is nothing in it to even arouse inner hostility, but rather perhaps pity.

This is how a religious Supreme Court justice, who does not belong to any extreme camp, interprets the appalling comments written by a rabbi at a time when murders in the name of the halacha were becoming increasingly rife. But the majority prevailed, and Rabbi Elba was convicted.

Along with the increasing tendency of the extreme religious Right to legitimize the murder of "goyim," another trend gained currency within broader circles: blatant repudiation of the authority of the state and its democratic institutions. According to those who subscribed to this view, neither the government of Israel nor the Knesset had the authority to make political decisions that contravened halacha, as interpreted by the rabbis of the religious Right. Obviously, these interpretations dealt with manifestly political issues, first and foremost that of the future of the occupied territories. What was involved was an attempt to appropriate the right of the country's democratic institutions to decide in matters of greatest significance on the public agenda. During the struggle of the religious Right against the Rabin government and the Oslo agreements, this trend was most vividly manifested in the rabbinic decision published by a large group of rabbis, including the most prominent rabbis of religious Zionism. This decision appealed to religious soldiers to refuse orders if they involved taking part in the implementation of the agreements with the Palestinians. The publication of this rabbinic decision aroused sharp criticism, and even some leaders in the National Religious Party (NRP) appealed to their constituents to disregard it. But, ultimately, such reservations were not expressed, and even the leadership of Bnei Akiva, the youth movement of the NRP, even decided to adopt the rabbinic decision. Those who attempted to defend the rabbis' position tried to create an impression that their decision concerned only a situation involving the evacuation of settlements, and presented the refusal to obey such an order on the part of a religious soldier as conscientious objection. Yet from the wording of the decision, it is clear that it deals mainly not with the possibility of evacuating settlements, but with that of withdrawal from permanent army bases—or, in other words, redeployment according to the Oslo agreements. In this matter, a manifestly political position by all accounts, the rabbis decided, leaving no room for the independent discretion and conscience of the religious soldier:

> We determine that it is forbidden according to the Torah to evacuate army bases and hand them over to the domain of gentiles, since this would involve the cancellation of a positive precept [the commandment to settle the land], as well as endangering lives and the very existence of the state. . . . A permanent army base also constitutes a Jewish settlement in every meaning of the word. . . . Therefore, in answer to the question, it is manifestly clear that every Jew is forbidden to take part in any act that will lead to the evacuation of a settlement, camp, or installation, as ruled by Maimonides (Laws of Monarchs, 3:9), that even if the king orders one to transgress the laws of the Torah, he is not to be heeded.[22]

It is against this background—halachic justification of murder and delegitimization of the states' institutions—that the campaign against Prime Minister Rabin began to gain momentum in an unprecedented manner. This campaign grew out of a public protest—legitimate in and of itself—on the part of the entire Israeli Right against the Oslo agreements. The religious and haredi right spearheaded this protest, and many of its representatives supported the offensive and seditious slogans that accompanied it. Clearly, not all harsh and intense expressions of protest against the Oslo agreements, led by the Rabin government, can be considered sedition. But this definition should apply to all those who decried Rabin and his government as traitors, enemies of the people, and collaborators

---

22. *Gilayon Rabbanei YESHA*, 25, Tammuz, 5755 (Heb.) (the regular newsletter published by the Rabbis of Judea and Samaria, vol. 25, July 1995).

with the enemy. Accusations of this type, especially when they are aimed at the prime minister, cannot be considered legitimate criticism, nor are they mere invective or abuse—they are, in fact, a sentence of death. An ordinary traitor may be arrested and judged by law; not so in the case of someone at the head of a government, who holds the fate of the country in his hands. If the prime minister of Israel is in fact a traitor, leading the country to disaster, the self-evident conclusion must be that he be slain in order to save the country. All that is needed to arrive at such a conclusion is to take the accusation of treason in all seriousness and to demonstrate a willingness to sacrifice oneself for the sake of people and country.

This message—that the government of Israel and its head, who took the difficult route of mutual recognition and peace process with the Palestinian leadership, are a gang of traitors—was conveyed systematically and consistently. From an infinite number of examples, one may quote the incitement broadcast on Arutz 7, the settlers' radio station, which received extensive support and backing from the leadership of the Right.

Adir Zik, an Arutz 7 commentator and well-known right-wing activist, repeated again and again in his commentary that Yitzhak Rabin was a traitor, and his government a "treasonous government." In order to make it clear that this was no mere hyperbole on his part, Zik quoted the dictionary definition of "treason," as well as paragraph 97 of the Israeli Criminal Code, which provides for the death penalty or life imprisonment for treason. "His punishment— make note of this listeners—is death or life in prison." Professor Hillel Weiss of Bar Ilan University, a member of Professors for a Strong Israel, declared a short time before the assassination that he was looking into the legal possibilities of having Yitzhak Rabin and Shimon Peres stand trial for treason. Unlike many other inciters, who following the assassination tried to obfuscate their previous allegations and deny their part in the incitement, Hillel Weiss declared publicly—after Yitzhak Rabin was dead and buried—that he did not retract his previous comments. Professors for a Strong Israel gave him their full backing.

The perspective that regards the evacuation of parts of the historic land of Israel as tantamount to treason has very deep roots in the philosophy of the Right, particularly in that of the religious Right. On November 4, 1985, exactly ten years before the assassination, the Council of Jewish Settlements of Judea and Samaria confirmed an official resolution warning of the possibility that an Israeli government could hand over parts of Judea and Samaria to a foreign sovereignty—Palestinian or Jordanian—in part or in full. Such a government was to be considered illegitimate and treasonous:

> We will consider any Israeli government which commits one of the abovementioned crimes to be illegitimate, just as Charles de Gaulle considered the Vichy government of Marshal Petain, when he betrayed the French people by signing the surrender of the majority of historic France.

This decision, which was no more and no less than a license to kill, and a stamp of approval for rebellion and civil war, was criticized by many of the settlers as well. Ultimately, the council passed a resolution that was supposed to mitigate the previous one, but that did not in fact include any qualification of it:

> The Council of Jewish Settlements of Judea and Samaria adopts the position of the plenum which states: No one has the authority to hand over parts of the Land of Israel or to surrender sovereignty.

The phrase *surrender sovereignty* reappears in the comments of the Israeli Right in discussing the future of the territories, which even the Likud government did not annex or apply Israeli sovereignty to, and whose inhabitants until the Oslo agreements were in fact subjects of a military occupation government, devoid of rights. No one seemed to have let on to the settlers and their supporters that the forceful subjugation of one ethnic group by another is not exactly what is generally thought of as sovereignty.

In any case, the claim that the surrender of territories was tantamount to treason, and the analogy to Marshal Petain became the standard fare of many in the Right and a permanent constituent of public Israeli discourse. With the beginning of the Oslo process, this point was driven home with immense force. The analogy to Marshal Petain was particularly attractive in regard to Yitzhak Rabin. Rabin had been the chief of staff during the Six-Day War, not unlike the hero of Verdun. Thus, Ariel Sharon could claim that "this government is worse than Petain"; MK* Rehavam Ze'evi dubbed the government a "Vichy government"; and Refael Eitan, a former chief of staff and the leader of a right-wing party, claimed that "these people [the members of the Rabin government] are quislings." Comparisons were also made to the Judenrat of the ghetto. At a session of the opposition parties on September 5, 1993, MK Uzi Landau developed this concept: "There too, the leadership of the ghetto assisted in implementing the liquidation plans." MK Benny Begin observed that "caution should be exercised when making such comments," but MK Landau answered that "this is exactly the comparison that should be made." Ariel Sharon took the trouble of explaining that the actions of the Rabin government were worse than those of the Judenrat during the Holocaust: "What is the difference between the community council in the ghetto and the government? There the Jews were forced to cooperate with the Nazis—and here the government is doing everything of its own accord."

Whereas the general political protest against the Rabin government was infused with accusations of treason and historical comparisons to traitors and collaborators, in the religious Right more specific designations were used, taken from Jewish tradition. The laws of *rodef* (pursuer) and *mosser* (informer) were invoked. These are clearly defined halachic categories, which describe a situation in which there is a dispensation, or even an obligation, to physically harm—or kill, if necessary—a person who poses an immediate danger to an individual or to the public. The killing is justified as self-defense. The report of the Shamgar commission, which investigated the Rabin assassination, quoted the assassin's words during his interrogation by the Shin Bet:

> Without a rabbinical decision or the invocation of the *rodef* law where Rabin was concerned by a number of rabbis that I know about, I would have found it difficult to kill him. If I had not had the backing, and if many additional people had not been standing behind me, I would not have acted.

---

*Member of the Knesset.

Later, after the public debate concerning the halachic stamp of approval for the murder had begun, the assassin, during his questioning by the fact finders for the commission, denied that he had been influenced by a rabbinical opinion, claiming that he had committed the act "of his own volition and discretion."

The interrogation of the assassin is of great importance:

> Yigal Amir: I would not have done all that I did were it not for my religious obligation to defend the Land of Israel from the mosser, Yitzhak Rabin, as explained by numerous rabbis who fear for the fate of the Land of Israel and the Jewish people. I did it for God, people and country . . .
>
> Q: Where did you get the halachic authorization?
>
> Yigal Amir: From my own knowledge and from religious leaders.
>
> Q: Can you give thenames of these religious leaders?
>
> Yigal Amir: No.
>
> Q: Why?
>
> Yigal Amir: Because.
>
> Q: Can you state that they were unequivocal in their decision?
>
> Yigal Amir: Yes.

In his interrogation, Dror Adani, Amir's accomplice, among other things, said:

> The law of *rodef* applies to both Rabin and Peres, meaning they are both deserving of death. If we had seen that Rabin went easily, we would have continued with Peres. . . . When Yigal Amir spoke to me of the law of *rodef* applying to Rabin, that he should be killed . . . I wouldn't have done it, but as far as the *Shulchan Aruch* [the Code of Jewish Law] and the rabbis are concerned, Rabin was designated a *mosser,* and as such, he was deserving of death.[23]

Following the assassination it was claimed, of course, that no rabbi would seriously discuss the question of applying the laws of

---

23. *Yedioth Aharonot,* 11 December 1995.

rodef or *mosser* to Yitzhak Rabin. But about nine months before the assassination, three rabbis—Dov Lior of Kiryat Arba, Daniel Shiloh of Kedumim, and Eliezer Melamed, the secretary of the the Council of Rabbis for Judea and Samaria—appealed in a letter to four well-known rabbis in the country, including the chief rabbis and members of the Council of Torah Scholars, in which they raised the issue of the law of *mosser* in all seriousness.

The difficult question is what would be law according to halacha concerning the government if it continues to implement the abovementioned agreement in Judea and Samaria. For where the individual who commits an act posing a danger to another individual is concerned, there are clear laws set out by Maimonides . . . but the law concerning elected representatives who commit such an act by virtue of their official position must be clearly defined. . . . And even if this act is defined as *mesira* [informing], it seems that it is impossible to decide that any person be permitted to kill or harm elected leaders, because nothing can be more detrimental to the public welfare than chaos, in which everyone does as he sees fit. In any case, it is possible that Torah sages and leaders should alert the prime minister and his government, that if they continue to hand over the residents of Judea and Samaria to foreign rule, according to halacha it will necessary to put them on public trial and have them punished by law in a rabbinical court, or having no other choice, in a secular court of law. Do leaders, rabbis and politicians have an obligation, at this difficult time, to forewarn the prime minister and his ministers, that if after the bitter experience of the Gaza and Jericho agreement, they continue implementation in Judea and Samaria, there will be no choice but to apply Jewish law to them, specifically the law of *mosser*— as one who endangers Jewish life and property, handing them over to gentiles?

At the end of the letter, the authors write:

And let no rabbi say that the subject of this question is opprobrious, because the question troubles and pains the hearts of many Jews in Israel and in the Diaspora, and many of them have been giving this question significant thought.[24]

The final comment shows just how topical the subject was in certain circles—completely contrary to apologetic claims voiced following the murder. The discussion of the possibility of placing Rabin "on trial" seems puzzling: It is clear that no civil court or rabbinical tribunal could be authorized to try anyone according to the laws of *rodef*. Moreover, the very essence of the concept of *rodef* is not a matter of trial and punishment, but rather execution without trial, inasmuch as the law itself is intended to provide an immediate solution to the existence of a real and present danger. To understand the intensity of the lethal codes obscured in this letter, one should read Maimonides on the topic of the laws of *mosser* in Chapter 8, in "Laws Applying to One Who Causes Injury or Damage," the section to which the three rabbis are referring to:

> It is permitted to kill a *mosser* in any place and even at this time when rulings on capital offenses are no longer passed. And it is permitted to kill before he has a chance to inform, for after he has said the words "I hereby hand over this person's body or money," even a small amount of money, he has sentenced himself to death. He should be warned and told not to go through with the denouncement (or handing over). If he responds insolently and says, "No, I shall hand him over," it is a mitzvah to kill him, and he who does so first is worthy of merit.

The practical significance of the letter by the three rabbis is that it is in fact a proposal to warn Rabin that if he persists in the implementation of the Oslo agreements—as he indeed did—his verdict will be death. Lacking such a warning on the part of "rabbis and politicians," the authors of the letter do not favorably consider the possibility of allowing "any person" to kill "public leaders" because such an act might lead to "chaos." It can be assumed, however, that if the contents of this letter had become known to Yigal Amir, the natural conclusion he could have drawn from it was that the rabbis indeed believed that the laws of *mosser* applied to Yitzhak Rabin,

---

24. The letter was published in *Ha'aretz*, 23 November 1995, in an article by Nadav Shragai.

but that they did not have the courage to say so frankly and openly. After all, this is, in fact, exactly what Dror Adani admitted in his interrogation. In any case, it is perfectly clear from the wording of the letter that the issue of the laws of *mosser* and *rodef* as they applied to Yitzhak Rabin were seriously considered in certain circles. During the stormy protest against the second Oslo agreement, in the period prior to the murder, when the incitement was at its height—when demonstrators stood in front of the prime minister's house shouting that he would soon be hung like Mussolini together with his wife in the city square—Rabbi Hecht of New York, a well known Orthodox figure, expressly stated in an interview with Israeli television that the laws of *mosser* applied to Yitzhak Rabin, and even quoted Maimonides that "it is a mitzvah to kill him, and he who does so first is worthy of merit."

At the "conference of soul-searching of religious Zionism," held a few days after the assassination, Rabbi Yoel Bin Nun declared that he knew who the rabbis were who had decided that the law of *rodef* applied to Yitzhak Rabin. He added that if these rabbis did not resign their public positions by the end of the seven-day mourning period, he would reveal their names and demand that they be excommunicated. His words aroused a storm of protest, and he became the target of vicious condemnation. Rabbi Avigdor Nebentzal, the rabbi of the Jewish Quarter of the Old City of Jerusalem, told the Jerusalem newspaper *Kol Ha'ir* (November 10, 1995), that he did not believe that Rabbi Bin Nun would carry out his threat because if he did so, the laws of *mosser* would apply to him as well. Ultimately, Rabbi Bin Nun refrained from naming the rabbis but, at the same time, he did not retract his accusation. The police investigation, during which a number of rabbis were called in for questioning—an act that provoked vociferous accusations of "religious persecution"—did not lead to indictments, inasmuch no proof of this specific ruling could be found.

This attempt to disdain any responsibility for right-wing militancy was not confined to Israel's Orthodoxy. In the wake of Rabin's assassination, Henry Siegman, former executive director of the American Jewish Congress, delivered this bitter comment on the attitude of American Orthodoxy:

> The notion that Orthodoxy itself is in any way implicated in this tragic event will be rejected, of course, by the Orthodox

community. But on some level they know this to be true despite their denials.

This is evident from the fact that even those within the Orthodox community who are most outspoken in condemning this act do not question the Orthodox bona fides of the rabbis who offered religious justification for the act or of the young men who committed it.

The Orthodox community accuses them of misapplying Jewish law, not of no longer being Orthodox Jews. If these same rabbis had ruled that the *halacha*, or Jewish law, permits riding a car on the Sabbath or eating nonkosher food, they and their disciples would have been instantly drummed out of the Orthodox community.[25]

The so-called soul-searching in the religious Zionist camp, proclaimed so widely after the assassination, was pathetic. Moderate religious leaders, who even before the assassination had come out firmly against violence, racism, and extremism—such as Rabbi Aaron Lichtenstein and Rabbi Yehuda Amital, the heads of the Meimad movement—made incisive and courageous comments, but they were the minority. The National Religious Party establishment turned the much-vaunted breast-beating into a campaign of self-righteousness and settling accounts with the Left and the media. The polemic against the critics from without—some of whom were indeed guilty of making sweeping accusations against religious people in general—was more important to many than a sincere reckoning. It was claimed that the extremists constituted merely a handful of radicals among the Right, "weeds," so to speak—a lunatic fringe—and no real effort was made to explore what had promoted this seed's growth. No condemnation was directed against known inciters, like Adir Zik and Hillel Weiss, nor against the Kahanist elements. No regrets were expressed. Occasionally, a murmur of dissent could be heard when attacks were made against Rabin's widow. This was seen as going too far. In *Nekuda*, the journal of the settlers of Judea and Samaria, a reader wrote: "True, many of us do not have a very high opinion of the widow of Rabin—of blessed memory— but to take joy in her grief? That is just too much." The cover story of that issue, celebrating Netanyahu's victory in the election, was

---

25. "In Wake of Assassination," *Jewish Week*, 17 November 1995.

devoted to "The people who brought victory." According to *Nekuda,* the people deserving of kudos were the activists of the extreme Right, and others of their ilk, among them Adir Zik himself, granted a place of honor in the annals of the heroic battle against the government of Israel.

This total denial of moral and educational responsibility for what had happened was clearly the dominant aspect of the official "soul-searching." There were, however, other voices. The comments by Rabbi Zvi Tau, one of the heads of the Mercaz Harav yeshiva, constitute a prominent example. Rabbi Tau is an important rabbinical authority, unquestionably identified with the religious Right, although considered relatively moderate, especially after he intensely attacked acts of murder committed by the Jewish underground. A few days after Rabin's assassination, Rabbi Tau met with a group of friends from the settlement of Keshet in the Golan Heights. His comments at that meeting were recorded and later made public:

> Everyone is concerned with our image; everyone is concerned with the question of whether Rabbi Yoel Bin Nun will name the rabbis or not, harping on it day and night. . . . The question is if that is in fact the problem; or whether the problem is inside, and instead of dealing with it, people are concerning themselves with "how to deal with Rabbi Bin Nun."
>
> . . . There is a virus raging among us. We have all been affected by it. One person pulled the trigger and killed the prime minister, and many more cursed him, calling him all kinds of terrible names. Even more killed him in their hearts. It is time for a complete overhaul. Sometimes a person acts knowing that he is fulfilling the expectation of the community he wants to belong to. There are rabbis who didn't think their words through. . . .
>
> I do not want to be a prophet of doom, but do not think that what happened will remain an isolated incident. For quite a few people, the shot that was fired was merely the opening shot. The assassination was what they were waiting and hoping for. For them, the murderer is a "Jewish hero."[26]

---

26. Zvi Tau, *Meimad* 7 (May–June 1996).

Rabbi Tau's observations are indicative of the terribly difficult and paradoxical situation to which the nationalist extremism has driven the religious Zionist camp. The hatred for the "goy" (i.e., Arabs) engendered hatred for those Jews trying to make peace with the Arabs, undermining the traditional values of respect for the state and love for fellow Jews. Among those who attributed religious sanctity to the State of Israel and considered it "the harbinger of our redemption," there arose manifestations of shameless and arrogant contempt for the state, to the point of their adopting the anti-Zionist lexicon of the ultra-Orthodox. The state did not live up to the Messianic-nationalist expectations they had had of it. Their contempt for secular democracy, as a form of government styled after the "ways of the goyim," further deepened the ever-growing rift within the nation. Similarly, there were those among the extreme religious Right who, during the virulent protest against the Oslo agreements, declared the traditional religious-Zionist prayer for the welfare of the state null and void because the institutions of the state were mentioned in it. Thus, we see how the radical negation of the fundamental aspiration of Zionism—the reinstitution of the Jewish people as an equal member of the family of nations—led ultimately to a confrontation with the moral values of Judaism and the Zionist state itself. The assassination of the prime minister was the ultimate manifestation of this confrontation.

Do the voices among the religious-Zionist camp that call for genuine soul-searching herald the return to the golden mean, from which it has deviated so tragically since 1967? Indeed, we have come a long long way since the historic event of Basel, 1897, from the time when Dr. Theodor Herzl first verbalized his national-moral theme—to the assassination of a prime minister of the Jewish state.

Let us now return to the question raised earlier. How indeed did a religious minority succeed in dictating its point of view to a large secular population—the overwhelming majority of the country— that did not share it? Of course, this is not the first time in history, nor will it be the last, that an aggressive minority has managed to prevail over an unorganized majority. But the success story of the religious Right in Israel—both the nationalist and haredi versions— has certain unique characteristics that bear pointing out. First, there is the growing political power of the religious population, in all its various shades, clearly evident in the results of the 1996 elections.[27] This increase stems both from demographic trends resulting from one of the highest birth rates in the world, and from a religious reawakening among many secular youth. Translated into the language of politics—both in the old election system of proportional elections, and in the new system of direct elections of the prime minister—this burgeoning power means complete dependence of both the Right and the Left on this camp. This dependence is growing because the Right and the Left are able to join forces to stress their common interest. The secular Right accepts the dictates of Gush Emunim, even when it does not agree with them, because their alliance with it is vital. The same is true for those voters who give the Right its power: They are willing to forgive the settler or haredi extremists their "lapses" in return for maintaining greater Israel. One fact or another, the support for more extreme views is no more than an instrument in the struggle against the leftist-dovish camp. One thing cannot be ignored: To a fair extent this majority was sustained by the overall disappointment with the Arab response to the peace process. This included the lack of normalization with Egypt and the continued manifestation of public hatred of Israel among the Egyptian intelligentsia, even after all the territorial and other differences between Israel and Egypt were settled. The same can be said for the Palestinian response to the Oslo agreements: Along with the positive steps of cooperation and rapprochement, there continued incitement, terror, and the protection and provision of asylum for murderers. Although a clear majority of Israel's citizens were willing to make peace in return for painful concessions—as was the case immediately following the signing of the Oslo and Cairo agreements—a series of murderous terror attacks followed, perpetrated by the Hamas and the Islamic Jihad, and this, in fact, increased support for the peace naysayers and the extremists of the religious-nationalist camp.

---

27. In the 1996 Knesset elections, the haredi parties received 14 Knesset seats, 10 of them going to Shas; the National Religious Party won 9 seats. These 23 Knesset members—out of 120—were elected in part because of the new election system, but it is that which makes these results all the more authentic. Voters were now free of the tactical considerations and implications their votes would have on the election of the prime minister.

But beyond all these explanations, there is another, even more fundamental one. From the outset, Gush Emunim and its allies did not attempt to affect the day-to-day life of the secular majority. Its demands were always directed at the government, and these concerned land, permission to build settlements, and budgets. It did not seem as if these demands would affect the country's destiny. Unlike the haredi camp, Gush Emunim did not assail the use of public transportation on the Sabbath; nor did it fight to have sports stadiums moved, or to have the playing of football on the Sabbath banned. It allowed the secular majority to live its life in peace, enjoying its live-and-let-live way of life, demanding loyalty in only one area, which included settlement of the land of Israel, noncompromise with the Arabs, and opposition to "defeatism."

This, however, does not imply a new willingness to share life with the secular population; on the contrary, Gush Emunim settlements are based on a religious lifestyle and exclusively religious education. But this isolation is part of a long and sad process of separation between the religious and secular populations in Israel, certainly does not adversely affect the secular majority.

Yet this isolationist mood entails not only Gush Emunim's willingness to turn a blind eye to the instances of heresy and desecration. Something much deeper and more fundamental is involved: the elevation of the commandment to settle the Land of Israel not only to a supreme level, but to a position that is unique, so that it supersedes all other commandments. This makes it permissible to ignore sins and prohibitions, no matter how severe. Anyone who supports its politics and settlement policy receives not only Gush Emunim's indulgence, but also the esteem and reverence of its leadership, with total disregard of any other halachic aspect. On the other hand, the fanatics of Gush Emunim shun observant and God-fearing Jews if they belong to religious peace movements like Meimad.

Receptions of the type normally reserved for eminent Torah sages have been held in Gush Emunim yeshivot for public figures who have never seen the inside of a synagogue. There is nary a sin—not even the eating of nonkosher food in public in an army camp—that can diminish the veneration and regard Gush Emunim accords its secular partners. The religious population gave Benjamin Netanyahu its complete and unconditional support, even though he is as far from religious observance as is conceivable.

Even worse: Although Gush Emunim's people themselves are exceedingly meticulous in their religious observance, they do not hesitate in providing ideological justification for disregarding sins and heresies. Thus, for example, Rabbi Moshe Levinger of Hebron said:

> We have found in our history that Omri, the father of King Ahab, merited being crowned king of Israel although his sins were weighty and he spread idol-worship among the people. And why? Our sages say: because he built a city in Israel— the city of Samaria! It would be a good idea for the ministers of the Israeli government to pay heed to this.[28]

What is a nonobservant Jew supposed to conclude from these comments? According to writer Ehud Ben Ezer, the answer is:

> Secular Jews, who constitute the overwhelming majority of the Jewish people today, are considered to be on the level of Omri, of whom it is said that he did evil in the eyes of the Lord, more evil than all that were before him. But if we abandon our opposition to settlements in Samaria, we are destined to merit the crown of Israel.

The application of quotations from the sages—the Talmud is virtually saturated with aphorisms of this type, enabling one to pick and choose from among them according to personal preference— reflects religious indulgence for the secular public: Its sins will be cleansed if only it supports the establishment of a city in Judea or Samaria. Everything else will be forgiven and forgotten.

The alliance between Gush Emunim and large sectors of the secular public was hence based on mutual convenience, and its continued existence is dependent on it. Moreover, the position of Gush Emunim and its partners—according to which everything hangs on "a city in Samaria," simultaneously bestowing the crown of the Torah on Omri and Netanyahu both—is also explained by an evasion of the real struggle over the soul of Israeli society. Because, in the real arena, that of religious faith and observance, the secular

---

28. In an interview with Refael Bashan, *Yedioth Aharonot*, 8 June 1976.

population would not concede its lifestyle, the battlefield was transferred to the political arena. The Torah, even the Jewish people, have been placed on the back burner. The Land of Israel has been elevated to a position of sanctity, and as long as the people support this sanctity, it is of no consequence if they are adulterers or public desecrators of the Sabbath.

This alliance of convenience between the "Synagogue militant" and the nonfanatic seculars came gradually to an end as the truth became apparent: There is a way out; there is a possibility to make peace with the Palestinians and, thereby, with a large portion of the Arab world. There is indeed a Middle East that is, if not new— Shimon Peres's unfortunate phrase—certainly different; there is a chance to extricate the Jewish state from a vicious circle of ever more costly wars. There is a chance for all that, but the settlements—all least part of them—are an almost insurmountable obstacle.

Suddenly, the contrast between the two interpretations of Zionism was dramatically lightened. But when, finally, the secular peace-seeking public woke up from its slumbering indifference, the political and demographic reality had altered drastically. Rabin was murdered, and his testament was rejected by a substantial majority of Jewish voters in the elections that took place a short time after that event in Tel Aviv's city square.

8

No More Sabras

The mold into which the native-born Hebrew was cast had been shaped before his birth. He was destined to be everything the Diaspora Jew was not: a rooted peasant, a native son, an earthy tiller of the soil. The first generation of Hebrew children born in the new land were called Sabras, after the local cacti. With their birth a cult was born: the cult of the Sabra, the prickly pear that is rough on the outside but which has, if you manage to cut through the thorns, a sweet heart inside. The Sabras grew up with this image in their minds, implanted by their Diaspora parents. Upon his immigration to Palestine, Uri Zvi Greenberg, one of Israel's leading poets, described in a poem written in 1928, a seaside scene where "Jewish mothers have brought their children to the sun, to tan and redden the blood that paled in all the ghettoes of the Gentile world."[1] Indeed, the Sabras were often described as the children of the newly cherished sun. In a poem devoted to the Sabra, the poet Yaacov Cohen wrote:

> *We are what we are, Sabras*
> *Simple folk*
> *Sons of the sun and honest are we*
> *ours is a wild charm*
> *And he who understands us*
> *will love us.*[2]

---

1. Uri Zvi Greenberg, "Le'iladim" (To the Children), *Yedioth Aharonot* (Tel Aviv), 8 October 1976.
2. Yaacov Cohen, *Ha'aretz* (Hebrew Daily) (Tel Aviv), 11 November 1946.

Love indeed surrounded the Hebrew-speaking native-born. Their every word was recorded with amazement, their virtues extolled with a fondness rooted in the great Jewish yearning to put an end to exile. The Sabra will not only be a new man, a super-Jew, but will also put an end to his parents' helplessness. One of the first Sabra protagonists in the new Hebrew literature was Amram, in Joseph Chaim Brenner's novel *From Here and There*, written in 1911. In the story the boy's unarmed father is murdered by an Arab thief. A certain verse from the Bible remains imprinted in Amram's mind: "If the thief is found breaking in, and is struck so that he dies, there shall be no bloodguilt for him." He hears about the custom of blood vengeance among the Arabs. The Jewish state of total helplessness finds expression in Amram's thoughts:

> Had it been he, Amram, who had found the thief he would have torn him to pieces like a fish. And when he grows up he would become the chief watchman in the settlement. He would kill all the thieves . . . for the thief there is no blood-guilt . . . his blood required no vengeance . . . but . . . but— Father? Father was not a thief. Father was a saint. Everybody said that. . . . His father had been killed on the road. On the road. From the neighboring village. Father had not been "breaking in." On the road. And why, then, not redeem his blood? Why was the blood of his sainted father not being redeemed? Was there no one to do it?[3]

In the last chapter, the boy and his grandfather, having buried Amram's father, stand "on guard for life," and the book ends on a note of anticipation that Amram, the native-born, will avenge his father's blood: "The account is not yet settled." The grandfather, who has lost his son, pins his hopes on the grandson of his dreams.

Paradoxically, the image of the native son was linked from the outset to the very past he was supposed to shake off. The Jewish parent was the negative image, but his humiliation and degradation had to be avenged; the new Sabra is born with an un-Jewish image, but his very raison d'être is to build a home for menaced Jews.

---

3. Joseph Chaim Brenner, *Mikan Umikan* (1911) in *Ktavim* (Writings), vol. 2 (Tel Aviv, 1946), 336.

This ambivalence toward their parents' past is not uncharacteristic of any first-generation immigrant. What was unique about the Sabra mentality was the absence of any society, any culture, into which the Sabras could assimilate and whose ways they could emulate. Once the gate east toward the local Arab society was found shut and locked, they had to form their own personality and create their own society. According to the Sabra mystique, the native-born had therefore to grow up without any reference to a Jewish past, without ancestors, without any literary pedigree. The Sabra was born into a vacuum with no father image, only an abstract, communal "I" posited as a paragon and linked to a Jewish heritage mainly by the urge to reject it. Thus, in one of the most famous biographies depicting the prestate Yishuv, Moshe Shamir's loving memorial to his dead brother Elik, the opening phrase is: "Elik was born from the sea." Indeed, in most Sabra literature written in the 1930s and 1940s, the absence of parents and family is perhaps its most conspicuous feature. Sabras are on their own, and their allegiances are divided between their commitment to Zionism and their love for each other.

The epic heroes of S. Yizhar, a leading Sabra author, strike roots in the arid ground, with none of their sustenance being derived from the wellsprings of previous generations. In the words of one critic, they are in a state of "eternal adolescence." They are men who refuse to part with their unripe youth and their childish egocentrism. Indeed, for the archetypical Sabra the adolescent state is a comfortable one: It suits his inability to adopt the image of his father, as well as his difficulties in creating an independent maturity for himself.

This childishness and egocentrism—apparent even when the Sabra is prepared to lay down his life for others—are found in practically all Sabra literary heroes up to recent years. The Sabra is an eternal child because there is no father in whose footsteps he can follow and because the Sabra prototype is a childish figure created and fostered by this very nonexistent father. Sabras refuse to grow up mainly because they are happy the way they are.

In Moshe Shamir's classical Sabra novel, *He Walked Through the Fields*, Uri is the expected prototype: a boy who never grew up, who is full of endearing perplexity, whose relationship to the people around him is somewhat vague and hazy. He dies carrying out the supreme mission, sacrificing himself for his comrades; yet through the entire book he hardly changes and his reactions to the people and events surrounding him remain passive and quiescent. Countless novels, plays, and poems depict the new Hebrew, the boyish man, the parentless comrade, the inarticulate hero whose encounters with the world in which he lives have the ring of primal experience. If his parents suffer from the pain of severed roots, his new earthy rootedness is coupled with a constant search for "meaning," with which he is intellectually unequipped to grapple.

It may be argued that this literary prototype never truly did justice to the young generation of the native-born. Contrary to the literary image, the Sabras did have parents—many of them Yiddish-speaking immigrants who brought with them the customs and mementoes of the old world. Whereas the fictional Sabra usually lived on the land, working the soil, most Sabras even in prestate times—were born and bred in urban communities and acquired urban professions. Unlike their cult counterparts, the young men and women of the Yishuv had to grow up, attain maturity, face reality, and, in the end, become parents themselves.

Indeed, contemporary readers scanning the Sabra literature of the forties and fifties are bound to acquire an ambivalent attitude. On one hand, the reader is captivated by the intense experience of the Sabra environment, the sense of fraternity and total devotion to the Zionist cause; on the other hand, the reader must wonder where all the others are? the non-kibbutz types, the non–socialist-youth-movement youngsters? the non-Ashkenazi? the new immigrants? the non-Sabra native-born?

Sabra literature did not reflect reality, but created its own myth: the myth about the first generation of the native-born whose idealism and self-sacrifice inspire Israeli society to this present day. Needless to say, as Israeli society became more open and heterogenous, cracks began to appear, until finally the myth was smashed the smithereens. In contemporary Israeli literature new non-Sabra Israelis raise their solitary voices. In Hanoch Bartov's book of essays, *I Am Not the Mythological Sabra,* he derides the very attempt to create such a stereotype in a society in which every tenth Israeli has arrived just yesterday and calls upon the myth makers to shy away from their immaginary creation and return to the "real Israeli, to the equivocal Jew."[4]

---

4. Hanoch Bartov, *Ani lo haTsabar haMitologi* (I am not the mythological Sabra) (Tel Aviv 1995), 46–47.

Side by side with the heroic figure of yesteryear, new literary protagonists appear: the weak-minded, the marginal, the "others." In recent years, new voices are heard: the Sephardi, the women, the new immigrants from East and West. New and harsh criticism is leveled against the cult itself, which is seen as an expression of an Ashkenazi elite, pampering its own sons, oblivious to others. The famous 1948 war generation is, in retrospect, indeed pitiful. The constant wailing about the elders; the soul-searching and sterile debates; the preverted love affair with a brutal Soviet Union without even mentioning its terror and persecution of the Jews; the egocentricity and total ignorance of the newcomers—all these are easy targets for today's observer.

In retrospect, it is easy to understand why the Sabras failed to penetrate the leadership of the fledgling state. As the historian Anita Shapira notes,[5] most of them, the few thousands who emerged from the Palmach—the top units of the Haganah—could have led a society marked by rapid changes and massive immigration. That so many of the Palmach Sabra leadership sided with the left made their way into the top echelon even more difficult.

In the past much has been made of the paralyzing impact of the founding generation. We shall deal with this later, but it should be noted that the present-day revisionist view of the Sabra stereotype explains one aspect of this failure. Preoccupied by issues that were of no relevance to the emerging state—why was the Palmach disbanded? how to strengthen links with the World of Tomorrow (i.e., with Stalin's Russia?)—they really had nothing much to say about the real issues of survival—military, economic, and social. Their inclusive ethos, and disregard of immigrants from Muslim countries, was bound to have deep consequences, which were to emerge years later.

But all this was still to come. When we return to the fomative years, we realize that a much more significant failure marked the Sabra mentality—the failure to realize that the days of hubris, the superiority over the inferior stepbrother, the Diaspora Jew, were over.

Throughout the formative years of Sabra culture, in the 1930s and 1940s and up to and including the first years of statehood, the image of the new Hebrew was always juxtaposed against his shadowy kinsman, the Diaspora Jew. It was this contrast that gave

---

5. Anita Shapira, "Dor Ba'aretz" (Native-born generation), *Alpayim* (Quarterly) 2 (1990): 201.

sustenance to the Sabra's self-image. The depth of this attitude can be fathomed by the fact that it survived the Holocaust and extended to the refugees from the death camps who clamored to get into the closed Sabra society. In their book, *The First Million Sabras,* Margalit Banai and Herbert Russcol described "this still unsettled breed, this still inchoate genus," and made the following observation so common in fifties and sixties, so rare and outrageous today:

> The Sabra's complex feelings toward Jews abroad are colored by the fact that he can never grasp, although he knows the sad answers, why six million Jews let themselves be murdered by the Nazis. He never can understand why they did not die on their feet. This haunts him. It is a slur on his honor. It accounts for the one profound, centrifugal trait of the Sabra: his readiness to act to defend his freedom.[6]

This statement was not unique. At least in the initial period of statehood, such preposterous statements, actually accusing the Jews of going to the gas chambers like sheep to the slaughterhouse, abounded in Sabra literature.

Indeed, while the Jews were being led to their death, they were being accused by some Yishuv leaders of shameful passivity. Thus, Yitzchak Greenbaum, in charge of the Yishuv's rescue operations, commented that the news about the Jewish uprising in the Warsaw Ghetto lifted a weight from his heart: "We could not understand up to now how the Jews of Poland were going to death like sheep to the slaughter. Did the [Nazi] hangmen succeed in murdering their souls before they led their bodies to be slain?"[7]

Such utterances represented an extreme position, but the general sentiment of the Yishuv was that rebellion was a means of saving Jewish honor, and the victims' passivity puzzled and disturbed the native-born.

The Sabras' attitude toward the refugees of the Holocaust was tinged by these sentiments. Ehud Ben Ezer commented that "the Sabra detested the Jewish 'refugees,' who arrived after the

---

6. Margalit Banai and Herbert Russcol, *The First Million Sabras* (New York: Hart Publishing, 1970), 11.
7. Quoted in S. B. Beit-Zvi, *Ha'tzionut Hapost-Ugandit Bemashber Hasho'ah* (Post-Ugandan Zionism in the crucible of the Holocaust) (Tel Aviv, 1977), 386.

Holocaust, who did not even speak Hebrew, whose shorts reached their knees and whose manners were a sign of weakness and effeminate frailty."[8]

Many novels describe this clash. In Shamai Golan's *The Death of Uri Peled,* the protagonist comes to the country as a young escapee from the Holocaust. Like many new immigrants, he acquires a Sabra name as well as Sabra mannerisms. Nevertheless, he is viewed with suspicious disdain by the homogeneous native society he encounters. His friend, a fifth-generation Sabra, harangues him:

> The fighters of our War of Independence died for you, so that this land could absorb the likes of you—refugees who arrive from many exiles. We spilled our blood for this country, and you, I'm telling you, don't you now turn it into a pigsty with your swinish galut wheeling and dealing.[9]

In these typically harsh words is the very duality, the ambivalence, that characterized in those early years the mentality of the Sabra: He is ready to die for those he despises. The same attitude pervades many children's books on which the young are reared today. The Jewish immigrant boy, seeking the company of the healthy Sabras, is always portrayed as a pale weakling, gradually losing his ashen look and acquiring true manly Sabra qualities. Occasionally, there is some feeling of remorse among the local boys when their nastiness toward the newly arrived orphans is overdone. One such story tells of the typical Jewish boy: "pallid, wearing strange clothes . . . his seemingly bloodless face round like a girl's . . . his hair well combed above his white and smooth forehead." In short, the very opposite of the sun-tanned macho gang that accords him a typical welcome of ridicule: "My word, he is funny." The galut boy, who "squirms and shakes all over" when he hears the sound of a plane in the sky, becomes friendly with only one of the boys, "who is also somewhat strange." In his eagerness to be accepted by the Sabra gang, the refugee boy claims that he can swim like everybody else. To prove this, he dives into a pool and nearly drowns; he is saved in the nick of time by his stunned companions.

8. Ehud Ben Ezer, "Portsim unetsurim" (Besiegers and besieged), *Keshet* (summer 1968): 128.
9. Shamai Golan, *Moto Shel Uri Peled* (The death of Uri Peled) (Tel Aviv, 1971), 9.

The companions are ashamed; such remorse is rare in early Israeli children's literature.[10]

These random illustrations underscore the Sabra's initial feeling of superiority over his allegedly negative Jewish twin. The "negation of Exile" is expressed, in Sabra folklore, by a paternalistic attitude, oscillating between pity and contempt, toward the typical representative of that Exile. In the fifties, when the refugees from Nazi Europe were sharing the crowded transition camps with the refugees from Islamic repression, the Sabra cult reached its zenith and the Canaanites, who rejected the very nexus between Jews and Israelis, were reaching the peak of their influence. For a time it seemed that Sabra chauvinism was impervious to what had happened to European Jews.

Some of the refugees, in typical Jewish fashion, assimilated into this brash environment with great vigor, and a few even managed to out-Sabra the local specimen. Suppressing their nightmarish memories, parentless and homeless in a society dominated by familial ties, these refugee children acquired new Sabra names and personalities. Some became Sabra gurus, offering morsels of native humor and folklore. Dahn Ben Amotz, the classic refugee-turned-Sabra, described this process. After changing his galut name for the obligatory Sabra Hebrew name, he was born anew:

> With one blow I severed my links with my private past, to such an extent that I began to be born in Palestine—to invent a new identity, to deny any connection with my factual biography. With time the new identity I acquired became my authentic identity. . . . Within a few years, my Hebrew became more Sabra-sounding than that used by the native-born. Camouflaging my true past had to be perfect if I wanted people to believe my invented past.[11]

Thus, like assimilated Jews before him, Dahn Ben Amotz became more Israeli than the Israelis: "It was I, like other refugee children, who first shook off a literary Hebrew replete with galut European

---

10. Amiram Amitai, *Milchemet Hasheluliut* (The Battle of the Puddles) (Tel Aviv, 1968), 36–46.

11. Dahn Ben Amotz, *Ziyunim Ze Lo Hakol* (Tel Aviv, 1979), 116.

images, and when I began writing I resorted to the spoken substandard Hebrew which became an integral part of my identity."

The Holocaust and father's home were being blotted out of memory and replaced by all the paraphernalia of the new culture: the youth movement, folklore, kibbutz life, uninhibited camaraderie, toughness mitigated by the famous below-surface sentimentality.

But this heyday of Sabra consciousness was not destined to last. Even before the Six-Day War, cracks began to appear in the seemingly solid wall. The Jewish fate, ostensibly excluded forever from the sunny shores of Israel, seemed to creep through the back door of Israel's external conflicts. Dormant memories of the Holocaust surfaced from the limbo of repressed nightmares into an awakened realization that the unthinkable did take place and that some explanation for it had to be found.

The newborn Sabras, the ex-refugee orphans, were beginning to relive what they could no longer suppress: childhood in the shtetl; the last mementoes of a family that had disappeared into the abyss; survival in the face of annihilation and death. The nightmarish screams, up to then muffled for shame that the Sabra gang would hear, began to acquire literary manifestations. In 1963 a play called *Children of the Shadow,* written by Ben Zion Tomer, an orphan-turned-Sabra, depicted for the first time the clash between Israeli society and the newcomers. The play's protagonist, like the author, is an acculturated Sabra flaunting a classic Sabra name, Yoram. But behind this healthy, earthy mask, in constant terror, lies Yossele, the real Yiddish name of the "child of the shadow." Yossele-Yoram is ready to look inward beyond the Sabra mask, face his past, and recall half-forgotten memories. The play ends with Yossele-Yoram, having survived the crisis of this new recognition, acquiring a new, balanced self-awareness of himself as a composite personality combining traditionally Jewish with Sabra traits. The Sabra hero, the super-Jew, is no longer the opposite of the inferior Jew. *Children of the Shadow* opened the gate to a flood of such suppressed memories. Out of the newly acquired Hebrew names emerged the old galut names; Yiddish phrases cropped up; a mother's last look registered; childhood scenes in the old country were recreated. The past could no longer be pushed aside.

In Aharon Appelfeld's short stories and novels, the pre-Holocaust galut home is seen not only with pangs of nostalgia but with love for a lost happy childhood; the new Israeli environment cannot compensate for the intense feelings aroused by these resurging memories of the loved home that went up in flames.

The ashen world of Auschwitz began to reemerge in Sabra literature in the sixties. And so the galut began to creep onto the literary scene: first through childhood memories of the immigrant-turned-Sabra, then through a reexamination of the very attitude toward the "inferior stepbrother." A new trend, termed "neo-Jewish," began to manifest itself in the writings of native-born, authentic Sabra authors. In this new school, the galut existence is rarely shown in a negative light. On the contrary, in many of these new writings the galut Jew appears as a forceful character and traditional Judaism is portrayed as a powerful and consistent antidote to the Sabra's perennial perplexity. Occasionally, the roles are reversed: The galut Jew represents the stable element, the ability to weather the vicissitudes and vagaries of time and place, and the Sabra is depicted as the weak man whose disappointment with Israeli society is coupled with an immature helplessness that long ago lost its endearing qualities.

In *Nor the Battle to the Strong,* a novel by Ehud Ben Ezer, an Israeli student goes into a depression while serving his annual reserve duty in the army. He runs amok straight into the invisible enemy's fire. But before his death, he mourns his fate and bewails the tragedy of his country: "You said: a new truth. But we were cheated and became slaves to the sword, not its masters." And the heresy continues: "I wish I were unrooted, like a Jew, and not belong so much, because the roots entangle my legs and ensnare me."[12]

Israel Segal, brought up in an ultra-Orthodox home, gone secular to become an author and television personality, exemplifies this move back to Jewishness. In his book depicting the post–Six-Day War period, a Sabra officer still utters the old rhetorics. "This war erased finally the stain of the Holocaust, wiped off the spit which covered our faces since the catastrophe in Europe." The author himself totally rejects this view and in an interview expounds the opposite: "I am for the Galut, for the Jewish personality which grew up, separate and different, in Europe."

Such sentiments, echoing the very idea against which Zionism waged unrelenting war, could have been written only after the cru-

---

12. Ehud Ben Ezer, *Lo Lagiborim Ha'milchamah* (Nor the battle to the strong) (Tel Aviv, 1971), 104.

cial disillusionment with the Sabra myth. When Beth Hatefutzot, the Museum of the Diaspora, opened in Tel Aviv in 1979, it began to attract young Israelis eager to absorb the wealth of material attesting to the vast richness of Jewish communities in galut.

The search for Jewish roots acquired new meanings when Poland opened its gates to Israeli youth. Thousands of schoolchildren have visited the death camps and come back with the sights deeply embedded in their memory. In the West, as in Israel, the Holocaust became an indelible part of contemporary consciousness only in recent years, but in Israel this new awareness has erased past conceits.

In a series of polls the new generation of Sabras demonstrate this change of heart and mind. In his research, Yair Oron found that the Holocaust has become the major element in the new Jewish-Israeli identity—both collectively and individually.[13] Of those polled, 77.4 percent of the secular students and 88.7 percent of religious students, are proud of the Jews' conduct during the Holocaust, and only a small minority, less than 5 percent, share the former generation's shame at their so-called passivity.

Thus has Israel come full circle: In the forties, Haim Hazaz, a noted author, wrote that when a man cannot be a Jew anymore, he becomes a Zionist. Now, many young Hebrews believe that their traditional secular Zionism, with its emphasis on normalcy, has reached a dead end and that Hazaz's dictum is refuted and reversed by experience: When a man cannot be a Zionist anymore, he reverts to being a Jew.

Nothing demonstrates this point more dramatically than what might be called "the game of the name." Since the Second Aliyah, changing a galut-Yiddish name into a Hebrew name became a cherished practice of the new Hebrews. It was more than a mere act of immigrant acculturation. By acquiring a Hebrew name, the galut Jew transformed himself into a new being, shorn of the humiliating load of the past. By reverting to biblical names, the names of the Hebrew kings, prophets, and soldiers, the new Hebrews were embodying that wish to forget their Diaspora existence, the very essence of Zionist philosophy. Even in picking the new names, especially first names, the new Hebrews were careful to avoid names that had galut connotations. In the Yishuv such typically Jewish names

---

13. Yair Oron, *Zehut Yehudit-Israelit* (Jewish-Israeli identity) (Tel Aviv, 1993), 107. The poll was conducted among students in teachers colleges.

as Abraham, Isaac, Jacob, Moshe, Aaron, Sara, Rivka, and Rachel became rare; in their place were names Diaspora Jews never used or rarely resorted to: Amos, Yoram, Nimrod, Uri, Yuval, Amnon. The two-syllable name, with the accent on the second syllable, became the staple hallmark of young Hebrews, and its very sound pronounced a rebellion against the foreign-sounding, Yiddish-tinged names of the parents' generation.

The trend, which began with the pioneers of the Second Aliyah, acquired pace in the twenties when David Ben-Gurion became secretary general of the Histadrut. In 1922 the first general census of Histadrut members was taken, and Ben-Gurion used this opportunity to cajole many members into adopting appropriate Hebrew names. After he became prime minister in 1948, Ben-Gurion used his authority and influence to effect the massive conversion of names in the young country's political and military establishment. For Ben-Gurion himself (né Gruen) the new Hebrew name signified more than mere renunciation of galut: It was an act of rebirth, for, as Ben-Gurion himself used to say, he had been born anew in Palestine and his galut childhood did not count as part of his life.

Under Ben-Gurion's leadership, a new unwritten rule was formulated: Senior officers in the army and in the government bureaucracy had to adopt Hebrew names. Thus, men and women of advanced age acquired a new Hebrew mantle upon entering office. Golda Meyerson lived for fifty-eight years under the name she had been born with. Upon becoming foreign minister in Ben-Gurion's cabinet, she turned into Golda Meir. In similar fashion, Pinhas Kozlowsky became Minister of Finance Sapir; Yigal Sukenik became Chief of Staff Yadin; Zalman Rubashov became President Shazar; Shimon Persky became Labor leader Peres. In the 1950s, under the directives of Moshe Sharett, who at the age of fifty-five forsook his well-known family name of Shertok, no diplomatic passport could be issued to a bearer of a non-Hebrew name, and the Foreign Service in its entirety—Teddy Kollek being the single inexplicable exception—had to acquire new Hebrew names, relinquishing, occasionally, proud age-old Jewish family names. Officials pleading special attachment to their family names were not spared. In the army, the rule was less severe: High-ranking officers such as Chaim Laskov and Ezer Weizman were allowed to keep their non-Hebrew names, the first pleading orphancy, the second an attachment to his great uncle, Chaim Weizmann.

Dahn Ben Amotz, the classical Sabra on whose slangy maxims generations of young Israelis were nurtured, underwent a double transformation. He arrived in Palestine from Poland bearing the almost unbearable Yiddish-sounding name of Moussia Tehilimzeiger. Within days, he was renamed Moshe Sheoni—an impossible attempt to Hebraize an untranslatable name. Later, in 1945, when he deserted from the British army and joined a kibbutz, a new name was adopted for the purpose of obtaining a false Palestinian identity card. It was with this Sabra name that Dahn gradually became the mythological Sabra trendsetter. Of the Tehilimzeigers, none survived the Holocaust.

But this great wave of name changing receded with the new soul-searching mood of the sixties. No longer was the verbal transition regarded as symbolic of the rebirth of Israel. The old names signified the very civilization destroyed by the Nazis, and relinquishing the verbal mementoes of this civilization lost some of its former attraction.

Expressions of this new attitude often appear in contemporary literature. In Yitzchak Orpaz's novel *A Home for One Man*, the protagonist, Izzi Ornan (a more Sabra-Hebrew name is hard to find) is portrayed at the beginning of the book as a true Tel Avivian submerged in the typical day-to-day problems of secular Israeli society. His uncle, whose spiritual and actual language is Yiddish, symbolizes the link with traditional Judaism. Before his death, this uncle castigates his Sabra nephew: "Remember where you came from; Sternharz is a name which one should not be ashamed of."

Sternharz is the galut name of the Sabra protagonist before being Hebraized. The uncle's last wish is not forgotten. The nephew proceeds to recall and relive his forgotten past. Jewish tradition is symbolized by a pair of Sabbath candlesticks that the nephew has inherited from the dead uncle and in which he sees the road back to his forefathers' belief. And shortly after the publication of this novel the author added his original Jewish name—Auerbuch—to his acquired Hebrew name.

The poet Avoth Yeshurun—again, as Hebrew a name as can be imagined—writes: "I've changed my name, I've changed my tongue, I've changed my town." His father then appears to him in a dream and fails to recognize him. The son cries out: "I, Yechiel Alter of old/ Avoth he did not recognize." And the poet wonders:

> *How did I come*
> *To think of changing my name,*
> *Which cannot be changed?*
> *Why do I long*
> *After the name my mother gave me*
> *And called me?*
> *My name was the only thing*
> *She left me, she left me.*[14]

And, similarly, writes Aharon Komem in his poem "My Mother":

> *The name Kominkovsky*
> *lasted for years . . .*
> *My mother called me*
> *in my name*
> *I—in her proper name*
> *only on distant envelopes*
> *and on mourning notices*
> *which she will never read.*[15]

From a research study that analyzed two million first names, some interesting findings emerge. From 1882 to 1920, classical and biblical names abound. Between 1921 and 1944, a new native Hebrew fashion brings non-Jewish original Hebrew names into fashion. Finally, in the third stage, the trend is toward English-sounding Hebrew names, often made up to sound bilingual: Gaie (Guy), Ron, Li-on (Leon), Tom, and Ro'iy (Roy).[16]

The new Sabra can henceforth resemble his Jewish cousin living in the Diaspora in first and family names alike. No more inferior stepbrother, the Diaspora Jew can now be emulated.

---

14. Avoth Yeshurun, *Sha'ar Knissah, Sha'ar Yetsi'ah* (Entrance gate, exit gate) (Tel Aviv, 1981), 61. Author's translation.
15. Aharon Komem, in *Alpayim* (Quarterly) 12 (1996): 137. Author's translation.
16. Sasha Vitman, "First Names as Cultural Indices: Tendencies in the Identity of Israelis 1882–1980," The Pinchas Sapir Center for Development, Tel Aviv University Publications, 1985.

By the time the new mass immigration from the former Soviet Union and from Ethiopia begins to arrive in the 1990s, all such attempts are forsaken. Most immigrants retain their names—both family and individual—and no attempt is made to cut them off from their mother tongue and culture.

But it is not only this new equality with the former "inferior stepbrother" that dented the old myth; further blows landed on the hallowed stereotype. In the late sixties—again, after the Six-Day War—a new phenomenon raised its head: a movement of *hozzim b'teshuvah,* of repentants, or "born-again" Jews. The movement became significant not only because it reversed the regular Israeli trend of moving away from religion, but mainly because it involved a large number of classic, secular Sabras, among them famous artists and entertainers. These individuals were not content with a flight into the yeshiva but insisted on joining the most Orthodox and reclusive segments in the religious community. Their act became symbolic: Out of the cafés of Dizengoff Street, out of the most permissive circles of the Sabra environment, they crossed over to a society barely associated with Israel, resembling, as it does, the ghetto-like shtetl existence. The typical Sabra was transformed into the galut image of his forefathers. The Sabra grandson took over the shape of his grandfather, that very grandfather against whom his father had staged his Zionist rebellion. In one case, this transition acquired nationwide visibility. Uri Zohar, an entertainer and actor, had been for many years synonymous with Sabra humor and folklore. With Dahn Ben Amotz, he created a whole language of Sabra quips and aphorisms. His very appearance on television, where he had his own show, bespoke Sabra-ness. Then, before his admiring audience, Uri Zohar—again, the unmistakable Sabra name— changed his persona. The Sabra hero was transformed into an Orthodox Jew: first the skullcap, then the side curls, finally the beard and bearing of an Orthodox, grandfatherly person. After he left public life and television, Uri Zohar completed this metamorphosis from sandal-shod native son to heavily garmented, bent shtetl chasid.

Occasionally, these Sabras-turned-chasidim join the most militant Orthodox groups of the Mea Shearim quarter in Jerusalem, from which they emerge to throw stones at cars traveling on the Sabbath. From the heartland of Israel they have traversed all the way to the non-Zionist shelters of galut within Israel. Just as their fathers ran from Jewish isolation, seeking participation in current history and culture, so do these Sabra grandsons seek refuge from current history in a haven where Judaism, unaltered by the outside world, reigns eternal.

At the other end of the ethnic spectrum, within the Sephardic community, a massive return to religion suddenly emerged as a powerful social, educational and political force. This force is led on the spiritual side by the charismatic Rabbi Ovadia Yoseph, and on the political side by an astute leader, Aryeh Der'i. Low-income groups in development towns and poor urban neighborhoods flocked to the new Shas Party and to its own independent, but publicly financed, ultra-Orthodox school network. These Sephardic Jews, who remained on the lower rungs of the social and economic ladder, found solace and pride in their rediscovered old beliefs and rites. They responded both to the party—growing dramatically from five Knesset members in 1992 to ten after the 1966 elections. They too, together with their Ashkenazi counterparts, detached themselves from the Sabra culture.

Sabra secularism suffered a further blow from another direction: Gush Emunim, devout in its religious-nationalist tradition, sought to continue the Zionist pioneering spirit that in the past had been associated with the Left. Its members adopted the casual, sandal-clad look, the songs, the folklore associated with the old Palmach-type Sabra. Thus, a new skullcapped Sabra came into existence, continuing, as it were the old tradition. The resemblance was superficial and misleading; reality enforced a contradiction between the two opposing political camps. But the idealism, the readiness for self-sacrifice, was still there and moved an old stalwart of the Left, Yaacov Hazan, to admire the resemblance of the Gush to his old flame—the socialist Kibbutz of yesteryear.

This new type of religious Sabras established a fact: The native-born culture gave birth to not one but two identities, and these two fight over Israel's soul.

Let us now return to the beginning of this chapter and ask ourselves why, despite all these transmutations and transitions, the original Sabra image continues to engage so much attention. Why should we harp, time and time again, on the 1948 war and its typecast heroes? Why bother with the Sabra thing?

The answer lies in an inchoate sense of continuity between the symbols of 1948 and our present day. Added to this is a new, mature understanding that Israeli society is torn by two contradictory forces: that which draws generations of new immigrants into the very heart of Sabra culture and the centrifugal force that leaves outside this idiosyncratic culture large segments—parts of the Sephardic community and the ultra-Orthodox. The cohesive, acculturating force of the original native-born nucleus, not self-evident in a formative society that increases eightfold in less than fifty years, overcomes seemingly unbridgeable contrasts, but leaves outside its zone ever-growing enclaves whose political clout is becoming stronger.

And there is another open question: Why was the Sabra generation so late in reaching political leadership? Only during Rabin's second government did the native-born generation take its place in the composition of the cabinet. Linked to this question, and more enticing, is the failure of the two prototypical Sabra leaders to make a difference when in power: Moshe Dayan and Ygal Allon, both highly intelligent and almost legendary in their reputation, demonstrate this failure.

To many, Dayan personalized the Sabra, the new Jew, landed in the Labor-led government directly after his meteoric military career. His road to the top was paved with popularity; he lacked only one quality: leadership. He ended his life and political career while heading a two-member party in the Knesset and while his inheritors kept arguing about the meaning of his political will and testament, assuming such existed.

This militarily courageous man, who did not flinch in face of danger, who could make fateful decisions in battle, moved on Israel's political stage, Hamlet-like, without being able to make a lasting decision. His whole political career abounds in perplexing inconsistencies and ambivalent ditherings, which invariably ended with his accepting the authority of his "elders": Ben-Gurion, Eshkol, Golda Meir, Begin.

Dayan had some helpful ideas and instincts in setting goals for the nation: the opening of bridges linking the newly occupied West Bank with Jordan; opposition to death sentences for terrorists; his willingness—declared and taken back within days—to withdraw unilaterally from the Suez Canal during Israel's occupation of the

Sinai. But after all was said and done, his main contribution was to obfuscate the dilemmas facing Israel. One day he declared that Sharm-el-Sheik was more important than peace and sank billions in the Sinai; then he said the exact opposite and was instrumental in bartering the whole of the Sinai—including, of course, Sharm-el-Sheik—for peace with Egypt. Did he really believe in a "benign occupation" of the West Bank and the Gaza strip? Did he really convince himself, as he convinced others, that trucks carrying the West Bank's tomatoes over the Jordan bridges would be a substitute for a political solution?

Dayan's story symbolized the Sabra failure, primarily because of the determination he had exhibited as an army leader. The same is true of Yigal Allon, the classical Sabra leader of the Palmach, the elite crack force of the Haganah. Unlike Dayan, he formulated a strategic plan, named after him, stipulating the division of the West Bank between Israel and the Palestinians, but he never had the stamina and determinaton needed to transform this plan into a political platform. At various stages in his career he, like Dayan, gave in, with or without dissenting mutterings, to the wish of his elders. He opposed, at least ostensibly, the establishment of settlements in the midst of urban Arab areas, but actively supported bringing armed religious and fanatic settlers into Hebron. Finally, this otherwise brilliant person ended his career by abstaining on the crucial Knesset vote ratifying the peace treaty with Egypt.

This abstention spoke loudly and attested, again, to the familiar apparition: a dramatic discrepancy between military capability and political impotence. Dayan and Allon are not alone in exemplifying this discrepancy. Yigal Yadin, Meir Amit, Aaron Yariv—all excellent men, all coming into politics with impeccable army careers, all bearing the obligatory Hebraized Sabra two-syllable names—became political failures, not because they were not given an opportunity to succeed, but because when given the opportunity, they had nothing meaningful to say.

Sociologist Yonathan Shapiro, an astute observer of the political scene, explained the origins of this apparition of the manly Sabra who is a political neuter:

> This placed the native-born in an extremely difficult situation. Unlike the young Jews who had grown up abroad in confrontation with the older generation, incapable of finding

a solution to the Jews' worsening situation, the native-born found themselves confronting an older generation imbued with success at having accomplished its goals. . . . In consequence, the young people did not challenge the Zionist and Socialist theses of the generations of the founders. The native-born youth were thus unable to crystalize into generation units with nuclei groups capable of adopting independent world views. However, when they grew up, they found that the organizational and political structures set up by the elders were closed to them. For lack of any other alternative, they were compelled to organize themselves but they were an abortive generation without an independent world view . . . conspicuous in its weakness and sterility.[17]

Thus it was that from the early days young leaders opted for a military career as a vehicle leading them upward. In the underground and in the army, the native-born found a way of life after their own hearts. Indeed, the central experience that connects the early formative years with Israel today is the double experience: army and war. The 1948–49 war was traumatic: the six thousand—mostly young—who died in battle constituted 1 percent of the population. This sacrifice created its own collective memory, as well as its own myth and antimyth. We are dealing with a bloodletting equivalent to that suffered, in an equivalent time span, by Britain, France, and Germany in World War I. One must remember that this bloodshed came in the wake of the Holocaust and Jewish losses at the hands of Palestinian Arabs during the Mandatory period.

Hence the myth: The lost generation of the War of Independence whose absence in the formative years, explains, or seems to explain, the failure of the Sabras to acquire a leadership position. The countermyth relates to others who died in battle: not the Sabra heroes, but the faceless, often nameless, unsung new immigrants who were sent to the battle straight from the boats bringing them to the shores of a beleaguered nation. They died, "without nuisance, without making life difficult to others, without slowly killing those who remember."[18] Indeed, although the share of casualties among those

---

17. Yonathan Shapiro, "Generational Units and Intergenerational Relations in Israeli Politics," *Israel: A Developing Society* (The Hague, The Netherlands: Van Gorcum, Assen, 1980), 168.
18. Poem by Aryeh Sivan, *Ma'ariv,* 8 May 1981.

who landed in Palestine after 1947 is lower than the share among the veterans, the losses of the new immigrants—the heroes of the antimyth—cannot be thus measured: three out of ten of the post-1947 immigrants who died in battle were parentless or had no kin in the new country.[19]

This myth and antimyth, which continue with amazing intensity to the present day, provide another reason that the early days are still part and parcel of contemporary Israeli consciousness.

Indeed, if one may speak about Sabra culture, war and death are its central themes. The 1948 literature and poetry created an inter-generation partnership, because death in war—which was supposed to end with every Israeli victory—is an ongoing common lot.

Their arduous service in the army plays a major role in the life of young Israelis. It sucks their physical and mental energy; it provides an alibi for refusing to enter other—political and social—commitments; it is also a source of great satisfaction, for in such service the young can exhaust their hunger for glory and their need to be in a tight and mutually supporting group. Military duty enhances the qualities for which the native-born is famous: The army becomes the group, the mission, the folklore, the destiny, the threat of death.

Danger of death is indeed a constant companion. Far from ruthless fearlessness, Sabra writings manifest a sense of deep futility and resigned despair, perhaps singular in its intensity. In vain will one look for anything resembling flag-waving patriotism. Many Sabras write "war poems," and in a great many of these, they foresee their own death. But unlike Rupert Brooke, who in World War I wrote, "If I should die, think only this of me:/ That there's some corner of a foreign field/ That is forever England," the Israeli poets find no such consolation. Death in war is seen as wholly arbitrary. Thus wrote kibbutz member Yosef Sarig a short time before he died in the Yom Kippur War:

> *My death came to me suddenly*
> *And I cannot remember whether it happened*
> *In the thunder of fire or between*
> *The screaming walls of steel.*

---

19. Emanuel Sivan, *Dor Tashach* (The 1948 generation) (Tel Aviv, 1991), 27.

> *Or perhaps in white, in the finally*
> *Silent white.*
> *Now*
> *I do not remember.*[20]

And another poet, who died in the War of Attrition along the Suez Canal, Be'eri Hazak, predicted his own death in a tank in the form of a radio dialogue between God and himself:

> *Please shut your eyes now.*
> *I hear you now. Roger.*
> *You can finally die.*
> *Bereaved Father, I can feel no longer,*
> *The tears of winter will say kaddish over your grave.*[21]

The sentiments expressed by these astounding poems, not written for publication, extend beyond mere private anxieties. Even when expressing political dissent, Sabra authors write about their own predicted death. Poet Meir Wieseltier writes about his hypothetical death in a terrorist act and demands that this death not be exploited to undermine his political belief:

> *If I die one day from a bullet*
> *Of a young Palestinian killer, who will*
> *Cross the Northern border or from the blast*
> *Of a hand grenade*
> *Or from the explosion of a charge*
> *While staring at the price of cucumbers*
> *In the market, do not dare say*
> *That my blood furnishes proof*
> *Of the justice of your errors*
> *That my torn eyes strengthen you in your blindness.*[22]

---

20. Yosef Sarig, "Moti Ba li Peta," in *Makom Shel Esh* (Tel Aviv, 1975), 84. Author's translation.
21. Be'eri Hazak, "Ribono Shel Olam," in *Shdemot,* no. 53 (Tel Aviv, 1974), 127. Author's translation; for another translation, see *Lines Cut: Posthumous Poems of Four Young Israelis* (Tel Aviv: Hakibbutz Hame 'uchad Publications, 1981), 65.
22. Meir Wieseltier, "A Sonnet Against Those Who Exploit the Spilt Blood," *Siman Kri'ah* 11 (May 1980): 87.

This constant foreboding stems not only from the fear of imminent death; the tragedy emanates from deeper sources. The secular native-born finds himself torn by the existential dilemma characteristic of contemporary Israel. He is the product of prevailing Western culture, and with his Occidental counterparts he shares modern interests and attitudes. His head reaches to the heights of secular modernity: the attraction of the sciences and the arts, the pleasures and discontents of twentieth-century civilization. Yet his legs straddle a land subject to an ancient dispute. His heart is torn between the obvious need to defend his home, private as well as national, and the dark suspicion that this battle is acquiring, in spite of himself, the character of a religious war. Had he been fanatically religious, were he ready to give his life for the Tomb of the Patriarchs in Hebron, it would all have been much simpler. But his universal-secular upbringing makes it far from simple. Hence, the sense of futility, of frustrated lives terminated by an irrelevant death. This does not mean that he has doubts about the justice of his own cause or that he will not go to war, fight bravely, and be ready to make the supreme sacrifice, as he has always done in the past. But if the songs he prefers tend to be rather melancholy, it is perhaps because of this vague feeling that he finds himself stranded in a nightmarish existence. The Arab is not a fellow victim, as the 1948 literature suggested, but a permanent, and perhaps incorrigible, enemy. Across the barbed wire, over the border, lie not only tanks and minefields but also the "Lands of the Jackal"—to use Amos Oz's phrase—where unmitigated hate threatens to engulf the tiny island of Israel with its dark waves.

The peace process, first with Egypt, then with the Palestinians and with Jordan, was supposed to end all this. It may still do that. But the Arab animosity is still there, deeply embedded. In any case, terrorism will continue to threaten, under best of terms, the lives of Israelis. There is hope for a better future, but there is also a deep, ever-present anxiety: Iran and Iraq loom beyond the borders with their missiles and madness—1948 is not really so far away.

There is another reason that 1948 and all it entails are important. The army experience deepens and enhances the trait forged then in Sabra reality and folklore: *re'ut*—more kinship than friendship. "Sentiment" *(re'ut)* was, initially, a Palmach song that mourned the fallen "handsome generation" who died in the war. It was Rabin's favorite song. And it became, understandably, the hymn of the youngsters who lit candles, quietly lamenting the death of Rabin, one of the last remaining heroes of that war.

This *re'ut*—this kinship, this subtle brotherly love—has indeed become the most visible Sabra quality. Such kinship is a mixed blessing; painful when absent, infuriating when excessive, it has become an integral part of both fact and fiction. Members of the Sabra group, the *chevreh*, demand total loyalty and involvement in each other's life.

This honeycomb nature of Sabra society is an obtrusive fact of life, routinely celebrated, and ridiculed, in Israeli literature. Thus, Amos Kennan, a noted satirist, wrote a grotesque obituary for Dani, a Sabra who took his own life:

> Once there was a tragedy. The entire gang went out of town to attend the wedding of one of its members, and Dani was left by himself. All evening he walked the streets alone and didn't meet anybody. This made him despondent. He killed himself for this reason, and to this day no one knows how he managed to do it all by himself.[23]

A similar mood of in-group obsessiveness pervades Moshe Shamir's homage to his brother Elik, the Sabra "born from the sea."[24] This book achieves a truly classic description of a new type of hero: the kind-hearted, grassroots Sabra, the child of the sun and soil of Eretz Israel. Yet what most typifies Elik as a person is that he is an integral part of a close-knit whole. He lives and breathes with his group, at the agricultural high school he attends, in the underground, or on a visit to the big city. Elik and his friends, discover that they are not interested in anything except each other, that the place of the individual is increasingly being taken by companionship, and that without the group and its camaraderie life has no meaning.

Since those days, Israeli society has been radically transformed. It has grown in size and lost its family ambience. It has also become more open, more divided, more antagonistic. Contemporary Israeli

---

23. *Ha'aretz*, 6 June 1952.
24. Moshe Shamir, *With His Own Hands*, tr. J. Shacter (Jerusalem, 1970), 1.

prose and poetry deal with the individual, often the odd man out. But that small nucleus, the brotherly group, the *chevreh,* is still there, binding Israelis together—even when they live elsewhere—often exasperating but always there.

It is quite conceivable that the advantages and disadvantages of Israeli society, its capacity to absorb immigrants from different cultures so quickly, its attractiveness as well as its obnoxiousness, are intertwined with the myth of the Sabra. The myth is gone and buried, but still it rules us from its grave. Perhaps the survival of the Sabra ideal is due to a search for a fleeting moment when nightmare gave way to the dream and its children. And perhaps there is a simple need for an ever-present figure serving as a guide in perplexing times.

9

Post-Zionism
and Anti-Zionism

During the final two decades of the twentieth century a revived attack was being waged in Israel against classical Zionism. Offensives were launched from three directions: from within the camp that passes itself off as Zionist and from the two non-Zionist, or in their more virulent strains, anti-Zionist, camps: ultra-Orthodox Judaism and the post-Zionist intellectuals.

The nationalist-religious attack against Herzlian Zionism seemed to be waged right under Zionism's very nose, appropriating the Zionist flag and symbols. Nevertheless, it is completely alien to the foundations of Zionism, on both the Right and the Left, including classical religious Zionism. Zionist ideology has always been based upon a moral and universal foundation. It sought to establish a national Jewish homeland that would embody virtues of peace and justice; it would never be founded on hatred, violence, or racism.

When we come to the non-Zionist camp, the story is quite different. There is nothing new about ultra-Orthodox opposition to Zionism. It already existed at the dawn of the national Jewish awakening, even before the Basel Congress, subsequently growing more virulent. At its core, ultra-Orthodox objection to Zionism revolves around one basic theme: The Jews should wait for the Messiah's arrival before reestablishing their national center. Any mortal initiative of "forcing the Messiah's arrival" is liable to invoke God's wrath. Even an event as cataclysmic as the annihilation of Europe's Jews, many of whom heeded their rabbis' advice and chose not to emigrate to Israel when it was still possible—did nothing to moderate the ultra-Orthodox, anti-Zionist polemic. On the contrary, the Holocaust provided a new, insidious argument against the Zionists: Forcing the Messiah's arrival, extremist elements claim, was what incurred God's anger, explaining why he remained passive while a million and a half Jewish children were butchered, murdered, burned, and gassed, and while the God-fearing Jews of eastern Europe were sacrificed at the altar. The Shoah was the punishment meted out by heaven upon the Jewish people in retribution for transgressions committed by the Zionists. They had profaned the Holy Name with their rebellious disregard for God's will, seeking to usher in the redemption without his help.

Rabbi Avraham Yeshayaha Karelitz, the sage known as the Chazon Ish, "vigorously rejected Zionism, holding it responsible for the Holocaust."[1] Ultra-Orthodox literature on the subject, at least among the extremist elements, is particularly vicious. One ultra-Orthodox author puts it this way in his book (the title of which says it all), *The Crimes of Zionism in the Destruction of the Diaspora:* "At least the Nazis said what they had to say out in the open, whereas these Zionist criminals masquerade as lovers of Jews, with love for their people on their lips and Hitler-like hatred in their hearts. With great cunning, they managed to block all possible salvation efforts."[2]

Some of the opinions expressed by ultra-Orthodox writers, especially those affiliated with the leader of the Lithuanian Jewish community in Israel, Rabbi Eliezer Shach—on the issue of Zionist responsibility for the Holocaust are incredibly venomous. Writes another ultra-Orthodox author: "That which the heads of Zionism inflicted on European Jewry during World War II cannot be described as other than killing in the proper sense of the word. These Zionist leaders were, 'the criminals of the Holocaust who contributed their part to the destruction.'" The author goes on to say that the hands of Zionist leaders "are stained with blood, and the foundations of the Zionist walls are laid with [the bodies of] the children of Israel destroyed in the Exile. Not only did they [the Zionists] not raise a finger, but they actively sought to impede any

---

1. *Encyclopedia Hebraica*, vol. 30, 234 (Heb.).
2. S. Shalmon, *Pishei Hatsionut Behashmadat Hagolah* (The crimes of Zionism in the annihilation of the exile) (Jerusalem: Haredi, 1990), 69.

salvation efforts."[3] The Zionist leaders—and especially Chaim Weizmann, Moshe Sharett, Rabbi Stephen Wise, Nahum Goldman, and basically the entire leadership of the Yishuv and of American Jews—are besmirched with all possible invective: Ben-Gurion[4]— "pervaded with a hatred of Judaism"—is compared to Hitler; the leadership of the Labor Party and the Left "deliberately dispatched millions of Jews to their destruction," while blocking "the escape routes of European Jews."[5] The sickening verbal abuse continues ad nauseam.

What is the cause—if one can speak in such rational terms—of these unspeakable accusations? Aside from the general abhorrence for all things related to the alleged secular, heretical, atheist Zionism, the Holocaust is used to back up what has been the primary ultra-Orthodox indictment of Zionism since its inception: According to the Babylonian Talmud's tractate of Ketubot, three oaths were taken at Mount Sinai before God Almighty: two by Israel and one by the other nations of the world. God made Israel swear "not to rise up on the wall" (taken to mean that Israel should respect the boundaries set between it and the nations of the world, boundaries that enforce Israel's subservient role among the nations) and "not to rebel against the nations of the world." In return, God made the nations of the world swear "not to enslave Israel too much."

Taken together, these three oaths form a quasi-covenant between Israel and the nations of the world—the goyim—among whom they were dispersed. The ultra-Orthodox assert that Zionism violated the Covenant by its attempt to hasten the end, rebelling against the nations of the world, and in so doing absolving the goyim from their

---

3. In Moshe Scheinfeld, *Srufei Hakivshanim Ma'ashimim* (Victims of the gas chambers accuse)—Evidence, Documents and Testimonies on the Criminals of the Holocaust (Jerusalem, 1998), 6. The book, which has gone through several editions, was published by Torah Scholars Group, affiliated with Agudat Israel Youth, a group that joined forces with the Belz and Satmar Hassidim to disseminate the most ferocious propaganda regarding Zionist responsibility for the Holocaust. This book, and the book by Shalmon noted in the preceding footnote, which also went through several editions, are the most widely disseminated books on this subject within the ultra-Orthodox community. They were joined, primarily since the 1980s, by a series of articles appearing in some of the ultra-Orthodox press, which use the same terminology and level the same accusations.
4. *Hadashot shel Shabbat* (Sabbath news), 21 April 1989, in an interview with Ya'akov Segal.
5. This translated excerpt appears in Dina Porat's "Amalek's Accomplices—Blaming Zionism for the Holocaust: Anti-Zionist Ultra-Orthodoxy in Israel During the 1980s," *Journal of Contemporary History* 27 (1992): 695–729.

oath not to persecute the Jews at an intolerable level—"too much."
From this point it is only a short leap to the next conclusion:
Zionism exploited anti-Semitism, using it to impel the nations of the
world to banish the Jews from their home countries and bring them
to the land of Israel. The ultra-Orthodox allegation is that the object
of bringing Jews to the land of Israel justified the means of collabo-
rating with the Nazis. Dina Porat, of the Department of Jewish
History at Tel Aviv University, expands on this in her enlightening
article:

> Thus, the accusers formulated a kind of causal nexus with its
> own intrinsic logic: secularism, the mother of all sins, leads
> to nationalism; the striving to attain national statehood
> leads, in turn, to sacrificing the Jews who are not needed to
> attain this goal, namely, the ultra-Orthodox. This, in a nut-
> shell, is the theological and substantive groundwork on
> which the accusations against Zionism are based. The per-
> son most responsible for furnishing the theological argu-
> mentation against the very essence of Zionism was the
> Satmar Rabbi. Those who followed in his footsteps did not
> dwell on these questions at length, focusing instead on
> polemics based on certain episodes, repeatedly and exten-
> sively used as evidence.[6]

What are the specific claims lodged against Zionism? The main
argument is that in distributing the handful of immigration certificates it received from the British government on the eve of World
War II, the Jewish Agency discriminated between different categories of Jews. The small quantity of certificates was distributed at
the start according to a quota system, and in spite of everything, the
ultra-Orthodox Agudat Israel received between 6 and 8 percent of
the meager total. Moreover, there was an Aguda representative on
the joint rescue committee that allotted these few certificates.

When the true dimensions of the fate of European Jewry came to
light, the quota system was immediately dropped. Anyone who
could be saved was given any available certificate. Even still, the
quota was never filled until the end of the British Mandate. Several

---

6. Porat, "Amalek's Accomplices," 707.

rabbis and Hassidic leaders were saved thanks to the haven offered by the Zionists, including the Gerer Rebbe, Rabbi Avraham Mordechai Alter, and the Belzer Rebbe, Rabbi Issachar Dov Rokeach, who arrived in Israel in early 1944, just ahead of the Nazi invasion of Hungary. The Satmar Rebbe, Yoel Moshe Teitelbaum, managed to get out of Nazi Europe by way of the "Train of the Privileged," which was organized by Rudolf Kastner, a Zionist activist in Budapest, through which a few hundred Jews were saved from the Nazi clutches.

The second allegation is diametrically opposed to the first claim— that is, that Zionism collaborated with Nazism. This line of thought accuses the Zionist leadership of provoking Nazi Germany. That is to say, Zionism provoked Hitler and brought on the destruction of European Jewry by declaring an economic boycott of Germany after Kristallnacht, the Nazi-orchestrated pogrom against Jews that occurred in late 1938. The allegation is that on the eve of the war, Weizmann declared war on Nazi Germany in the name of the Jewish people. "Without a doubt," wrote one author, "Weizmann thereby intended to endanger the Jews as much as he could." Furthermore, another ultra-Orthodox author wrote that when Jewish representatives in Switzerland informed Weizmann about what was taking place at Auschwitz, they said that he was "very pleased, as it will help us get a state."[7]

The third accusation is that Zionism thwarted salvation efforts because the rescue of ordinary Jews—as opposed to the immigration of like-minded pioneers to Palestine—did not serve its goals. Interestingly, there is significant overlap between allegations of this sort lodged by the ultra-Orthodox and by the non-Zionist intellectuals, which is discussed in detail later. One prominent accusation relates to the Europa Plan, an affair that is referred to so frequently that it has taken on the dimensions of an ultra-Orthodox myth, constituting ironclad proof of Zionist guilt.

The Europa Plan was the brainchild of two larger-than-life characters who engaged in a desperate attempt to save the Jews of Slovakia: Rabbi Chaim Michael Dov-Ber Weissmandel and Gisi

---

7. The first quote appears in Shalmon, *Pishei Hatsionut,* 29. These ideas, first expressed by the Satmar Rebbe, are supported, as noted by Dina Porat, by revisionist German historian Ernst Nolte (see Porat, "Amalek's Accomplices, 707") The second quote appears in A. Y. Rotter, *Sha'arei Aharon* (Gates of Aharon) (Bnei Brak, 1982), 69.

Fleischmann. Coincidentally or not, the two were related. He was a sworn anti-Zionist rabbi, the son-in-law of the leader of Orthodox Slovakian Jewry. She was president of the Women's International Zionist Organization, a brave, heroic woman who personally conducted negotiations with Eichmann's agent, and who was eventually murdered in Auschwitz. The plan called for a suspension of the transfer of Slovakian Jews to Auschwitz in exchange for bribes offered to Dieter Wisliceny, Eichmann's henchman in Slovakia.

Ultra-Orthodox detractors claim that an appeal for funding to cover the bribes was rejected by the Jewish Agency, and that the representative of the Zionist organization in Geneva, Nathan Shwalb (later Dror), not only refused to endorse the deal but added that Jews had no right to offer bribes to goyim who are killing Jews. "We must do all we can so that the Land of Israel becomes the State of Israel." All nations were shedding their blood in the war, "and if we don't make sacrifices, how can we earn the right to come to the [negotiating] table? And if that is so, it is foolish and even impudent on our part to ask the nations who spill their blood to allow us to bring their money into their enemies' country in order to protect our blood: our land can be acquired only by our blood."[8]

Shwalb repudiated this damning accusation, providing a sworn affidavit that there was absolutely no truth to the allegations or to his supposed letter. Extant correspondence between Shwalb and the Yishuv leadership does actually indicate that he issued repeated requests for money for Weissmandel and Fleischmann's plan. In fact, the Jewish Agency, together with the Joint Distribution Committee, did transfer, albeit belatedly, an advance payment on the bribe.

In spite of all this seemingly incontrovertible proof of Zionist efforts on behalf of Slovakian Jewry, the saga of the Europa Plan has become a sweeping *j'accuse* against Zionism. The ultra-Orthodox omit all aspects of the story not germane to their version of events: Weissmandel's partnership with the Zionist Fleischmann; the actual

---

8. Excerpted by Dina Porat, *The Blue and the Yellow Stars of David: The Zionist Leadership in Palestine and the Holocaust, 1939–1945* (Cambridge, Mass.: Harvard University Press, 1990), 177; originally appeared in Chaim Michael Dov-Ber Weissmandel, *Min Ha-Meitzar* (In distress) (Jerusalem, 1960), 92. Here Schwalb is allegedly quoted from memory by Weissmandel.

role played by Shwalb; the widespread skepticism—among Zionists, non-Zionists and the Allies—claiming that the entire scheme was a fabrication; and the difficulties in transferring the money. All of these details have been discarded, leaving only two protagonists in the ultra-Orthodox myth. Rabbi Weissmandel, who, even after he escaped from the train to Auschwitz and was saved, persisted in his hatred of Zionism. In the ultra-Orthodox fable, he is the symbol of everything that is innocent and righteous, ever-faithful in his Jewish belief. The counterpoint to Weissmandel is the Zionist establishment, whose representative, Shwalb, is the embodiment of evil and malice.[9]

How can anyone account for this virulent ultra-Orthodox attack, which continues to charge Zionism of having an alliance with Hitler? How is one to reconcile this attitude with the very different state of mind among the secular public, which has managed to put the concept of "denigrating the Diaspora" behind it, and which over the years has come to grips with the loss of European Jewry as a whole, including its religious and ultra-Orthodox components? In her aforementioned article, Dina Porat offers several explanations. Although each of the reasons provides a partial answer, they do not add up to a whole and cannot excuse or explain the rabid vehemence of this hatred.

Not all of the ultra-Orthodox factions participate in this crusade. Shas, the ultra-Orthodox Oriental Party, is careful not to join in the fray. The most outspoken sources of hatred are elements close to and supported by Rabbi Eliezer Shach, the head of the Ponevezh Yeshiva in Bnei Brak and leader of Lithuanian ultra-Orthodoxy in Israel. Contemporary manifestations of the ultra-Orthodox allegations appear in *Yated Ne'eman,* a weekly "Lithuanian" journal, as well as in literature put out by those close to the Belzer Rebbe. The Belz-affiliated weekly, *Hamachane Hacharedi* (The ultra-Orthodox

---

9. In his book *The Seventh Million—The Israelis and the Holocaust* (New York: Hill and Wang, 1993), Tom Segev also levels criticism on the delayed transfer of funds by the Agency leadership, but neither he nor others accept the "facts" presented by the ultra-Orthodox. In summing up the affair, he writes: "There is no way of knowing if the Europa Plan ever really had a chance. Perhaps not. The only thing we may be sure of is that, had the leaders of the Jewish Agency been quicker about sending the money to Bratislava, they could have bought themselves the right to look following generations in the eye and say without hesitation: We did what we could, we did not miss any opportunity" (pp. 92–93).

camp), edited by Rabbi Israel Eichler, is a principal campaigner in his community's denunciation of Zionism's role in the Holocaust.[10]

Blaming the Shoah on the Zionist "partners of Amalek" (Amalek was the tribe that waylaid the children of Israel as they made their way from Egypt through the desert) seems to serve an important objective of the Ashkenazi ultra-Orthodox camp. The genocide of European Jewry must pose several painful questions to the ultra-Orthodox Jew, even if he is God-fearing, believes in the Torah, and upholds all of its tenets: How are we to comprehend the destruction of the pious Jews of eastern Europe in view of their unmitigated faith? How can we explain God's alleged anger? How is it that the last cries of the Jews in the gas chambers did not reach the gates of heaven? In order not to lose our sanity—or, worse yet, our faith—can we perhaps explain that the murder of children in front of their mothers was actually God's punishment for sins committed by secular and Zionist Jews? Or were these, in fact, the penultimate days before the Messiah's arrival?

For their part, the Zionists have their own account to settle with the ultra-Orthodox—for forbidding their flocks to leave Europe and emigrate to Palestine when it was still feasible. Even later, after the Final Solution was already under way, the rabbis continued to do their best to pacify their followers, assuring them that all would be well and that there was no need to become alarmed and flee. The best-known instance concerns the immigration from Budapest to Israel of the Belzer Rebbe, his brothers, and the rest of his family in January 1944, three months before the Nazi invasion of Hungary. In a sermon delivered by the rebbe's brother, Rabbi Mordechai Rokeach, one day, before leaving for Palestine, he soothed his worried Hasidim, counseling them thus: "Stop focusing your attention

---

10. See Porat, "Amalek's Accomplices," 707–711. Rabbi Schach, the supreme rabbinical authority of the majority of Ashkenazi ultra-Orthodox Jews in Israel, has never personally or directly expressed himself in this manner, but did write in the ultra-Orthodox weekly *Yated Ne'eman* (A sure foundation) that "the Holy One Blessed be He kept the account, one by one, a long account stretching over hundreds of years, until the account reached six million Jews, and this is how the Holocaust took place. . . . And if we refuse to accept it as a punishment, it is as if we do not believe in the Holy One Blessed be He, God forbid" (excerpted from Porat, "Amalek's Accomplices," 711). Professor Menachem Friedman, a researcher of ultra-Orthodoxy, believes that the prevailing opinion among the ultra-Orthodox is that Zionism was responsible for the Holocaust. See "The Haredim and the Holocaust," *Jerusalem Quarterly,* 53 (winter 1990): 86–114. See also the divergent opinion expressed by Porat in "Amalek's Accomplices," 727, n. 54.

on the Exile, and start to act as if all the troubles were already over and the Redeemer was standing just beyond our walls, with Redemption at hand." He added his prediction that Hungarian Jewry could expect "goodness and all that is good, and that goodness and kindness will be the fortune of our brethren the Children of Israel in this country."[11]

In contradistinction to these remarks are those we read with pain and horror, the incredibly harsh words dictated by the wife of the rabbi of Stropakov to a prisoner of the Sonderkommando just before she was gassed by the Nazis:

> Behold, I foresee the end of the Hungarian Jews. The government has allowed large segments of Jewish communities to escape. The Jewish public sought the advice of the sages, and their advice was always to remain calm, not to worry. The Belzer Rebbe said that Hungary would suffer anxiety only. And now the bitter hour has arrived, when the Jews cannot rescue themselves. Indeed, the heavens concealed the truth from them, but they themselves [the rabbis] fled at the last moment to Eretz Israel. They saved their lives, but abandoned the people like sheep for the slaughter. Master of the World! In these last moments of my life, I beseech you to forgive them, for they have profaned Thine Name greatly![12]

Like the Belzer Rebbe, Rabbi Yoel Teitelbaum—the Satmar Rebbe—also left his flock in Europe. Teitelbaum left Hungary aboard the train of privileged Jews that was arranged by the Zionist Kastner. Along the way, the train was delayed at Bergen-Belsen, and there were fears that the passengers would not be permitted to leave. In an effort to settle the crisis, the Rescue Committee of the American Orthodox rabbinate instructed its delegate in Switzerland to contact the representative of Messerschmidt in Switzerland in an effort to save the Satmar Rebbe from death in Bergen-Belsen. The

---

11. The story of this sermon, as well as other evidence of the soothing statements offered by contemporary ultra-Orthodox leaders, are presented in Mendel Piekarz, *Hassidut Polin* (Ideological trends of Hassidism in Poland during the interwar period and the Holocaust) (Jerusalem, 1990), 424–433. The rebbe and his family were in Budapest en route to Palestine.
12. Excerpted by Porat, "Amalek's Accomplices," 424–433; originally appeared in Piekarz, *Hassidut Polin,* 413.

Orthodox delegate gave assurances that his organization was interested exclusively in Rabbi Teitelbaum, adding, "We have no interest
in the other people who came with the Hungarian transport to
Bergen-Belsen."[13]

Obviously, the Belz and Satmar Hasidism and the ultra-Orthodox
press do their best to refute these facts, which were recorded and
publicized as the events unfolded. In their place, an altogether different version of what occurred has been fabricated: The rabbis and
sages did not flee; rather, they fulfilled their mission and then went
on to revive the world of yeshiva learning and Torah study in the
Holy Land. We are told that the ethical world of ultra-Orthodoxy
contradistinction to the Zionist criminal, exacts its revenge on the
murderous Nazi enemy by renewing the world of the destroyed
European communities in the Holy Land.

Nonetheless, the question remains: Why does a substantial segment of the ultra-Orthodox world feel the need to wage this campaign of incitement against the same Zionism that provided a haven,
saved its spiritual leaders, and brought the surviving remnant of
European Jewry to the chosen land? Why do they vilify the same
Zionism that supports and continues to support the ultra-Orthodox
establishment and that absolves its sons from military service? What
is the source of their compulsion to wage this insidious propaganda
war against Zionism? There is no rational answer to these questions.

The anti-Zionist smear campaign continues apace even as the
ultra-Orthodox community in Israel flexes its political muscles as
senior partners in the government coalition. Rabbi Yitzhak
Scheinfeld of the ultra-Orthodox "Kol Chai" radio station was
recently quoted in a televised interview as saying that "a few Zionists
believed that in order for the State of Israel to arise there had to be a
Holocaust." However, Scheinfeld did not stop there, but went on to
attack all Zionists, claiming that Zionism had hoped for "some
measure of Holocaust." These harsh statements prompted the inter-
viewer to leave the TV studio, overwrought with anger and disgust.

Following the deadly terrorist bombing in Mahane Yehuda market in July 1997, the following statement appeared in a popular
ultra-Orthodox newspaper:

---

13. Yehuda Bauer, *Jews for Sale? Nazi-Jewish Negotiations, 1933–1945* (New Haven, Conn.:
Yale University Press, 1994), 223.

Therefore, the call issued while we are still suffering the fresh pain of terrorism, that "we have to declare war on terrorism" is just stupid. What war? War with whom? Haven't there been enough wars in the State of Israel since Zionism intruded its way into our lives here? Tens of thousands of Jews have been killed in these wars, and not a single one has solved the existential problems of the people of Israel. On the contrary, war has simply led to more war. Anyone who believes that terrorism stems from the Oslo Agreement must recall that these agreements themselves are rooted in the Intifada which led to the Madrid Conference, which is rooted in the Camp David Accords, which is rooted in the Yom Kippur War, which is rooted in the Six Day War, which is rooted in the Sinai Campaign, which is rooted in the fedayeen terrorism that began after the Arab refugees were expelled in the 1948 war and the 1948 war itself was a result of the pogroms and riots that began [sic!] with the Zionist immigration, which declared a war to conquer the country and employ only Jewish laborers.[14]

In some inexplicable fashion, there seems to be no contradiction between this broadside against Zionism—alleging that it has been the cause of all of Israel's troubles, including the Arab pogroms and riots, which seemingly, had never taken place before Zionism's arrival in Palestine—and fervent support by the ultra-Orthodox parties for the most fanatical brands of Israeli nationalism.

Indeed, during the 1990s the ultra-Orthodox attacks took on a renewed significance: first, because, as we have seen, the ultra-Orthodox rank and file and its leadership underwent a process of nationalist radicalization, forming alliances with the nationalist right wing; second, because the ultra-Orthodox has grown more powerful, spreading their its far beyond the Old Yishuv. For example, in the 1996 elections, Shas had unprecedented electoral support, and its ten-member faction became the third largest in the Knesset.

One might have expected that the Sephardi Shas constituency, the majority of which is only moderately Orthodox, would moderate the latent anti-Zionist feelings of the party's rabbinical and lay

---

14. *Hamachane Hacharedi* (The ultra-Orthodox camp), 7 August 1997.

leadership. Indeed, on the charge of Zionist guilt for the Holocaust, Shas has not staked out a categorical position. On the other hand, it has embarked on a very harsh attack against the political underpinnings of Zionism itself. In speaking of what he calls the injustices and the discrimination suffered by Oriental Jews, member of the Knesset and former cabinet minister Aryeh Deri expressed his party's bitterness against political Zionism: "The great Zionist vision has failed. Now the secular are frightened that the Shas constituency will affect the secular character of the State. The real Zionists are us—the observant Oriental Jews, the same folks whom the establishment calls primitive."[15]

Attacks against Herzl and his successors, when instigated by leaders of the Oriental ultra-Orthodox camp, have contemporary political repercussions. The anti-Zionist assault tears down the external trappings of unity—symbols embraced by Right and Left alike such as flag, anthem, and national days of mourning. Moreover, there is a continued increase in the number of pupils who attend haredi schools, and who are thus excluded from the Zionist credo shared by the majority of Jews in Israel. The unavoidable side effect has been a steady decrease in the number of young men enlisting in the Israel Defense Forces (IDF) and the number of individuals acquiring the skills necessary in Israel's modern society. The increased Oriental ultra-Orthodox influence has also had an impact on the political balance of power. Shas supporters would undoubtedly prefer the Right over the secular Zionist Left, and Shas supporters will vote en masse for the right-wing candidate for prime minister, as 90 percent of them did in the 1996 elections.

As we shift focus from the ultra-Orthodox offensive to that of the post-Zionist academics, we no longer have to contend with widespread populist influence. The latter group lacks an electoral base and does not wield the sort of influence that might convince large blocs of voters to move from one side to the other. If the post-Zionist opinions and literature have had any effect on the stalemate between Right and Left, it is, strangely enough, in strengthening the Right. This is not because the target of sharp attacks by the post-Zionist academics is the Israeli Left—past and present—but because its members' extreme opinions make it that much easier for the Right to portray the Left as contaminated with post-Zionism.

---

15. *Yedioth Aharonot,* 4 April 1997.

Former Prime Minister Benjamin Netanyahu chose to launch an attack on the post-Zionists at the opening of the autumn session of the Knesset (October 28, 1997): "Even in an era in which people are speaking of post-Zionism . . . we are still surrounded on all sides by those who challenge our basic right to live here. And if we voluntarily relinquish this right, it will be taken from us."

In political terms, the two assaults on Herzlian Zionism—the ultra-Orthodox and the post-Zionist—have identical results: the weakening of the moderate camp that set into motion the Oslo Accords, mutual recognition between the PLO and Israel, and the initial stage of the pullback from territories occupied in 1967.

Political commentator Moshe Koppel analyzes the partnership between the ultra-Orthodox and the post-Zionist Left and finds that "this common perspective on the failures of Zionism does not reflect the mere shared contempt for a common enemy," but also a rejection of the use of religion as an element of modern nationalism.[16]

Post-Zionism is a common name given to a series of new approaches that began to emerge among a group of "new" historians and "critical" sociologists during the 1980s and 1990s. Members of this group are typically young, perceive themselves to be innovative and revolutionary, and are characterized by their dismissal of previously accepted Zionist history and sociology and, at times, by their willingness to renounce any and every precept of Zionism. Only a few of the writers have a Marxist or neo-Marxist worldview. Most, if not all, are adherents of what are called postmodern doctrines. Especially popular is the concept that there is no such thing as objective history—a monolithic set of truths for which the traditional researcher strives, even though it is not always within reach. Instead, history consists of a series of historical versions—"narratives"—that reflect the perspectives of other groups to which mainstream history has not provided a mouthpiece. The modern historian is supposed to render his opinion on all these narratives. He cannot simply content himself with providing testimonial evidence and documentation, as there is always a suspicion that these standard devices of "old" historians were determined unilaterally by the members of the elite, and that their recording of history was dictated by their standing in society.

---

16. *Jerusalem Report,* 8 August 1997, 55.

There is no one post-Zionist approach. The mildest form of criticism is based on the very success of the Zionist experiment: Inasmuch the day draws near when most of the Jewish people will soon be living in Israel, Jewish communities are no longer in a state of distress, and anyone who wishes to immigrate to Israel has already done so or can soon do so, the time has come to complete the process of normalization—Israel should become a nation devoid of any Jewish uniqueness. The State of Israel will no longer be a democratic Jewish state, but a nation like every other, just another country that exists for the benefit of its citizenry, without any special or official connection to the Jews of the Diaspora. This approach considers the Law of Return to be an anachronistic law for which there is no practical or ideological need. Moreover, it is a discriminatory law that infringes on the equal rights of Israel's Palestinian Arabs.

Like the Canaanite movement of the 1940s and 1950s, advocates of this type of post-Zionism see a critical need to cut off formal contacts with Diaspora Jewry. But the approach is unlike that of the Canaanites in that there is no ambitious Hebrew imperialism afoot here, nor any dismissal of the separate identity of the Arabs. The opposite is the case: there is desire to lay the foundations for coexistence based on universal principles of equality and brotherhood.

Still, advocates of this approach do not deny the legitimacy of the Jewish nationalism that brought about the establishment of Israel. They do not demand that the emotional and familial ties between the Jews of Israel and Jewish communities abroad be cut off. They maintain that these ties should continue in the same manner as is customary in other immigrant societies, where the "old country" or the "home country" evokes a special feeling. But such sentiments, so argue the critics, do not justify the Law of Return. Thus, we read how Hanoch Marmari, editor of *Ha'aretz*, proposed to set a time limit on the Law of Return, asserting that it should lapse twenty-five years after Israel's fiftieth anniversary: This would be the "day that the work of the Zionist movement would be completed; it would be able to dismantle itself knowing that its mission had been crowned with impressive, albeit incomplete, success."[17]

---

17. *Ha'aretz* (Hebrew daily) (Tel Aviv), 11 November 1994.

Similar ideas can be found in the writings of Boaz Evron, a noted author and intellectual. He provides deep insights into his way of thought and how he views the Israel of the future—a country combining secularism, democracy, and full equality. His book ends with "predictions for the future" regarding the decline of non-Orthodox Judaism and the eclipse of its connection to Israel, because of the lack of any ethical content aside from its veneration of Israeli power mongering. However, a short while after the book's publication, Israel was inundated by the mass immigration of Jews from the former Soviet Union. A significant proportion of the immigrants were not ideologically driven, but many were motivated by the spiritual reawakening of Soviet Jewry. This rejuvenation of Jewish identity was an unexpected development that took place despite a decades-long Communist attempt to expunge any trace of Judaism and suppress any connection to Zionism.

Evron is a serious scholar, but this sort of conjecturing does not always pass the test of a uniquely Jewish reality. In fact, the post-Zionism argument is not new. Only a short while after the establishment of the state voices were already calling for abolishment of the Law of Return. Before these ideas could even be seriously debated, there always seemed to be another wave of immigrants arriving at Israel's shores, discrediting the claim that no further immigration could be expected. Still, there is no doubt that in its current form, the Law of Return can and will be the cause of problems, both in terms of those seeking to manipulate the law to their advantage and use it to acquire Israeli citizenship, and those who will be discriminated against and denied citizenship because they are not considered Jewish.

Those who assume that the Law of Return will someday be abolished do not necessarily consider this harmful to the principles of equality and the democratic character of the state. Anita Shapira, a historian with a classical Zionist perspective, does not dismiss the possibility that in the twenty-first century the citizens of Israel will, of their own free will, abolish the Law of Return.

The post-Zionists have not adequately delineated their scenario. Will the futuristic state they envision have Jewish symbols such as the Sabbath and holidays, a flag and an anthem—or will all these have to vanish so that the state can belong fully and absolutely to all its citizens? Or will the repeal of the Law of Return be sufficient?

Will the country continue to be called "Israel"—a term pregnant with national and religious significance, not unlike "the Land of Israel"? The flag and the national anthem are also rooted in a national and religious tradition, although this connection seems to be conventionally accepted even in the most enlightened countries— countries where Jews live under flags adorned with crosses without feeling that their rights have been compromised.

Even in those countries in which there is separation between religion and state and which do not have an official state religion, there is occasional need during troubled times for religious symbols. On the eve of Paris's fall to the Nazis, members of the National Assembly marched through the streets to the Notre Dame cathedral for a prayer session, crying out to God for help, pleading for the same sort of miracle that saved Paris in World War I at the Battle of the Marne. The hymn "Onward, Christian Soldiers" has been played and sung in the United States on numerous official occasions and was given prominent play at the signing of the Atlantic Charter between Roosevelt and Churchill in 1941.

In short, the claim is that Zionism succeeded so well in its enterprise that there is no longer a need for it. There is no indictment here of an immoral inception, neither is there any attempt to retroactively deny the righteousness of its desires and struggles. Of course, the assumptions on which the claim is based are certainly open to question. If there are no longer any Jews living in distress, the Law of Return may be regarded as useless, but also as harmless to the principle of equality. Laws of repatriation—return to country of origin— are on the books in other countries, including Greece, Armenia, and, first and foremost, the Federal Republic of Germany.[18] Based on the latter law, hundreds of thousands of refugees of ethnic German origin or who simply belong to the "German culture" have been granted the right to immigrate and file for automatic citizenship. Meanwhile, the applications of others have been turned away, even those of second- and third-generation immigrants, whose naturalization as German citizens is habitually denied. In spite of the existence of the European Convention on Human Rights and the

---

18. Article 116 of the Basic Law defines a German as a German citizen or someone who had been admitted to the territory of the German Reich within the frontiers of December 31, 1937, as a refugee or expellee of German stock *(Volkszugehoerigkeit)*, or as a spouse or descendant of such person.

European Court for Human Rights, Germany has never been called upon to annul its own "Law of Return" on grounds that it harms the universal principles of equality, which is the argument adopted by those wishing to repeal Israel's Law of Return. The right of a state to differentiate between groups of potential immigrants and citizens was expressly recognized in the United Nations Convention on the Elimination of All Forms of Racial Discrimination, ratified in 1965. The convention explicitly states: "Nothing in this Convention may be interpreted as affecting in any way the legal provisions or States Parties concerning nationality, citizenship or naturalization, provided such provisions do not discriminate against any particular nationality."

The Law of Return is but one example of the problems posed by post-Zionism. There are few, if any, societies whose identity is not founded on a joint cultural motif and shared heritage. Even the image of the United States, embraced by many Israelis as a suitable model, is not as simplistic as imagined. In any case, there is no possible chance to apply this type of model in the Middle East, a region where two monotheistic religions and nationalist movements are clashing with each other with such tremendous force. Yearning for this sort of ideal society, in which human beings are autonomous, and in which the governing framework is devoid of any of the trappings of a common cultural heritage and religious tradition, is the result of a utopian vision that has nothing in common with reality. Perhaps it is worthwhile considering that most European countries, in spite of their extraordinary willingness to surrender partial sovereignty to the European Union, do not conform to this radical universalistic model.

But can one even begin to compare the United States or countries of western Europe to the Middle East? Is it not obvious that Israel has a unique attribute—Jewishness—that sets it apart from every other country? Is not this attribute its very raison d'être?

Another problem arises from the assumption that there is no longer any need for Israel as a safe haven from anti-Semitism. In fact, post-Zionist academics claim that anti-Semitism no longer exists. Both the concept and the actual manifestation of it are no longer part of the lexicon of the egalitarian world in which they live. True, we are witnessing nowadays a steep decline in acts of anti-Semitism, and where it does persist, it is considered aberrant. Other forms of xenophobia, primarily in Europe, are much more popular. Yet only someone who does not know, or does not want to know, the history of this phenomenon—exceptional in its hatred and durability—would rule out the possibility that this age-old monster, the evil twin of Jewish survivability, may once more rise up like a phoenix from the ashes. We have already witnessed this sort of ebb and flow in the past. A person would not be considered unduly pessimistic if he expressed concern that anti-Semitism might rise again. Witness the National Front in France, desecration of Jewish cemeteries in various countries, expressions of chronic anti-Semitism in eastern Europe, the diabolical diatribes of Louis Farrakhan in the United States, and the dissemination of anti-Semitic literature in various countries. All these are evidence that even if such incidents take place at the fringes of society, fear of anti-Semitism hardly qualifies as paranoia.

The post-Zionists repudiate and overlook all such apprehension. Because their interest in Judaism is minimal or nil, the issue does not bother them at all, and they either repress or rebuff any discussion of hatred of Jews, as in their view it does not and cannot constitute a sufficient motive for Jewish nationalism.

However, the mistake of the post-Zionists is more general in scope. They discount the Jews' yearning for a national existence, even when stripped of its religious context. This fundamental lack of understanding, completely ignorant of what is actually happening among Jews, was also widespread among the Canaanites. The post-Zionist movement, like that of the Canaanites, is radical, led by intellectuals, and exists in a world of simulated reality in which the group's ideological concepts must be imposed on the real world. Completely disregarding even the most obvious gains realized by Zionism, the post-Zionists fail to properly appreciate the inherent strength of the Jewish people's will to survive and their desire to maintain and preserve Jewish identity. This subject will be discussed at greater length later in this chapter.

The second school of post-Zionist thought, which, like the first, does not deny Zionism's legitimacy, makes an accounting of the acts of injustice committed against the Arabs and the historical suppression of these acts. The most prominent representative of this school is Benny Morris. His research has focused on the subject of expulsion of Arab residents and the obliteration of their villages—all in contradistinction to traditional Israeli history.[19] Morris has made extensive use of documents held in the Israel State Archives that had been sealed for thirty years. As post-Zionist ideology has evolved, there has been an inclination to view the official versions of the War of Independence in a different light. Israel's early contacts with the Arab states have been reconsidered, as have seizures of abandoned property and confiscations of assets in the years after Israel's establishment. In other words, there is an attempt to reassess past events on the basis of recently unearthed facts and updated revisionist analyses. This latter phenomenon has become stylish elsewhere as well, including the reappraisal of the Cold War during the 1970s and 1980s among American historians, a perspective that has itself been reexamined in the wake of the collapse of the Soviet Union and the opening of its archives, and reassessment of the actions of the Vichy regime during World War II—initially by non-French historians and later by the French themselves.

There is no question regarding the importance of this endeavor. Israel is certainly strong enough to withstand inquiry into its recent past, even if some harsh truths are exposed, and even in spite of the fact that no similar process takes place on the Arab side. In contemporary Israel, it takes no feat of special courage to question the past. Ours is an era in which myths are being shattered on a daily basis; critical articles and books are constantly appearing, charging that everything the Israeli pupil takes up in school is wrong and deceptive.

In such times, a reverse sort of courage is needed: the ability to stand up and say that there were swamps in the Jezreel Valley; that the Jews settled a poor and sparsely populated country; that the Jews were victims of acts of murder and massacre; that in the War of Independence, the Yishuv had no allies, was practically unarmed, and had to fight off well-disciplined and well-equipped Arab armies; that the Zionist movement accepted the United Nations' partition plan, whereas the Arab states and the Palestinian leadership rejected it and invaded Palestine in order to wipe out the Yishuv; and, finally, that were it not for the Arabs' attempt to destroy Israel, the painful Palestinian refugee problem would never have been created.

---

19. Morris's principal work is *The Birth of the Palestinian Refugee Problem, 1947–1949* (Cambridge: Cambridge University Press, 1987).

There is nothing wrong per se with the act of reexamination. Indeed, it is abundantly clear to any intelligent investigator that there is always another side to tell. The Palestinians suffered greatly; aside from willful flight in war, there was also forced expulsion of Arab residents during the war and, worst of all, even after the war ended in Israel's victory. During the early days of the State, especially in the 1950s, Israel acted foolishly and unjustly, setting up a military government in Arab-populated areas of the country, expropriating and seizing large tracts of land. Arab villages were destroyed even after the Supreme Court ruled that their residents should be permitted to return. The Iqrit and Bir'im affair, in which Arab residents were prevented from resettling in their villages along the Lebanese border despite promises to the contrary, still calls for these promises to be fulfilled. The brutal raids on Qibiya and Kafr Qasim, two West Bank villages in which Israeli reprisal raids during the fifties got out of hand, were inexcusable. Following the Six-Day War, villagers in the Latrun enclave and elsewhere were deported with unjustified and unneeded cruelty. Harsh discrimination against Arab Israelis was the norm for decades; only in recent years, and especially during the tenure of the Rabin government, has a reverse trend taken root and, in the realm of education, has affirmative action been initiated.

All of the aforementioned events have taken place, yet there are differences of opinion on their depth and breadth. The precise account of the wartime deportation is the subject of factual and analytic controversy. Benny Morris's rendering of history has been countered by eyewitnesses and historians alike.[20] One example of the post-Zionist reworking of history is the allegation leveled by Ilan Pappé, who quotes documents to support his contention that Israel

20. The leading critics of post-Zionists are historians Efraim Karsh, author of *Fabricating Israeli History: The New Historians* (London: F. Cass, 1997); and Shabtai Teveth, author of "The Palestine Arab Refugee Problem and Its Origins," which appeared in *Middle Eastern Studies* (April 1990): 214–249, as well as the book *Ben-Gurion and the Holocaust* (New York: Harcourt, 1996). In his book and articles, Karsh refutes Israeli historian Avi Shlaim, who in his book *Collusion Across the Jordan* (Oxford: Clarendon Press, 1988), claims that Golda Meyerson (Meir) and King Abdullah of Jordan agreed on a division of the spoils—the Palestinian state—between the colluding parties, Zionism and Jordan. In a survey of post-Zionist literature, *The Economist* also refutes Shlaim's allegation in its July 19, 1997, issue, p. 82. *The Economist* ends with this observation: "Nobody can deny that, whatever the original intentions of Zionism's leaders, their project turned out to have calamitous consequences for the Arabs of Palestine. It may be that by accepting their portion of the blame, Israelis find it easier to reach a reconciliation with the Palestinians. But not, it is hoped, by rewriting their country's history."

was militarily superior to the armored Arab armies invading the country. It is questionable whether this opinion was shared by the defenders of the Negev settlements, the forces that broke through the siege around Jerusalem or the fighters at Kibbutz Deganya on the shores of the Sea of Galilee, who stopped the Syrian armored force with Molotov cocktails at the gates of their settlement.

Indeed, the methodology of certain post-Zionist historians changes when they attack Israel. In scrutinizing Israel's wartime actions, there is no subjective relativist examination of the Israeli narrative, which maintains that in the 1948 war Israel was David against the Arab Goliath, qualitatively and quantitatively out-matched. All of a sudden, one finds no narratives whatsoever—only old documents and statistics, which, in fact, do not even prove the post-Zionist allegation. If Israel really had proven military superior-ity that could have been discerned in advance, why then did the leaders of the Yishuv so greatly fear the repercussions of declaring the establishment of the state? And how is one to explain British intelligence assessments, which stated that the Yishuv would be unable to withstand the combined onslaught of the Arab armies?[21]

Granted, Israelis are not, and never were, angels, and there is no denying that during and after the War of Independence many wrongful acts took place. But the argument with the post-Zionists does not turn on this matter. Israel's history is replete with such rev-elations, and there has been a constant struggle, partially successful, to redress the wrongs, even before the post-Zionists began to point their accusatory finger. The fact that Benny Morris revealed supple-mentary details of the events, harsh as they may be, does not con-stitute grounds—not by this writer, at least—for condemning him, but rather for praising him.

The argument revolves around how these revelations are to be interpreted. Do these acts prove that Israel was conceived in a state of original sin and, as a result, Zionism failed? If so, has the time now come to abandon Zionism along with its hidden agenda?

---

21. In *Secret Channels: The Inside Story of Arab-Israeli Peace* (London: HarperCollins, 1996), Egyptian historian Mohammed Heikal sharply refutes the picture drawn by the critics. In this book he describes total Arab and Palestinian refusal to come to terms with the very existence of Israel up until the 1980s: "As late as the spring of 1988, Arafat told President Mubarak of Egypt that he would sooner cut off his right hand than accept United Nations Resolution 242 (which required, among other things, the recognition of Israel's right to exist)" (p. 9). "Palestinian public opinion was fiercely opposed to ceding territory to the invader, a principle which all Palestinian leaders upheld until 1988" (p. 52).

War—and all the more so a war like Israel's desperate War of Independence—is hell; there has not yet been a war in which horrible acts did not take place. Nor are we aware of the wartime birth of any other new nation that was not attended by the same sort of circumstances experienced by Israel. According to the strict standards to which Israel is being subjected, not a single country—certainly not any of the newer nations of the world—would be found innocent of charges of oppressive treatment and disgraceful conduct.

The post-Zionist narrative is deficient for yet another reason. Under the guise of adopting the Palestinian narrative, the New Age radical academics omit any reference that might embarrass the Palestinian side or that strengthens or justifies Israel's position during its initial years. There is almost no reference at all to the following facts: Arab riots against the Jews, including the massacre of the defenseless inhabitants of Hebron in 1929; bloodthirsty cooperation between Haj Amin el-Husseini and the Nazis, and the incendiary racist statements broadcast over Radio Berlin, calling for the murder and destruction of the Jews of Palestine; readiness of the vast majority of Zionist leaders to accept any compromise proposal that would partition the contested country between Arabs and Jews, and the steadfast refusal by the Arabs to agree to any partition, even to the Peel Commission Plan, according to which the Jews were to receive a minuscule portion of the country; unconditional Arab boycott of negotiations with Israel; and other facts that tarnish the pristine nature of the Palestinian "narrative"—the magic word that is supposed to silence any rational response offered by the other side.

We have arrived, then, at the third version of the post-Zionist critique, one that actually crosses the line into the realm of ordinary anti-Zionism. There is a significant difference between revisionist criticism, sharp and unfair as it may be, and a one-sided approach that uses every possible contrivance to portray Zionism and Israel as tainted from the moment of their births. Those who take this approval, these radical opponents of Zionism, are not interested in exposing past injustices and seeing to their present-day rectification. Rather, they are set on a head-on assault against the very existence of a national homeland for the Jewish people. At this point, the post-Zionist assault becomes anti-Zionist propaganda, representing an ideological worldview; this is quite different from academic research, critical though it may be.

Neither is this new history but, rather, old propaganda. One of the staunchest spokesmen in this vein is Ilan Pappé of Haifa University, who elucidates this point in his article "Post-Zionist Critique on Israel and the Palestinians." Pappé presents a survey of the post-Zionist attack, explaining that it has succeeded—within the academic world, at least—to shatter Zionist conventions. However, he bemoans the fact that even such progressive movements as Peace Now refuse to endorse the all-out attack on the essence of Zionism. Pappé complains that "every attempt to discuss the essence of Zionism . . . has been denounced as a typical intellectual exercise on the part of self-hating Jews in the service of the enemy." Pappé explains that opposition to post-Zionism "has not come from the Right in Israel, which has a very limited representation in the Israeli academia, but from the Zionist Left. Although this Left accepts criticism of post-1967 Israel, the period 1882–1967 is off limits." Far from being an exclusively academic exercise, the dialogue reverberates among much of the public at large: "It was only when anti-Zionist positions, such as ones held for years by the Communist party in Israel, were adopted by academics that fundamental changes occurred in the way Israelis perceived the 'Arabs' or the 'Palestinians,' or indeed the whole Zionist project."

Despite his disdain for Peace Now over its failure to hitch its wagon to the anti-Zionist convoy, he comforts himself that the Israeli press, in spite of conserving "the old prejudices and images of Israel and the Palestinians," serves as "the channel through which the findings and views critical of Zionist interpretations are conveyed to the public. It was through the press that the public became aware of the growing critique of Zionism among the different groups comprising the culture-producing community in Israel. Most of these groups have remained within the limited critique of Zionism typified by Peace Now, but they contributed to the decline of the Zionist myth and truth no less than their more radical and anti-Zionist colleagues inside and outside the local academia."[22]

In fact, there is nothing new here. The same allegations were made in the 1940s by the Arab-Jewish Palestinian Communist Party. Then, however, they were not a statement of home-grown ideology,

---

22. Ilan Pappé, "Post-Zionist Critique on Israel and the Palestinians," Part I of III, *Journal of Palestine Studies*, 20, no. 2 (winter 1997): 29–41. Incidentally, Pappé is stricter than the Israel Communist Party, which voted on July 5, 1950, in favor of the Law of Return.

but the usual propaganda emanating from the Kremlin. Lenin and Stalin rejected the right of the Jewish people to their own state, claiming that the mere concept of a Jewish state was a Zionist artifice. This controversy actually began not in the Soviet Union, but in the ideological clashes that divided nineteenth-century European Jewry even before the foundation of the Zionist movement. The Zionists and non-Zionists continued to lock horns until the entire community was lost in the Holocaust. Subsequently, the argument revived with the establishment of the Jewish state. The "new" historians and sociologists, who consider Jewish nationalism to be an artificial contrivance of Zionism, do not contribute anything new to the dialogue. Their sole claim to fame in today's post-Holocaust and post–Soviet Union world is to continue to make this claim, and at a intensity that is clearly in inverse relation to the cogency of their arguments.

It is hard to argue with the new historians, and it is nearly impossible to carry on a discussion with the critical sociologists, inasmuch as it is they who decree the rules of the game. They decide what constitutes a narrative—in itself a legitimate concept—and they decide what gets in and what gets left out of the various narratives. At times, the facts are important, especially when they help the critics to smash "the Zionist myth." At other times, they are deemed insignificant and are thrown onto the discard pile of deconstructionist relativism. They revile the historians and sociologists who preceded them, portraying them as tendentious academics who enlisted in the Zionist cause. Holocaust researchers such as Yehuda Bauer and Yisrael Gutman are assailed as "propagandists" for daring to rebuff the claim made by Yosef Grudzinsky regarding "the Zionisation of the Holocaust"—a loathsome, especially sickening expression, which, had it been written by a non-Jew, would have justifiably sparked universal outrage.

The main allegation leveled by the anti-Zionists is that Israel was born with two original sins: the sin of colonialism and the sin of Zionist behavior during the Holocaust.[23]

---

23. *Original Sins* is the title of a book by Benjamin Beit-Hallahmi (New York: Olive Branch Press, 1993), in which the author sums up his stand: "Zionism, at the level of an abstract idea of Jewish sovereignty and territorial concentration, cannot be faulted. We can ask whether it is practical but we cannot fault its morality. The trouble with Zionism starts when it lands . . . in Palestine. What has to be justified is the injustice to the Palestinians caused by Zionism, the dispossession and victimization of a whole people" (p. 66). For another endorsement of post-Zionist altitude, see Laurence J. Silberstein, *The Postzionist Debates* (New York: Routledge, 1999), in which the author enthusiastically espouses the post-Zionist critiquer of both second and third categories. See also Gershon Shafir, *Land, Labor and the Origins of the Israel-Palestinian Conflict 1882–1914* (Cambridge: Cambridge University Press, 1989), in which the author draws an analogy between the Zionists and European colonialists.

However, before we appraise the claims themselves, it should be pointed out that the assailants choose to arm themselves with jargon borrowed from contemporary idiom and from the period following World War II, when the colonies achieved independence, not without having to struggle to free themselves from their European masters and, likewise, the European powers freed themselves from their colonies. Transporting this terminology to the days of Herzl and the beginning of Jewish settlement in Palestine is a fundamental historiographical error, and can lead one to judge the history of long-past realities through the looking glass of a world that has a quite different set of standards and concepts. It is especially surprising that this error is committed so blatantly by practitioners of a school of thought that constantly emphasizes the subjective-relativist aspect of how factual truth ought to be considered. Geoffrey Wheatcroft, former literary editor of the London *Spectator,* relates to these allegations:

> It later became the fashion to denounce the whole Zionist idea as a form of colonialism, and to call all the Zionists imperial conquerors from the beginning. This was little more than a truism; as a judgement, it was not so much wrong as *prochronistic.* Herzl and his colleagues were not rapacious or brutal men, only men of their time. Once it became a serious enterprise and not simply a day-dream—*kein Märchen*—Zionism became patently a colonial enterprise. But then the time of Herzl's dream was the 1890s, the heyday of European imperialism. At the beginning of that decade, Africa had finally been partitioned, at the end of it Kipling would urge the Americans to "take up the White Man's burden" in the newly acquired Philippines.

Wheatcroft adds another point, ignored by the radicals:

> Herzl proposed no massacre or military conquest; but he did not give a second's thought to colonizing a country which then had few Jewish inhabitants. Quite apart from the historic claim of the Jews on the Land of Israel, even as Herzl wrote, millions of men were swarming across the world to settle in the Americas, southern Africa, Australia, all of them places which had not known a single European inhabitant

four hundred years earlier when Isabella expelled the Jews from Spain.[24]

When the new historians examine documentary evidence in support of their thesis that Zionism is a colonialist movement, they rely on terminology from the early 1900s. Herzl called his bank the Jewish Colonial Trust—need we say more?—because the first Jewish settlements were in fact called colonies and, superficially at least, resembled European settlements in other regions of the New World and Africa. But if a historian already finds the need to reach for a modern-day glossary of terms in order to judge the past, then he cannot legitimately stop there; he must deny the right to exist of every New World country conceived in a state of colonial illegitimacy.

The transfer of values and norms from one generation to the next is the sort of mistake made by the layman. If one takes these primitive analogies to their logical end, right-minded persons should forbid the staging of Mozart's *Magic Flute,* as it abounds with chauvinist and sexist references; change the name of the capital of the United States, as it pays homage to the memory of a slave owner; and boycott Winston Churchill, an incorrigible imperialist, who spoke in phrases like "this proud race." Clearly, this is not sensible. Moreover, the post-Zionists stop short at drawing analogies that do not serve their purposes. According to their views, all descendants of 1948 war refugees—some of whom left, some of whom were expelled—have the right of return. Yet this right is denied to Sudeten Germans, all of whom were expelled by Czechoslovakia after the war, after having been plundered, raped, and murdered. The perpetrators of these crimes were all granted clemency by Czech president Eduard Benes. Was it only because of the Sudeten Germans' collective responsibility for Germany's crimes? Why do not the millions of Muslim refugees who left or were expelled from India in 1948—that is, during the civil war that broke out following Britain's departure—have the right of return? Why? Because they do not have the privilege of their own narrative, and this privilege is preserved only for the Palestinians? Or is it because the Israeli Communist Party and the Soviet Union never supported the right of return of these individuals?

---

24. Geoffrey Wheatcroft, *The Controversy of Zion* (London: Addison-Wesley, 1996), 84, 85.

Based solely on external indicators, one can label the settlement of Palestine as a colonial movement, but this label has no real validity. There is not one colonial movement that bears any of the constituent elements that characterized the Zionist movement. Conversely, not a single significant attribute of European colonization of the New World holds true for Zionist colonization. First, there are no other instances in which members of one ethnic group remained faithful to a country from which they had been exiled so long before. There is no similar connection, no comparable yearnings, no sustained hope or prayer, no other case in which the country to which the immigrants came was so full of the relics—tangible and intangible—of that people's past. Nothing in the "colonial" world even slightly approximates the ways Jews revere their ancient homeland and past nationhood. Neither does the allegation that these deep feelings stem from the Bible—religious indoctrination, as the critics call it—stand up to the acid test of reality. The yearning for a return to Zion, or whatever nomenclature is used to describe it, has been shared by all Jews, religious and nonreligious alike. In fact, at times—such as during the Uganda crisis—it was the secular, even more than the religious, Zionists who remained loyal to the idea of reviving Jewish independence in their ancient land.

Again we witness an astounding phenomenon: Persons whose profession it is to describe and explain reality in professional terminology have chosen to ignore the facts in a wholesale fashion. Why do they not mention the waves of immigration that have continued unabated since the days of the original colonies, or the inner strength that drove Jews to reach the Land of Israel—some who did not have any other choice, some who came out of conviction and faith? The new historians seek to impose their personal opinions and preconceptions on this chapter of history. Their proffered explanation, that this climactic development in Jewish history is but the by-product of manipulation and agitation by the Ashkenazi Zionist elite, is nothing but a case of overindulgence by academic figures in their own propaganda. What we have here is an especially vulgar attempt to offer a cheap "conspiracy theory" to explain away a mighty historical phenomenon.

Frequently, anti-Zionists compare Jewish colonization of Palestine to that of the whites in South Africa, but this is a ridiculous comparison: The Dutch émigrés lacked any religious or cultural tradition to tie them to that particular land, and as far as we know never uttered a single prayer of "Next Year in Johannesburg." The same is the case for every other colonialist chapter in history. Shmuel Eisenstadt, Israel's leading sociologist, compares Zionist coloniza-tion to American society, inasmuch as both countries were founded by revolutionary ideologies. Neither merely sought to establish just another colony; both were committed to democratic ideals and the rule of law.[25] This analogy is not accepted by the critical scholars, since it does not serve their objectives.

The second difference between Zionism and European colonial-ism is that the Jews as an ethnic group did not have a country of their own. They did not have a France or an England, a Spain or a Portugal. Most of them could choose between only two options: remaining an unpopular minority, denied of rights, living among other nations; or attempting to achieve full emancipation in their own country. Not only did they not have a country of their own, they did not emigrate from any single host country, as was the case throughout colonialist history. Jewish immigrants arrived in Palestine from every Jewish community, East and West, leading to the foundation of a multicultural and multitraditional Jewish socie-ty. Furthermore, the settlement of Palestine cannot be explained on classical economic grounds, according to which both the colonist and his old homeland profit from the colonization process.

Third, there is no other instance in which, during the migration itself, the émigrés considered themselves to be a people realizing their right of self-determination. This is a basic human right with which the Left is supposed to identify. There is no other case of an ethnic group that claimed to lack any national homeland aside from the one to which it was migrating.

Fourth, Zionist settlement of Israel constituted an ideological, moral message. This message, and the attempt to establish a society of a new kind, also led the Zionists to adopt a unique attitude toward the Arab laborer: Instead of hiring Arabs as common labor-ers at low market wages, Zionism had the settler take on the role of common laborer—in what became known as the "Conquest of

---

25. S. N. Eisenstadt, *The Transformation of Israeli Society* (Boulder, Colo.: Westview Press, 1985), 152–153. The radical critique of Zionism is not a recent phenomenon. These ideas were first enunciated by Mazpen, immediately after the 1967 war. "Mazpen's critique of Zionism was formulated from a Marxist-Socialist perspective; see Silberstein, *The Postzionist Debates,* 85.

Labor" in the old-fashioned and politically nuanced jargon of the Zionists. Needless to say, this antiexploitive phenomenon—entirely and diametrically opposed to every colonialist precedent—is also subjected to anti-Zionist scorn, because the policy hampered the Arab worker's capacity to earn a living and his opportunity to reap the fruits of the Zionist investment.

In truth, there is nothing the Jewish settlers could have done to the Arab laborers that would have shielded them from post-Zionist critique. It is a catch-22: Based on the historians' parameters, the presence of cheap Arab labor constitutes an express indicator of oppressive colonialism. In this case, however, it is the Jewish laborer—not the opportunistic Jewish employer—who fills the role of oppressor. It makes no difference what the Jews do—they are always the oppressors. These second-rate analogies lead to additional internal contradictions.

There is no precedent or parallel to the Jewish settlement of Israel, because there is nothing else quite like the Jewish problem, or the Zionist solution for it. There is no other ethnic group that has the Jews' unique status among the nations; there is absolutely nothing that compares to the waves of hatred, even when they did not result in actual bloodshed, to which the Jews were subjected and from which they could not escape. There is no parallel to the collective memory of the Jews—religious, traditional, or freethinking—that bound them to their ancient land. Neither is there any parallel to the Zionist solution, which envisioned leading the Jews toward a normal state of affairs and set out to bring the Jews back to the Land of Israel, taking a path that was paved with blood, toil, sweat, and tears.

The new anti-Zionists make their arbitrary determinations by relying on theoretical equations borrowed from academia, without ever pausing to think through the prerequisite question: Can this formula explain such an extraordinary phenomenon? In their effort to overcome this difficulty and verify their claim that there is no such thing as the Jewish people, some writers are forced to rationalize why entire Jewish communities immigrated to Palestine, and later, to Israel. They can fudge the terminology—calling it not an "Ingathering of the Exiles" but a "nonselective migration," but the question remains: Why did these "nonselectives" migrate to a country that since its foundation has had compulsory military service and reserve duty, periodic wars, nearly continuous terrorism, much bloodshed, and which, early on, was abjectly poor? Why did the nonselectives do it, and why did they prefer a dangerous country over their native lands?

The "new and critical" academics have no answer aside from their Zionist conspiracy theory. What happened here, such critics say, was, of course, but another act of manipulation perpetrated by the Ashkenazi Zionist elite; it was they who prodded the Holocaust survivors to board the crowded Italian fishing boats and migrate to the Israeli state; it was they who planted the bombs in the Baghdad synagogue to motivate Iraqi Jews to forsake the rivers of Babylon and serve as pawns of the Zionist establishment; and this same establishment is accused of causing Yemenite Jewry to desert their villages and follow in the footsteps of the Iraqi Jews. As usual, there is no clear evidence to support these claims aside from rumors and self-evident facts such as, for instance, that emissaries from Israel believed that it was incumbent on the Jews to immigrate to Israel, and acted accordingly.

There is a substantial flaw in the argument of the anti-Zionists. If they cling to the idea of a society with universal and egalitarian values, then what wrongs were committed by the Zionist elite—capable of the most despicable acts—in luring or intimidating the Jews of Iraq and Yemen to migrate to Israel? In which society, in their opinion, did these individuals stand a better chance of cultivating these values: under Iraqi or Yemenite rule, or in Israel? Their response, of course, is that by their bringing in these nonselective émigrés, the authentic residents of the land—the Palestinians—were pushed aside, making them refugees.

There is something infuriating not only in this superficial, one-dimensional understanding, but also in how the anti-Zionists relate to the nonselective Jews as herds devoid of any will of their own. They were allegedly prodded like sheep to the sacrificial altar by the arch-Zionists, who had not have even the slightest twinge of emotion toward their own people aside from their wish to strengthen Israel. The principal question, to which the critics do not have a reply is, how could propaganda or manipulation impel hundreds of thousands of Jews to uproot themselves from their homes and move to a distant land known for its suffering and wars? Does not the mass immigration—in utter contrast to the claims made by detractors of Zionism—actually prove that, first, there was a "Jewish problem" both in the East and in the West and that second, there is an undeniable force of gravitation exerted by the new-old land?

All of these inherent contradictions pale in comparison to the anti-Zionist attack on the issue of the Holocaust and Zionism. In this fight, the academics have joined hands with ultra-Orthodox extremists. Although they may not have gone so far as to determine Zionist responsibility for the mass murder itself, some allegations are similar, or even identical.

First, the new historians seek to delegitimize the Jews' exclusive claim to the Holocaust, asserting that the episode is no different than other acts of mass murder. They claim that by assigning a unique Jewish identification to the Holocaust, the Zionists—as well as those non-Jews swayed by them—damage its universal significance.

How was Zionism to blame for the Holocaust? The accusations vary: The Zionist establishment favored strengthening the Yishuv over rescuing European Jews; its leaders preferred to grant immigration certificates to European Zionists; their disposition toward the Jews of Europe, including the survivors, was a combination of patronization, apathy, and alienation; immediately after the war, Zionist emissaries talked the displaced persons into immigrating illegally to Mandatory Palestine, in disregard of their own interest; and the Zionists distorted the history of the Holocaust by minimizing the role played by non-Zionists in the Warsaw Ghetto revolt. They, in effect, "Zionised" the Holocaust.

It should be noted that for some of the post-Zionists—certainly the anti-Zionists among them—the subject of Zionism's role in the Holocaust is of primary interest. Jewish-Israeli heritage is increasingly being forged, especially among young people, around the memory of the destruction of European Jewry. For example, the number of youth delegations visiting the death camps has proliferated of late, and during the author's tenure as minister of education, quite rapidly so. Alarmed at the prospect of the Holocaust serving as a rallying point for Jewish-Zionist identity, the post-Zionists would like to thwart its continued crystallization in the collective consciousness and to strip it of special significance. "The issue of the Holocaust," writes Anita Shapira, "confounds any attempt to draw simple analogies between the situation in Palestine and other colonization countries. Thus, the desire to neutralize that issue is part of the effort to create a seemingly autonomous Israeli-Palestinian narrative, independent of history, circumstances and the biographies of the players. This stance may be summed up in the words of Ilan Pappé: "'The State of Israel was created with the aid of Western colonialism. It intentionally uprooted the Palestinian population and justified this retroactively on the basis of Jewish 'uniqueness' resulting from the Holocaust."[26]

One may have assumed that in treating this particular subject, the new historians and critical sociologists would employ a more reserved and balanced tone than usual and curtail use of the quasi-professional newspeak in which they ordinarily express themselves. Yet the opposite is, in fact, the case: In discussing one of the worst disasters to ever befall the Jews—even assuming, as they do, that there is no such thing as a Jewish people—with memories still painful and witnesses still alive and hurting, the new historians show not even a modicum of restraint. In *The Blue and the Yellow Stars of David,* in which Dina Porat analyzes the behavior of the Zionist leadership during the Holocaust, the eminent historian reaches a point in her investigation at which she is simply unable to make her pen continue along with academic professionalism. A dam of tears bursts wide open, carrying the reader with it. This happens while Porat is describing how the British rulers thwarted efforts to rescue and bring to Palestine several thousand—by the end, several hundred—Jewish children:

> This is one of the instances where the historian feels that he just wants to throw aside all the principles and practices instilled in him by his mentors—the reserved, indifferent tone, the careful analysis of sources, the cautious arrival at conclusions—and instead just sit down and weep.[27]

Anti-Zionists have no such problem. They do not cry, they do not mourn; they simply persist in their critical appraisals, writing with

---

26. Anita Shapira, "Politics and Collective Memory," *History and Memory* 7, no. 1, (spring/summer 1995): 19–20. In the article, Shapira points out the inconsistency between the claim that discussion of this issue should be independent of the Israeli-Palestinian conflict and the claim that the Zionist movement did not do enough to save the Jews of Europe.
27. Porat, *The Blue and the Yellow Stars of David.* This passage appears only in the Hebrew version, which is entitled *Hanhaga be-Milkud, 1942–1945* (Cambridge, Mass.: Harvard University Press, 1990), 308.

cool and indifferent quasi-objectivity. From the safe vantage point of the present, they sit in judgment of leaders who were caught in the most distressful straits, the likes of which have no historical precedent. Here too we find not a trace of Zionist narrative, no accounts of the Zionists' dilemmas, nor any equivocation as to the authenticity of these critics' retroactively fabricated truths.

True to their methodology, the anti-Zionists rule out the mere idea that the Holocaust is uniquely Jewish; this uniqueness would further the Jewish-national thesis, thereby damaging the universalistic theory. However, any reasonable observer can see that there is no clash between the "narrow" Jewish context and the "wider" significance to humankind: The Third Reich viewed the Jews as the enemies of humanity; they had to rid the world of each and every Jew—for racial reasons—just as rats, which spread disease and infection, are exterminated.

Innumerable acts of murder were carried out in occupied Europe, including the systematic killing of gypsies, Russian prisoners of war, Polish intellectuals, and ordinary people whose sole transgression was not belonging to the master race or whose mere existence was at odds with the Germans' concept of an ideal society. Many were persecuted for their deviant political beliefs or homosexual practices; the "abnormal" and the "parasites" were enemies of the state. It is vitally important to recall these acts, not only because they actually occurred, but also out of respect for the victims' memory, and out of our obligation and sensitivity as Jews.

It is true that not all the victims of the Nazi regime were Jewish. However, only the Jews—assimilated, converted, half-Jewish, quarter-Jewish, babies, the old and the frail, in fact, anyone the Nazis wanted to define as Jewish—were defined en masse as an enemy whose punishment was utter annihilation. The universal message that the anti-Zionists are so zealous to uphold is by no means compromised by this incontrovertible fact. Professor Yehuda Bauer, an eminent Holocaust researcher, enumerates the chief elements by which the Holocaust stands apart from other instances of mass murder, including genocide:

First, the Nazis sentenced every person who had three or four grandparents whom they defined as Jews, to death for the crime of being born. There is no precedent for such a thing.

Second, their intention was to reach every single person who fit their definition as a Jew, everywhere in the world. This was unlike other acts of genocide that have taken place in specific countries or regions. The Nazis intended to carry out murder on a global, universal scale.

Third, every other instance of genocide involves a practical, political, territorial, geoeconomic, geopolitical, or military motive.

Fourth, the hatred of Jews goes back for thousands of years, albeit in forms that did not involve a program for mass destruction. Every other instance of genocide was the result of an emotional outburst or an idealized pretext for very practical intentions. The Holocaust was motivated first and foremost by the transformation of this age-old hatred into a murderous ideology, believed in by masses of humanity.

Fifth, the Nazis not only developed murder into an art form, but humiliation as well, which was evidenced particularly in the concentration camps. This is unparalleled by any other act of genocide. The Holocaust was, then, a unique case of genocide.[28]

Bauer explains that none of these reasons diminish or contradict the universal significance of the destruction of European Jewry:

> The contrary is the case: Precisely because the Holocaust focused on one ethnic group that was singled out because of its paricular history, it has implications for all humankind, for it means that such a thing could theoretically happen to others, albeit certainly not in the same manner. The utter destruction of a specific ethnic group in the Holocaust is the common denominator with which every human being may identify.

Neither the uniqueness of the Holocaust nor its universal significance is contingent or conditional upon concerns that this sort of episode might reoccur. The uniqueness and significance to humankind derive directly from what actually happened, not from a might-have-been or could-happen scenario. Nowhere else in authentic history is there anything approaching the systematic hatred and satanic destructiveness of all things Jewish such as took place during the Holocaust.

Yossi Grudzinsky, one of the post-Zionist academics, writing in

---

28. *Ha'aretz*, 30 May 1997.

Ha'aretz (June 6, 1997), ignores all these factors and seems to have no trouble issuing a shallow statement like, "The Jewish holocaust was a dreadful episode. But, sadly, there have been other dreadful episodes in modern history." As far as Grudzinsky and his colleagues are concerned, there can be no special Jewish claim of uniqueness. Yet there is an inherent contradiction in the anti-Zionists' argument: Here, inexplicably, there is no "Nazi narrative" to be included in the historical analysis; they ignore Hitler's *Mein Kampf,* imbued with an anti-Semitic obsession; there is no mention of the Nazis' anti-Jewish propaganda, which was always much more extreme than even their anti-Allies propaganda.

There is absolute disregard for the facts: Extermination of the Jews continued apace even when it exacted a military and economic cost to the German war effort and persisted even as Germany was crashing toward defeat. Not only were the Jews systematically annihilated, the Nazis also took pains to obliterate every trace of Jewish existence and culture.

As the Nazis saw it, Europe was hosting other racially inferior ethnic groups, and they were also targeted. We must remember them all and cannot forget the crimes against them. But at the same time we must also understand that the total war of annihilation was waged only against the Jews, because they were an "anti-race"— vermin that needed to be exterminated even at the expense of the national and military interests of the Third Reich. The "racial pollution" laws enacted at Nuremberg in 1935 targeted the Jews and the Jews alone. Germany and its satellites were seized with an anti-Jewish frenzy that was different from the acts of murder against other groups. In occupied France, for example, there were tens of thousands of black Africans. Nazi theory held that they were racially inferior, but they were never subjected to any special treatment. At the very same time, under the Vichy tricolor flag, French police were hunting down Jewish children, who were French citizens, and sending them to their deaths. In resolutions adopted at the Nazis' 1942 Wannsee Conference, at which the bureaucratic arrangements were made for the Final Solution, not a single Jewish community was left out, not even the two hundred Jews living in Albania.

None of this deters the anti-Zionist crowd. Not only is the Holocaust not unique, they say, it is not even as significant as we have been led to believe. In fact, Zionists are not the only group to commit the sin of dwelling on its unique significance. Others are guilty as well. Thus, we find one of the critics, Professor Henry Wasserman, writing:

> It is well known that insistence on the uniqueness of a phenomenon, even when it is done to formulate a universalistic significance, is a clear indicator of the thought patterns of modern nationalism, which makes much use of the unique attributes and suffering of "its" nation. For the most part, the overstated insistence on the uniqueness that is accorded to "the Holocaust" in Israel and various places around the world, fills local-national needs: American Jews need it to reinforce their Judaism, German historians need it as an effective tool for denouncing the real or imagined [sic!] nationalist Right, and Israeli historians are doing exactly what nationalist historians have always excelled at doing, attaching meta-historic significance to the sufferings of their people.
>
> The Auschwitz death camp, which was called "anus mondi" (the anus of the world) by both prisoners and warders, went through a process of significant change ("from impurity to holiness") that is quite common in the psychology of religion, and which constitutes an especially interesting chapter, as an example of modern collectivist psychopathology.[29]

Furthermore, the same historian says, it is a mistake to attach "'universalistic' significance to the devastation of European Jewry, as if we were discussing a historic episode as significant as (or even more significant than), say, the French Revolution, and which is perceived as a 'cultural rupture' with cosmic significance."

---

29. Henry Wasserman, "Goetz Aly Against the Uniqueness of the Holocaust," *Ha'aretz,* 8 September 1995. See the rebuttal by Yisrael Gutman, a Holocaust researcher and historian, in *Ha'aretz,* 29 September 1995. In his article, Wasserman describes the mass murder of Jews by asphyxiation in trucks at the hands of the Einsatzgruppen as murder by "conventional means," which preceded Auschwitz—the quintessential symbol of "the Holocaust." Yisrael Gutman points out the ignorance and erroneousness of this depiction, inasmuch as other death camps were in operation before Auschwitz, operating at the same time as the "conventional" murder. Gutman also says, choosing his words carefully, "One must be very thick-skinned" to use this term to describe the extermination of Jews by means other than gas chambers.

The war declared by Nazi Germany against the Jewish race, of which the prime symbol was Auschwitz, is not, then, the earth-shattering event we thought it to be. There is no Before Auschwitz or After Auschwitz. The "unicum of Auschwitz," as Primo Levi calls it, does not exist; neither does K. Tzetnik's "ashen planet." Nor is there a world after Auschwitz that no longer has poetry, as Theodor Adorno contends. The Holocaust is reduced to a "despicable crime," as Wasserman terms it, or a "horrible event," in Grudzinsky's view, and achieved its extraordinary significance only through the manipulation of three groups—Zionists, American Jews, and German historians—who attach modern collectivist psychopathological expression to an event that cannot even be considered a "cultural rupture."

Next come the passages that describe the Holocaust of European Jewry not as an act of mass murder carried out by humans against humans, but as an abstract concept that did not actually take place on earth. There are no murderers or victims, no real people—parents and children—who love and who die. Rather, it is an abstract collision of pseudo-Freudian, metahistoric forces—either postmodern or premodern, as the case may be—phrased in a cryptosociological jargon so jam-packed with scientific expressions that anyone not privy to the secret cannot help but be impressed that they must know what they are talking about. Thus, we find Ilan Gur Ze'ev writing about the annihilation of one-third of the Jewish people and of the massacre of one and a half million of their children:

> The holocaust is not merely a historical episode. It is first and foremost an expression of the fundamental histories of experience taking place in the dialectic between Eros and Thanatos, which we duplicate in an ecstasy that has been domesticated to a state of smug "normality."[30]

One reads these words and simply refuses to believe they were written seriously, that they are not some intentional parody raising sociological gibberish to heights of absurdity as yet unscaled by this sort of quasi-professional mumbo jumbo and meaningless psychobabble. But this is no parody. These words were written with abysmal serious-mindedness. They intend to prove yet again that the memory

---

30. *Davar* (Tel Aviv), 20 January 1995.

of the Holocaust is another Zionist-Jewish myth and that postmodern man must eschew this myth, adopting the ostensibly scientific, universalistic explanations as his new bible.

But where in this grand dialectical exercise do we find the bad guys? Gur Ze'ev has a clear response:

> The discussion of the holocaust cannot be disassociated from the evil Zionist-manufactured economy of myths, which is but an organ of instrumental rationalism and its representations in the technologies of progressive capitalism.

Gur Ze'ev does not explain precisely how this manufacturing of myths fits into the dialectic between Eros and Thanatos, but one may infer what he is after: Not only did the Zionists use the Holocaust for their own dark purposes, but they are guilty of the very same sin of which they accuse the Nazis—responsibility for the Holocaust that has consumed the Palestinians. Expelling Palestinians during the 1948 war and destroying their villages is no different from assembly-line murder.

Writings of this kind go further than anything written by the writers' Western colleagues. These young academics are unwittingly joining together with anti-Semitic "researchers" who seek to release themselves from a memory of a mass murder—a phenomenon that cannot be forgotten.

True, the academics in question do not refute the facts of the Holocaust. Instead, they refute its significance. They deny the fact that the Holocaust was more than a coincidental misfortune that took place in the mid-twentieth century, and that there is any connection between the various forms of anti-Semitism and the policies of the Third Reich. In a way, their denial of the Holocaust is worse than the primitive, openly anti-Semitic version of the neo-Nazis. In trying to disclaim facts that are accepted by the vast majority of humanity, Holocaust deniers have to overcome an absolute lack of credibility. Gur Ze'ev and his colleagues do not deny the facts, only their significance. As they see it, the Nazi crimes were unexceptional; after all, they point out, the Zionists themselves bear responsibility for a parallel holocaust. Gur-Ze'ev writes: "The same industry that has fabricated the Zionist subjective cannot abide Zionism's inclusion as a party responsible for the holocaust of the Palestinians—the authentic Jews of our time." Denial of the uniqueness of the Holocaust as compared with other historical acts of barbarity forms the nucleus of the "soft" Holocaust denial expounded by Ernst Nolte. It is no wonder, then, that some critical historians see fit to rebuke mainstream German historians who cling to anti-Nazi thought, and reject Nolte.

Furthermore, not only do the academics overlook the Nazi narrative and the facts concerning planning and implementation of the extermination of the Jews, but they also look the other way when it comes to the flip side of the Holocaust: the refusal of the free world to offer a haven to the potential escapees, even by those countries that were at the time hoping to attract capable immigrants. There can be only one explanation for this unwillingness to accept them: their being Jewish. The official delegate of the Australian government to the Evian Conference put it in no uncertain terms: The arrival of Jewish refugees in a land without anti-Semitism would bring with it the scourge of anti-Semitism. South Africa, which was encouraging whites to immigrate, rejected visa applications from Jews solely on account of their being Jewish. Several Latin American countries agreed to accept refugees, but on condition that they be either "farmers or Catholics."

The anti-Semitism pervading the British halls of power, even during the darkest days of mass murder, is simply astounding. The Bermuda Conference, which convened on April 19, 1943—the same day the Warsaw Ghetto revolt broke out—was ostensibly convened to do something to rescue the Jews. In fact, it was a joint act of fraud in which the governments of England and the United States conspired in advance not to lift a finger. Lord Halifax, the British ambassador to Washington, had warned the State Department that Germany was liable to "change from a policy of extermination to one of extrusion . . . and aim at embarrassing other countries by flooding them with immigrants." These appalling words, which testify to British-American apathy in the face of the Jewish genocide, are only part of a long series of indictments against the Allies, from which one clear conclusion arises: The Nazis exterminated the Jews and the West refused to grant them safe haven for the same reason—they were Jews.[31] As Chaim

---

31. The excerpt from Lord Halifax is from Porat, *The Blue and the Yellow Stars of David*, 140. Bernard Wasserstein's book, *Britain and the Jews of Europe, 1939–1945* (London: Oxford University Press, 1979), is full of similarly harrowing excerpts. One British Foreign Office official is quoted as saying: "If we open the door to adult Jewish males who cross over from enemy territory, this would result in an unstoppable flood (Hitler is likely to ease this situation)" (p. 204). In reply to an American petition to save the Jews of southeastern Europe, who in 1943 had not yet been sent to the death camps, British Foreign Minister Anthony Eden said, "If we do so, the Jews of the world will want us to do the same for Poland and Germany. Hitler is likely to be tempted by such an offer, but there are not enough ships and other means to care for the Jews" (p. 159). Similar details can be found in a book by David S. Wyman, *The Abandonment of the Jews* (New York: Pantheon Books, 1984).

Weizmann expressed even before the outbreak of World War II, the world can be divided in two: those who expelled Jews and those who refused to open their gates to them.

How do these facts jibe with "lack of uniqueness"? Exactly where is the "Zionist lie" here? The post-Zionists are not interested in facts of this kind.

Let us now examine the critics' indictments of Zionism and the Yishuv leadership during and after World War II. As in the reappraisal of the War of Independence, here too one has to differentiate between the critical need to disclose the truth—painful though it may be—and the ideologically motivated and propagandistic use made of this disclosure. The behavior of the Zionist leadership and the Yishuv as a whole at a time when six million Jews were dying is not only a legitimate subject for discussion, but in terms of historical accuracy, a crucial one as well. The question remains a festering sore on the collective conscience, and although it is unlikely that disclosure of the facts will fully assuage the pain, it is a legitimate and necessary subject for historical research. The discussion was initiated with the publication in 1977 of *Post-Ugandan Zionism in the Holocaust Crisis,* by Shabtai Bezalel Beit-Zvi.[32] Beit-Zvi took on the big questions, which until then had remained unasked: Did the Yishuv do everything it could to save the Jews of Europe? Did it make available all the resources at its disposal? Did the leaders cry out against the daily slaughter of their brethren? Or did the routine work of Zionist struggle and the emphasis on immigration—as opposed to salvation—prove too tempting to the Zionist leadership? Several important books have been written on this subject by Dina Porat, Tom Segev, Yechiam Weitz, and Hava Eshkoli (Wagman).[33] All try to provide answers to these questions, but the picture emerging from their collective research is somewhat complex and unclear. In Chapter 5, "The Holocaust and the Struggle for Israel's Independence," we saw how the Yishuv persisted in its rejection

---

32. Shabtai Bezalel Beit-Zvi, *Hatsyonut hapost-Ugandit beMashber haShoah* (Post-Ugandan Zionism in the Holocaust crisis) (Tel Aviv, 1977).
33. Porat, *The Blue and the Yellow Stars of David;* Tom Segev, *The Seventh Million.* Yechiam Weitz, *Moudaout veChosser Onim* (Aware but helpless: Mapai and the Holocaust, 1943–45) (Jerusalem, 1994); Hava Eshkoli (Wagman), *Elem—Mapai leNochach haShoah* (Silence: Mapai and the Holocaust, 1939–1942) (Jerusalem, 1994.)

of the Diaspora and its native egocentrism even after coming face-to-face with the reality of the Holocaust. The Jews of Palestine were unable to replace old truths with the unfamiliar new reality of genocide.

The anti-Zionist attack waged by these critical sociologists latches onto this particular issue in the hope of further disparaging Zionism and Jewish nationalism. As with their treatment of Israel's partial expulsion of the Arabs of Palestine during and after the War of Independence, we find an entire ideology built upon a nucleus of half-truths, all in the service of a clear political goal. Here, too, there is no logical consistency: Zionist leaders are accused of preferring the selfish interests of Zionism over the rescue of European Jews. This accusation falls apart when we compare the behavior of the small Jewish Yishuv living under hostile British rule, itself exposed, until the victory over Rommel in North Africa, to possible destruction and extermination, with the strong and highly influential Jewish communities in the Allied countries, especially in England and the United States.

If there was a Zionist failure—and there is no doubt in the author's mind that there was a failure to act promptly and quickly on the part of the Yishuv leadership—the failure of Diaspora Jewry in the free world was incomparably worse. Given their electoral strength and the fact that individual Jews were close to, and even part of, the governments in question, it is heartbreaking that the Jewish communities of the West were unable to effect any change in their governments' apathetic attitude to the fate of the Jews. They could not persuade them to even slightly open the sealed gates.

American Jews had an ostensibly friendly president, Franklin Delano Roosevelt, whom they supported without reservation. Roosevelt was surrounded by Jews: Henry Morgenthau was his secretary of the Treasury; Rabbi Stephen Wise was a close personal friend; and Bernard Baruch was a senior political adviser. Jews had tremendous influence in the media and were prominently represented in the Hollywood film industry. Nevertheless, in 1939 the United States refused to accept the *Saint Louis,* a ship filled with Jewish refugees fleeing post-Kristallnacht Nazi Germany. Denied port entry, the ship eventually had to return to Hamburg. Throughout the entire episode, American Jews failed to effect a change of policy, and their leaders did not intervene at the Bermuda Conference, which was supposedly convened to devise a solution to the Jews' suffering in Europe. Meanwhile, the cattle cars continued to make their way to the death camps.[34]

Australia and South Africa, two countries exceedingly interested in attracting new immigrants, were closed to Jews as a result of anti-Semitism at the top levels of government. Their Jewish communities did not raise any outcry. Until the end of 1940, Jews were still free to leave Poland—if only there had been a country to take them in! They were able to leave other countries, including Rumania and Hungary, even later still. But they had nowhere to go.

The Jewish settlement in Palestine, completely dependent on the good graces of the British government—which was always afraid of stepping on Arab toes, which viewed Weizmann's and Shertok's bothersome meddling as the pestering of "these moaning Jews," and which thwarted any attempt to rescue Jews—may have committed some sins of omission, but it did act. Its young men enlisted in the British army to fight the German enemy. The Yishuv waged a valiant effort to bring refugees to Palestine, by legal and illegal means. Young men and women volunteered to parachute into occupied Europe. In spite of the debatable efficacy of this courageous act, one can hardly dismiss the fact that a thousand young men and women immediately signed up for what was essentially a suicide mission.

If, in fact, there was a breakdown in the commitment to rescue European Jewry, it was of a general nature and more pan-Jewish than Zionist. By no means was it an outgrowth of the Zionist world-view. Rather, it may be attributed to a series of factors that can be explained only against the background of that period: inability to believe reports of what was happening in Europe; reluctance to make waves in the middle of a war the Nazis portrayed as being instigated by the Jews; lack of confidence in the ability to make any difference. Aside from these factors, there was a fair amount of

---

34. The British Foreign Office, pervaded by anti-Semitism, attributed great electoral power to the Jews, which was never taken advantage of. Lord Halifax, the British ambassador to the United States, wrote in late 1943 to the British Foreign Office: "It is now an election year, the Jewish voice is very important, and the administration would certainly not want to be identified with a British resolution, since all the Jews here, Zionists and non-Zionists alike, will consider it inhumane. For this reason, I have almost no doubt that if I act as I have been instructed in your telegrams, all of the blame for denying this request by the Jews will be placed on His Majesty's government"; see Wasserstein, *Britain and the Jews of Europe, 1939–1945.* Eventually, Halifax's concerns were for naught: The British position was accepted, the Jews remained quiet, and their voice was not important to anyone.

bureaucratic incompetence and entrenchment in routine patterns of thought and action. This especially characterized the large Jewish communities of the West and, to a lesser degree, the leadership of the Yishuv. Similarly, accusations that monetary transfers were often too little and too late hold true for the Jewish Agency no less than for the Joint Distribution Committee and the World Jewish Congress, which carried on their business-as-usual routines. None of these organizations were fully aware of the extraordinary circumstances that, in retrospect, called for the allocation of every possible resource toward the rescue effort. Furthermore, the Jewish communities of the world were reluctant to take a provocative public stand in favor of their beleaguered brethren, fearing that they might further reinforce the Nazi claim that this was "a Jewish war" and bring local anti-Semitism to a boil.

Dina Porat sums up the greatest tragedy of all: "The Jews of the free world did not consider Zionism and the Yishuv to be an address for coordinating rescue activities, and no other address presented itself."[35]

Detractors of Zionism make the mistake of considering Zionism a monolithic movement lacking any internal heterogeneity, individual voices, or segmentation. As Amos Oz has said, Zionism is the surname given to many different forms of the Jewish national ideology. We have already seen that policies formulated by Mapai (Labor), the Jewish Agency and the Yishuv's Salvation Committee headed by Yitzhak Greenbaum were attacked from 1942 onward by the Revisionist Right, the General Zionists, and some leaders of the religious camp. The right-wing newspapers called for the Yishuv to awake from its stupor and do everything in its power to save the Jews. The Stern Gang (Lehi) and the Irgun (Etzel) declared a rebellion against the British, determined to do what they could to force the British into abandoning their no-immigration policy. It was left to the Zionist Right in the United States, headed by Peter Bergson (a.k.a. Hillel Cook) and Shmuel Merlin, to realize that the policy of polite silence toward President Roosevelt and his government was not helping their European brethren. They organized high-profile demonstrations that contributed to greater public awareness in America of what was happening in Europe.

---

35. Porat, *Hanhaga be-milkud* (original Hebrew version of *The Blue and the Yellow Stars of David*), 474.

Anyone who accuses all Zionists, or Zionism as an ideology, of being party to a conspiracy of silence is consciously ignoring these facts, as well as the fact that the Zionist Right did not have any alternative plan for rescuing the Jews. If the critical historians were able to prove that the Zionist leadership, out of Zionist motives, prevented or actively blocked efforts to rescue Jews who might have been able to find safe haven outside Palestine, there would be substance to their accusations. However, there is no basis for this claim. Before the war, in 1938, Ben-Gurion did make an unfortunate statement that it was better to bring half the Jewish children of Germany to Palestine than all of them to England. But this expression remained just that and was never translated into action. The opposite, in fact, is the case; from the moment the facts about the extermination became known, the Zionist leadership took steps to rescue Jews without regard to where they might find haven.

The wave of immigrants arriving in Israel after Hitler's rise to power brought tens of thousands of German Jews who could find no other sanctuary, and who, had they remained in Germany, would have surely perished. The Yishuv leadership was prepared to entertain any proposal, enter any negotiation with the Nazis, in order to rescue Jews by means other than their immigration to Palestine. The best-known example is the mission undertaken by Joel Brand, known as the "Trucks for Blood" proposal, in which the Zionist leadership explicitly agreed to a condition that the ransomed Jews would not immigrate to Palestine. Even so, the British scuttled the deal, and it is still unclear whether Brand's operators actually had intentions of going through with the plan. Of the handful of schemes for rescuing European Jews—which were never implemented, because of to British-American collusion—none involved transfer of refugees to Palestine. Nevertheless, Yishuv leaders lent their support to each proposal but were unable to rescue the Jews, who had been abandoned by Britain and the United States.

In their articles appearing in the Israel press, the academic revisionists present a clear-cut image of the world: Zionist manipulators controlled the Jewish communities, who were devoid of independent thought; there were no Western intellectuals who chose to remain silent in spite of the unfolding reality; there were no anti-Semitic officials who could not think what might be done for "a million Jews" who could have been saved from Nazi Europe; there were no factions within the Zionist leadership; and there were no arguments between Right and Left. So what was left? There was what the revisionists call "Zionist manipulation" during and after the Holocaust.

Some of the allegations constitute legitimate criticism of policies pursued by the Jewish Agency directorate and Mapai leadership. This sort of criticism, with varying levels of severity, has been voiced by nearly every historian—old and new—who has studied the events of that difficult and dreadful period. The student of history is astounded to learn how much time and energy the Yishuv leadership squandered between 1942 and 1945 on—in view of what was happening elsewhere during those years—petty squabbles, quarrels, and even a totally irrelevant split in Mapai. None of this frenetic activity had anything to do with the tragedy taking place in Europe. How many words were wasted on meaningless issues, discussions, and discussions about discussions, at the very same time as the fate of an entire people was being sealed, including the families of the debaters! Reading through protocols of these pointless discussions, the observer is struck with a sense of utter helplessness.

This judgment is not limited to retroactive consideration of events of the time: There were some Mapai leaders who viewed contemporary events within a historical perspective. In January 1943, Yisrael Galili, a prominent figure in Mapai's leadership, cast aside any previous differentiation that may have been made between Diaspora Jewry and the Jews of the Yishuv. Looking out at the thousands of mourners who gathered in Tel Aviv once word of the genocide got out, he remarked to himself: "In my heart I was asking myself how the thousands of people in front of me were any different from the Jews of Europe. They were cannon-fodder who would be led like sheep to the slaughter. If an enemy broke through to the city, how would these thousands go out to meet him? These people were not trained. . . . All Jews, wherever they may be, share the same fate."

In 1943, historian Ben-Zion Dinaburg (Dinur), later a minister of education, said:

> Try to juxtapose the news about the annihilation of thousands of Jewish communities and the facts about the dissension and splits within the parties and factions day by day, and you will come to realize what a dreadful legacy we are leaving for our future.

> Future generations will examine and recount and record
> everything we say and do today . . . and I am very much
> afraid that the verdict of the next generation, the generation
> of our children, will be extremely severe.[36]

In truth, the verdict is not an easy one. Looking back, one can clearly see the mistakes that were made at time: Not enough funds were transferred, and there were delays in sending them on schedule; no special efforts were made to take action through the Madrid and Lisbon missions that tried to save Jews through those two neural states, perhaps because of an antifascist ideological reluctance; the Yishuv was too quick to accept the policy of duplicity and deception adopted by London and Washington; and, as stated earlier, excessive energy was wasted on partisan squabbles, including disproportionate arguing over the crucially important salvation committee in Istanbul, the only place with direct links to the Balkan Jewish communities. Certain questions remain unanswered: Why was no attempt made to send an emissary from Palestine to Poland? After all, the Polish government-in-exile in London—the first official source to disclose details of the extermination of the Jews—dispatched a number of emissaries to its occupied homeland.

These and other nagging questions remain an open, festering wound. True, the small Jewish settlement in Palestine would not have been able to save many Jews, but each and every opportunity to rescue even a handful of Jews, even through bribery or forged documents, should have been given highest priority. Neither is there any doubt that, at least in the initial stages of the war, the knee-jerk Zionist reaction continued to give precedence to immigration over all other considerations.

There are also extenuating circumstances. Clear evidence has been found that explains why and how Britain scuttled every plan to rescue Jews, and why there was never any chance for missions such as that of Joel Brand ("Trucks for Blood") to succeed. Toward the end of the war a genuine problem arose: Could Jews expect the Allies to sanction any deal—aside from offering monetary bribes—

---

36. Dinur's and Galili's remarks are excerpted from Porat, *The Blue and the Yellow Stars of David,* 254.

with Nazi Germany that was liable to extend the war through shipment of trucks and other means of assistance?

What does any of this have to do with the allegations concocted by the post-Zionists, motivated solely by their insatiable need to flay Zionism? Can anyone really imagine that the leaders of the Yishuv, most of whom came from Poland and Russia, were wholly apathetic to the murder of their friends and family—and, at times, their brothers, sisters and parents? One of the most problematic figures of the period (see Chapter 5) was Yitzhak Greenbaum, chairman of the Yishuv's Salvation Committee. He had been a prominent Jewish leader in Poland between the wars. His bizarre pronouncements on the issue of rescue were at the time bitterly denounced by the Zionist Right; today they are difficult to stomach. But this same Greenbaum had a son in Poland whose whereabouts were unknown (after the war it was revealed that young Greenbaum had been a *kapo* in Auschwitz). Can anyone imagine that Yitzhak Greenbaum knowingly and consciously turned down an opportunity to rescue Jews because he preferred to cling to the priorities of classical Zionism? And Hanna Senesh and Enzo Sereni, two parachutists who landed and died in Nazi-occupied Europe—whose families remained in Hungary and Italy—how should we classify them? As Zionists who were apathetic to the idea of rescue?

Even if we accept the facts brought to support them, some allegations leveled by the detractors of Zionism are simply inadmissible. In those days, Zionism was a national movement fighting for its independence, and when the Yishuv leadership received a limited amount of immigration certificates—"migration permits"—from the British government, it gave preference to young Zionists who would be able to strengthen the small and weak Yishuv. As the dimensions of the tragedy grew, this differentiation fell by the wayside and the non-Zionists for whom Palestine was their sole refuge pressed for and received their share of the handful of certificates that the British government issued with diabolical parsimony.

Does the Yishuv's preference for able-bodied Zionists over other, less productive Jews destroy a Zionist myth? Or does it in fact reinforce the myth, inasmuch as it highlights the fact that during those dark times, Jews had no other haven to turn to? Some revisionists—especially Yossi Grudzinsky and Henry Wasserman—claim that

Zionist historians have consciously ignored the contributions of non-Zionists in the ghetto revolts, and that particular injustice has been done to members of the Bund and their commander in the Warsaw Ghetto revolt, Marek Edelman. This claim, that Zionism obscured the role played by the Bund, is rejected out of hand by respected historians, who, unlike the critics, have access to the sources as well as knowledge of the source languages.

But let us suspend the factual argument for a moment. Let us suppose that this intentional omission of the part played by the Bund in the ghetto revolt is true and that the official, subverted-by-Zionism history treated the Bund and its leader—who stayed on in Communist Poland—unjustly. What does this have to do with the allegation made by the anti-Zionists? This sort of thing is the rule for national liberation movements: They fight their battles, glorify their leaders, and disregard their opponents. Surely we have to correct a wrong—if committed—and we must stress the cooperation that existed between all of the Jewish movements, including the Bund and the Communists, active in the underground opposition to the Nazi occupier. However, where is the significance in the claim being leveled against the Jewish national movement? And in spite of everything the post-Zionists would like us to think, the chief organizers of resistance efforts were, naturally, the Zionists.

Another example introduced by the critics is the Zionist refusal to evacuate Jewish children from the displaced persons (DP) camps and the persecution of Bundists that took place in these camps, according to Bund sources. Again, there is no genuine scholarly research here, just hearsay. Objectively, stories by Bundists, whose hatred for Zionism did not abate after the Holocaust, cannot serve as a sole historical source.

Again, let us assume that such things indeed occurred, that Zionism discriminated against the Bundists. Is it not obvious that every national movement, past and present, uses whatever influence and persuasion—not to mention pressure—it can muster to achieve its objective? Is there any national movement—not to mention one that lacks a territorial base, that is waging such a desperate fight after such a horrific tragedy—that has not lorded it over its own people in the course of the struggle? Were all the Irish polled when the violent Easter Rising conflict with the British broke out? And when the Palestinian leadership—so dear to the hearts and minds of the anti-Zionists—declares general strikes, be it under British rule or under Israeli rule, is every merchant asked for his opinion on the matter? And all this is in addition to the acts of violence and assassination committed by national liberation movements. After all, the more legitimate and noble the national movement is—that is, the harder it has to fight for the people it represents—the more resolute and even cruel it will be toward its internal adversaries. The injustice committed against the Bund by the Zionists—if true—is mere child's play compared with what has happened in other national liberation movements. This sort of preaching of ethical lessons to Zionism—when these lessons are simply intended to deny its legitimacy as a national movement—indicates, at best, extraordinary ignorance and superficiality. The truth is that a movement does not exist that has not hurt members of it own people—be they collaborators or those who simply refused to take part in the struggle—even more than the external enemy. In those terms, Zionism is exceptional and commands a higher moral ground. Again we come across a familiar tactic: the revisionists speak in the name of universal values and make free use of historical analogies, but when it comes to the Jewish people and Zionism, the general rules no longer apply. The radical academics set the most exacting standards, which apply to the Jews and the Jews alone.

Finally, there is one allegation that simply goes too far—that the mass immigration to Israel after the war was simply the result of Zionist manipulation, incitement, and acts of provocation. "Critical" descriptions of the Jewish DPs and refugees portray them as little more than a rabble. They lack any individual will of their own, simply doing the bidding of the Zionist emissaries. In fact, the relevant research and the personal experiences of the survivors tell a different story. One only needs to recall the contemporary circumstances: The Jews of Poland tried to return to their former homes after the war, where they came across the familiar old hatred, albeit enhanced by Nazi propaganda. The climax was the 1946 pogrom in Kielce, in which Holocaust-surviving Jews were massacred by local Poles. This pogrom provided a clear beacon of warning to the surviving remnant of eastern European Jewry.

Western countries, especially the United States, were stunned at the scenes awaiting American troops who liberated the concentration camps, and they opened their gates to small-scale immigration of Jews. Meanwhile, Mandatory Palestine remained sealed shut. The vast majority of surviving Jews remained displaced and homeless, subsisting on the aid and social welfare provided by various aid agencies. Nevertheless, in spite of all they had been through, their resolution and resourcefulness never failed them. Most were not Zionists by ideology, but reality, which has always been the midwife of Zionism, pushed them toward Palestine. The critical academics may prefer to dwell on themes such as Zionist agents crushing the Bund, or the "dispatch" of illegal immigrants to Palestine, but the picture is altogether different, as Yisrael Gutman writes:

> The picture of the DP camps and of the Holocaust survivors that one gets from the over-simplified, doctrinaire schema of "post-Zionism," or to be more precise, "anti-Zionism," is that of a human camp lacking any spine or will of its own, led by its nose . . . by a militant corps sent by the Zionist author-ities of the Yishuv. In actual fact, the survivors rapidly under-went a process of emotional and collective rehabilitation. This was reflected in their self-organization, their cultural and educational activity, their deeds and their yearnings.[37]

One small anecdote underscores this instinctive craving for Zion. During David Ben-Gurion's visit to a DP camp in Germany, a young girl approached him and asked in Yiddish if he was king of the Jews. Ben-Gurion answered that he was not, but the girl persisted. "Yes! They told me that you are the king! Take me to the Land of Israel right now!" Ben-Gurion turned his face aside—the only external indication that he was overcome by emotion.[38]

Writing in *Ha'aretz* (August 18, 1995), Ilan Pappé protested against Zionism's near-exclusive custodianship of the Holocaust. One of his contentions was that "only some of the Holocaust sur-vivors chose to come here, while a large portion preferred the United States and Australia, and even opted to remain in Europe."

However, Pappé's entire premise is weak. Israel and the Diaspora are not nearly so divided as he would like to think. The fact is that after the Holocaust, Western countries, for the most part, refused to

---

37. *Ha'aretz,* Culture and Literature section, 22 July 1994.
38. Tom Segev, *The Seventh Million,* 119.

offer a haven to the survivors; generally, those who did migrate to the West maintained a close connection to the State of Israel, and many became strong advocates for Israel. The vast majority of Zionists, including Herzl himself, never considered it incumbent on every Jew to immigrate. The World Zionist Organization, and later, the State of Israel fully accepted the idea of a Western Diaspora living side by side with Israel.

Most Holocaust survivors did not migrate to the West. They remained in the DP camps, awaiting an opportunity to leave for Palestine. This invariably meant additional suffering and tribulations along the dangerous routes that led to the coast of the Land of Israel, which for three long years after the end of the war remained hermetically sealed by the British. Many were imprisoned yet again in the British detention camps on Cyprus. The gates finally opened wide in May 1948, when the State of Israel was born.

Again and again we are treated to patronizing descriptions of thousands upon thousands of refugees who are devoid of any will of their own. They are manipulated by emissaries from the Yishuv, who put them on boats so they can serve Zionist interests in Palestine. Some of these emissaries from Palestine may have looked upon the survivors as a single bloc lacking any individual thought or feeling. But this image of a shell-shocked, dehumanized public waiting to be told what to do is but a figment of the new historians' imagination. Scholars who have conducted research into this subject consistently reach the opposite conclusion:

> When the emissaries arrived in Europe from Palestine, they found that the survivors had already organized themselves, from A to Z. A leadership class had already formed, they had already set up institutions and committees to manage day-to-day affairs, they had set up an astoundingly vibrant cultural life, and given thought to what they had gone through, as well as their views on Zionism.[39]

Nor do the statistics support the image of mindless, defeated masses shepherded by the Zionists to Palestine. Toward the end of

---

39. Hanna Yablonka, *Achim Zarim* (Alien brethren—Holocaust survivors in the State of Israel, 1948–1952) (Jerusalem, 1994), 4.

1945, 90,000 displaced persons were gathered in Germany, Austria, and Italy. Within eighteen months that number had risen to 250,000. The majority, 175,000, had gone from the Soviet Union to Poland at the end of the war, with the idea of resettling there. This very un-Zionist scenario was scrapped only after the Jews began to suffer from the intensified hatred that peaked in July 1946 at Kielce, in southeastern Poland, where 41 Jews were murdered in a pogrom. Polish Jews ignored the advice of Bund leaders to remain in their old homeland, choosing to flee to the DP camps in Germany. Any sane observer would be stunned by their powerful survival instincts and ability to organize themselves, as well as their readiness to undergo additional suffering on the way to Palestine. More than 50,000 men, women, and children attempted to reach Israel via the illegal immigration route arranged by Yishuv leaders. The extremely high birth rate in the DP camps and aboard the ships headed for Palestine—three times that of the Yishuv—is evidence of a strong will to survive and a determined resolution to begin a new life.

There are also several controversial accounts describing the attitude of Yishuv leaders and emissaries toward the survivors arriving in Palestine. In *From Catastrophe to Power: The Survivors of the Holocaust and the Emergence of Israel,* Idith Zartal scrutinizes statements made by Yitzhak Sadeh, the legendary Palmah commander, and Nathan Alterman, the famous Yishuv poet, in which she finds a patronizing attitude toward the illegal immigrants held aloft on the shoulders of Sabra-heroes.[40] Ben-Gurion, however, does not share such an attitude, choosing instead to raise the image of illegal immigrants jumping off ships and swimming ashore to a level of heroic bravery. Yet none of these portrayals purports to represent the survivors themselves. Throughout this literature, the Holocaust survivors are depicted as a herd lacking any will of its own. They are never seen as independent individuals willing to risk their lives to reach the Land of Israel. Thirteen illegal immigrants were killed and hundreds were wounded by British soldiers and sailors. But the story of the illegal immigrants—many of whom are still alive and available for interview by interested historians—is hardly told by the revisionists. The new history is written as if they are no longer alive;

---

40. Idith Zartal, *Zehavam Shel ha Yehudim* (From catastrophe to power: The survivors of the Holocaust and the emergence of Israel) (Tel Aviv, 1990), 489–501. (University of California Press, 1998).

instead, we are provided with documents that are supposed to speak for and about them. The reaction of the Yishuv is depicted by means of documentary evidence—not by extensive historic research, which would have provided a more reliable portrait of friends, relatives, and acquaintances looking forward to seeing their surviving loved ones. The entire historical episode is given such distorted, cursory treatment that the reader is left to wonder what happened to the new school of historiography—the one that was supposed to take up the case for "the other," the leaderless victims who do not record their own history.

Basing their research on Bund sources, some post-Zionist historians portray the Zionist emissaries in the DP camps as bullies who rule the camps with an iron fist, battling against the Bundists. The Jewish refugees, we are told, have a difficult time resisting the Zionist "incitement" and are hard-pressed to develop their own opinions on relevant issues. This terrible sin—although quite understandable, given the circumstances of time and place—has been dubbed "the Zionisation of the Holocaust." But what hope was the Bund holding out to the refugees? Putting down new roots in Europe? Just where in Europe were they supposed to settle? Who wanted them? Tens of thousands of Jews had tried to resettle in Poland, but were eventually forced to leave. Some immigrated to Israel in 1956–1957—in what was known as the Gomulka immigration—and others fled to the West, until there were practically no Jews left in Poland. In retrospect, then, the Zionists were right. The post-Zionist or anti-Zionist allegation is based on such flimsy logic that it can only be described as simplistic propaganda.

In truth, the dual attack on Zionism, by the ultra-Orthodox and by the cadre of "new" academics, is based neither on the facts nor on new discoveries. Rather, their attack takes cynical advantage of a tragedy that befell the Jewish people to settle political accounts with the only national Jewish movement that survived the Holocaust. Zionism took in the vast majority of the survivors, providing them with a home and giving them new hope: Never again would they be dependent on the good graces of others.

Indeed, there are cases of political exploitation of the Holocaust. The memory of the Holocaust is being devalued for political purposes. Menachem Begin's comparisons between Arafat in Beirut and Hitler in Berlin, and between the bombing of Beirut and the bombing of Dresden; Shimon Peres's especially bizarre description of the atomic bomb in Hiroshima as an "airborne Auschwitz"; the brutal use by the Israeli right wing of Judenrat to describe the Rabin government—all these debase the unique significance of the extermination of the European Jewry. But this sort of devaluation, which causes a natural revulsion, pales in comparison to the devaluation of the Holocaust that is hidden in untruths and camouflaged by a quasi-scientific doctrine. Primo Levi, a non-Zionist, provided the correct response to the baseless accusations of the post-Zionists:

> Here's what the state of Israel was intended for, and it was supposed to change the history of the Jewish people, but in a very precise sense: it was supposed to be a lift raft, the sanctuary to which Jews threatened in other countries would be able to run. That was the idea of the founding fathers, and it preceded the Nazi tragedy: the Nazi tragedy multiplied it a thousandfold. Jews could no longer do without that country of salvation. Nobody stopped to think that there were Arabs in that country. In truth there weren't very many. And it was considered a negligible fact compared with this tremendous driving force that was sending Jews there from all over Europe.[41]

No national movement is impervious to defects and mistakes, and Zionism is no exception to the rule. This holds true for every school of thought within Zionism as well. Zionism is not and cannot be immune to criticism, and its historiography is subject to constant reexamination. Thus, critical historians do not lack for sufficient causes to conduct this sort of reappraisal. Moreover, the historical schools of thought they purport to represent make it easy for them to disregard the accepted version of history that is made—and sometimes also written—by the leaders. Emphasis should be placed on those segments of the population—Jewish and Arab alike—whose perspectives have never been incorporated in political-diplomatic history.

---

41. Ferdinando Camon, *Conversations with Primo Levi* (London: Marlboro Press, 1989), 53–54.

The historians were given a golden opportunity to reinforce a trend already under way in Israeli society. In recent years, inroads have been made on the egocentric characterization of a one-dimensional, highly ideological Yishuv that considered the new Jew—the Sabra Israeli—to be the culmination of the Jewish evolutionary process. By properly investigating the historical foundations of this myth, the new historians may have contributed to a more complex, multidimensional perspective, which has come to include an ever-increasing awareness of "the other." Academics, whose natural inclination is neither to accept nor to consecrate the status quo, can play an important role in accelerating this process.

It is entirely natural that academics who specialize in history and the social sciences would emphasize the blunders of the past and the complex realities of the present and would grant expression to "the other"—Arab and Jew alike. Immersed in their heroic struggle to establish the state, Zionist leaders never paid any attention to the complexity of the society they led. In denying the legitimacy of the Exile, they reduced the status of the Sabra's "inferior stepbrother" in the Diaspora to a mere caricature. The European-born leaders of Israel, staunchly believing in the melting pot in which new generations would be formed, were not wise enough, during the years of mass immigration, to understand the need to preserve the distinct cultural uniqueness of the Oriental communities. The leaders of the Yishuv, who became the leaders of the state, lacked the sense and sensibility to grant full equality of rights to the Arab minority of Israel.

Zionism, then, had a lot to learn, and it has taken half a century or more for some of these issues to be thrashed out. One might think that this would prove to be a fertile area of research to the inquiring historian. However, the critical academics have generally not been interested in initiating new expositions of virgin historical territory. Their primary goal has been to unearth facts and documents that validate their personal ideology. Because most of them attack the Zionist idea itself and have thus alienated themselves from the vast majority of the Jewish public, they have had even less influence than other academics. In attacking their predecessors, they have received and continue to receive prominent exposure in the press and the academic world. But all this sound and fury has had no effect at all on the formidable challenges now faced by Israeli society, and certainly has done nothing to reduce the nationalist-religious–ultra-Orthodox threat from the Right. The opposite is the case, as noted at the beginning of this chapter: Unintentionally, the new historians play into the hands of the right wing. In their attempt to deny the real significance of the Holocaust, some have aligned themselves with dubious allies. The fact that most of their writings in Israel are published through the patronage of the mainstream Zionist movements only proves how much more open, and less doctrinaire, Israeli society is than that which they describe in their writings.

Reading through their articles and books, one cannot tell where they are heading. Until the Oslo Agreement, the slogan of the Left was "Two States for Two Peoples." Everyone immediately knows who one of the peoples is—the Arab-Palestinian people. In this case, it is all right to be a people with a right to self-determination. But who is the second people? If it is not the Jewish people, then who? Some revisionists openly acknowledge who that people is: all of the citizens of the state, in the same way as the United States is a country of all its citizens. Others are wary of issuing such bold declarations and are content with implied hints that lead in this direction.

But if this is what is meant by the second people, why should we need two states? Why not unite the two states—and, as long as we are at it, why not the entire Middle East—into one big secular, democratic country, not unlike the kind that used to be featured in PLO propaganda? After all, it is well known that there is no more secular and democratic a society than the Palestinian society, and the United States is the model that the entire Arab Middle East is yearning to adopt.

Moreover, the radical critics point out that the Arabs of Israel are part of the Palestinian Arab people. Indeed, this is how Israeli Arabs define their own national—as opposed to civil—status. If this is so, however, then there is no "Israeli people" that unites Arab and Jewish Israelis as a nation. If it is to be taken seriously, the principle of "Two States for Two Peoples" must also recognize the right of the Jewish people to self-determination. Herein lies the very essence of Zionism. Anyone genuinely interested in creating an "Israeli people" must, in the name of intellectual honesty, propose that Israel's Arabs, no more and no less than its Jews, should relinquish their present national identity. It must be patently obvious that not a single critic of Zionism would ever dream of supporting such an idea.

What would be the ethical, political and intellectual consequence of accepting the post-Zionist concept of an "Israeli people," in whose name its critics attack Zionism? Nothing but empty slogans.

Interestingly, this radical group has not yet come to terms with what the PLO took upon itself at Oslo: mutual recognition between the two peoples, so different from one another, who have fought for years over the same little hardscrabble piece of land and who now, let us all pray, have set out on the path of mutual recognition and conciliation.

10

A Home—Not a Temple

Within a fairly short period of time the majority of world Jewry will be living in Israel, and even today more Jewish children live in the Jewish state than anywhere else in the world. By the year 2020, 41.7 to 52 percent of the world's Jews will be living in Israel, both as a result of immigration to Israel and because of its greater population growth as compared with that of the Diaspora. This is this the victory of the movement that began as a small and quixotic trickle in the late nineteenth century, in the face of unprecedented hostility and violence. It is a great victory from yet another aspect: Zionism arose as a minority movement, surrounded on all sides by the bustle of competing movements and ideas. It cannot even be claimed that Zionism was unique in its being a national movement. Various other such movements, calling for cultural and personal autonomy for Jews within their mother countries according the ideas promulgated by historian Shimon Dubnow and by the Bund, the Yiddish-speaking Jewish workers' movement itself—both before the advent of political Zionism, and following it—also gave expression to Jewish nationalism. Today, after the slaughter of the vast majority of Europe's Jews, only two dominant Jewish factors continue to exist in Israel and the Diaspora: Zionist nationalism and halachic Orthodox Judaism. Nothing remains of Zionism's many opponents. Jews who want to remain Jewish, and who want their children to remain Jewish, have two means to express this desire: either through their faithfulness to the halachic civilization or in their affinity to Israel. Visit Jewish schools anywhere in the world where Jews reside and you are sure to find one of these two foci of attraction, and sometimes both. Jewish revolutionary movements are a thing of the past; belief in the enlightenment is no longer perceived as the solution to the Jewish problem. Assimilation has ceased to be held as a general philosophy, but rather as an individual determination of Jews who no longer wish to remain Jewish, either because of marriage to a non-Jew or as the result of a personal decision. Jews can now succeed and flourish in democratic countries without having to relinquish their Judaism. There are no Jewish communities that do not have ties to Zion and Zionism. What started out as an esoteric conference in Basel is today claiming a resounding victory. There is no longer any Judaism, excepting the haredi—ultra-Orthodox—type that is not Zionist. The non-Orthodox movements, representing the majority of Jews in the United States, adhere, both by means of their interpretation of Judaism and their loyalty, to the Zionist idea.

The claim that the Zionist leadership invented this survival impulse, the desire to continue this sense of belonging, as part of a world of demonic and imaginary manipulations, is not consistent with the facts. It is doubtful whether the Zionist renaissance, along with the revival of the Hebrew language, can be included in the sweeping theories generally used to define and explicate nationalism and national movements.

The argument itself borders on the absurd: The desire of the individual or of a group to belong to a larger group—whether tribal or national—cannot be quantified scientifically. Not all Jews wish to remain Jews, but for those who do, the State of Israel, in the national version—or the Holy Land, in the Orthodox version—has a central appeal that no theory can abolish. These are the facts of life, and if they are not consistent with the dogmatic doctrines of scholars, then this is where the rational debate comes to an end.

Is it at all possible to create a theory that binds Jewish history in all its incarnations to one central concept? Jewish nationalist Orthodoxy has an unequivocal answer: the Land of Israel, the sacred land that was promised to the Jewish people, belongs to the chosen people of the Covenant, according to the Torah of Israel by virtue of the commitment to the revelation at Sinai. Ahad Ha'am suggested a common link in the history of this unique people: Religious civilization was in fact just another incarnation of the national spirit, reflected in different periods in different ways. Such incarnations evince a continuous and uniform survival instinct. It all ultimately depends on certain axiomatic assumptions and a basic philosophy. Do you base your personal philosophy on a religious perception that sees Israel as a step in the direction of the creation of a "nation of priests, a holy people"? Is Israel's position among the nations of the world dictated by that same divine role, which divided the Jews from all the other nations, decreeing isolation and hostility between the chosen people and the Gentiles who do not know Him? Is Balaam's prophesy—"For from the top of the rocks I see him, and from the hills I behold him: it is a people that shall reside alone, and shall not be reckoned among the nations"—to be considered a curse or a guide for present-day Israel? Or is the primary point of departure perhaps the need, or the desire, to maintain the Jewish people in its own country—and this is the source of everything, including the relationship to the divine commands and the Messianic tradition? Or perhaps, as in Ahad Ha'am's view, biblical and halachic tradition must be seen as part of that same manifestation of a national entity, which takes on different forms and shapes with changing times and circumstances. Or perhaps we must go even further and take the State of Israel, or at least its secular aspect, not merely as a modern reincarnation of an ancient civilization, but as the creation of a new nation that has cast off its links with the old Jewish world, a satellite that has pried itself loose from the old launching pad of tradition– a butterfly, as it were, emerging from exile's cocoon.

The polarization within Israeli society has intensified the difficulty—formidable from the outset—of finding answers to these questions acceptable to all the trends, movements, and views prevalent in Israel and in the Diaspora. Political compromise is a fact of life, but ideological compromise has become almost impossible. Herzl and his nonreligious associates obscured the essential religious polemic because they wanted the rabbis to be active partners in Zionist action, and because adherence to religious tradition made it possible to skirt the issue of Jewish identity that is not religious. Today, however, there is no way to reconcile the contradiction between Dr. Theodor Herzl and Dr. Baruch Goldstein, a fervently religious physician who murdered scores of praying Muslims in Hebron, or between the Basel program and the settlers of Hebron. The Rabin assassination created a crisis in Judaism, not only because of the horrifying act itself, supported by a not inconsiderable number of people, but because it illustrated the depth of the abyss dividing the two mutually alien perceptions; that is, between humanistic, peace-loving and compromise-seeking Zionism, on one hand, and national-religious Messianism, which rejects the very principles and foundations of classic Zionist teachings, on the other.

The contradiction is fundamental, because it relates to the very foundation and guiding principles of the Zionist idea. This does not imply that anyone subscribing to the traditional Zionist school, surveying Jewish history from a national point of view—and in this respect there is no difference between Herzl, Ahad Ha'am, Jabotinsky, and Ben-Gurion—is ignoring the forces represented by the Jewish religion and halachic continuity in the life of the Jewish people. Moreover, people who adopt a Zionist-national viewpoint—rather than a religious one—do not necessarily have to adopt an Ahad Ha'am-type philosophy, which regards all the various historical incarnations of the Jewish people as manifestations of one unique national entity, which sometimes takes on a religious guise, only to divest itself of it when the time for nationalism has come. Despite the clarity of his formulation, Ahad Ha'am himself is aware of the less than rational aspect of his theory—the nonreligious continuity of a nation, whose very existence, struggles and survival in the past were inextricably linked with a monotheistic philosophy and a lifestyle based on the strict observance of the commandments of the Torah:

> History has not yet satisfactorily explained how it came about that a tiny nation in a corner of Asia produced a unique religious ethical outlook, which, though it has had so profound an influence on the rest of the world, has yet remained so foreign to the rest of the world, and to this day has been unable either to master it or to be mastered by it. This is a historical phenomenon to which, despite many attempted answers, we must still attach a note of interrogation. But every true Jew, be he Orthodox or liberal, feels in the depths of his being that there is something in the spirit of our people—though we do not know what it is—which has prevented us from following the rest of the world along the beaten path, has led to our producing this Judaism of ours,

and has kept us and our Judaism "in the corner" to this day, because we cannot abandon the distinctive outlook on which Judaism is based.[1]

Indeed, until recent times, there was no doubt among Jews and non-Jews alike that a Jewish civilization, which preserved its very uniqueness in a way foreign to the "rules of history," is explicable only in terms of a communion of religious beliefs and ethnic affinity. The idea of an independently secular Jewish nation is of relatively recent origin in Jewish history, but it has one major advantage: It is the only idea that can account for the survival instinct of the Jews as a nation and their will to perpetuate this existence.

But recognition of this historical process does not mean that we must accept a uniform and monolithic interpretation of the essence of the Jewish people, its traditions, and the forces motivating it from time immemorial to the present day. Even those who recognize the forces that created and formed Judaism in the past can take into account the unique and radical shift that took place once Jewish civilization ceased to preserve its separate frameworks and its close and confining ghetto walls. We often talk of the Zionist Revolution, because it articulated new goals and charted a new course for Jewish history. And, indeed, as we have seen in previous chapters, the term *revolution* is quite apt to describe the shift. This shift preserves the constant internal tension between the old and the new, perpetuation and revolution. Yet far beyond the tension, it was always clear to Zionist leaders that something essential was changing in the basic assumptions of Jewish existence, that no longer would a common faith determine the Jews' common fate, but, rather, that it would be governed by a new kind of existence, explicated and justified in secular-national terms, which they themselves recognized from their common past and heritage.

It was not Zionism, however, that created this shift. On the contrary, when Hovevei Zion (the Lovers of Zion) first appeared in eastern Europe—and in the West, Herzl had begun to dream his impossible dream—traditional Jewish civilization was already splintered and unsettled. Emancipation opened previously locked gates.

---

1. Ahad Ha'am, quoted in Arthur Hertzberg, ed., *The Zionist Idea* (New York: Harper Torchbooks, 1966), 71.

The vigor and forcefulness with which Jews stormed out of the ghetto into the new society, and the speed with which they were prepared to adjust themselves, their religion, and their lifestyle to the non-Jewish world offered ample testimony to the shakiness of the bulwarks of traditional Judaism. Even in eastern Europe, where the majority of Jews still clung to their religious traditions and their separate Yiddish language, the agitation felt by the free, enlightened, revolutionary minority found its impetus in a pronounced dissatisfaction with the prisonlike life represented by traditional Jewish civilization. There, too, the unrest found its first expression in a demand for Western-style emancipation—accompanied by a surprising and broad willingness among the new Jewish intelligentsia to assimilate into Mother Russia and join the Russification trend. When Zionism made its appearance on stage, it sought to save the Jews from this internal erosion. Thus, a new brand of Jewish secularism grew with its own independent values, which spurned both confinement and assimilation.

Side by side with Zionism, which started out as a thin trickle, toward the end of the nineteenth century a mighty stream of emigration from the Russian Empire and Rumania to the United States grew into a mighty flood. In its own way, this massive movement, having no ideological motive outside the traditional Jewish instinct to flee an affliction and find a haven, testified to the depth of the crisis of tradition in the Jewish communities of eastern Europe. Despite the fact that the immigration transferred large Jewish concentrations from one country to another, and although the vast majority of the immigrants gathered in a few large communities, traditional Orthodoxy could not maintain its hold in a new emancipated society, and within a short time Orthodoxy became the domain of a minority. It lost its former position of leadership to other groups eager to embrace the American ethos of a melting pot, equality of all races, and interreligious ecumenicalism. The very essence of this American ethos contradicted the traditional Jewish emphasis on exclusivity and uniqueness. This emphasis, which could thrive under the cloudy skies of the Pale of Settlement, wilted under an American sun radiating enough equality to enable Jews to escape both persecution and the shackles of an antiquated doctrine. In other words, when we claim that the emancipation created a rift in the history of the Jewish people and rescinded for most Jews many of the old tenets and the idea of Jewish exclusiveness, we are not making a value judgment, we merely are describing what actually happened.

These facts distinguish between two eras of Jewish history—before and after the emancipation. In the first era, despite their dispersal and the lack of a homeland, Jews kept their devotion to the laws and customs of their faith in a way that can only arouse astonishment and admiration. In the second era, this common denominator lost its binding force and a new pluralism arose, producing both assimilation and a new Jewish nationalism. This rift in history was not only a fact, but also a juncture, which created—if one may borrow a term from jurisprudence—a new basic norm.

As Yechezkel Kaufman wrote in response to the Ahad Ha'am theory concerning religion's being a manifestation of national self:

> The Jewish religion did not serve as a "means" in the hands of those who desired national existence to maintain the nation; nor was it an archive of "the baggage of exile" used as a means by the national survival urge. The Jewish religion was the *prime mover* in Jewish history, and it forced the Jewish people to isolate itself from its surroundings, to maintain its unique character.

This is the source of the difference between the changes undergone by the Jewish people in all its various incarnations in the Diaspora and the Zionist revolution, which desired to grant it a territorial basis, and turn it into a normal nation:

> This is something as yet not experienced by Judaism. The Jewish culture which had kept the nation alive until now had no need of a territorial homeland. It was a universal culture that could exist anywhere and under any circumstances. There is no proof that a territorial-national culture will be able to fulfill the role of the old universal Judaism.[2]

The answer to the question posed by Professor Kaufman is unequivocal: Zionism cannot fulfill this role, but it can function to

---

2. Y. Kaufman, *Golah ve'Nechar* (Exile and foreignness), vol. 2 (Tel Aviv 1961), 335.

preserve the Jewish entity by means of the Jewish state and the nexus with its Diaspora.

From this aspect, the new Jewish national emancipation, in all its various incarnations, forged a geological rift in Jewish history; Zionism is the juncture, the revolution that will bridge this rift by creating a new common denominator to displace the old religious civilization. This common denominator gives priority to the idea of a people, a nation—and its becoming a normal nation—above all others, because there is no possibility of creating any other common denominator for all Jews.

Bearing this in mind, let us examine the achievements and failures of the Zionist endeavor. Anyone who peruses the history of Zionism must be aware of the gap between lofty ideals and harsh reality. A considerable portion of the assumptions on which it was based turned out to be false, and many of its hopes—despite the formidable will to realize them—were but a dream. The vast majority of Jews did not immigrate to Israel, even after the newly established state opened wide its gates, but, as stated previously, the Jews of Israel—as a result of their vitality and their birth rate, and also because of the assimilation rampant in the Diaspora, will gradually become the largest concentration of Jews in the world. The establishment of the state did not extinguish anti-Semitism; yet despite this, Jews in the Diaspora have never been stronger, better established, or more respected than during the period of the flourishing of the Jewish state. Israel finds itself in a traditionally "Jewish situation" vis-à-vis the Arab and Muslim world surrounding it, but the peace process provides hope for the beginning of normalization in this area as well. Israel is not a "safe haven" for the Jews of Israel, who must constantly be on their guard against war and terrorism, but it has immeasurably been strengthened by the military struggle for its defense. One basic issue seems to be unsolvable; the "Jewish problem" of Zionism—if it can thus be termed—remains unchanged.

The former chief rabbi of Britain's Jews, Dr. Immanuel Jakobovits criticizes secular Zionism, which "led our people to believe that if we only had a state of our own, we would normalize the Jewish condition" and finally do away with anti-Semitism. The State of Israel has not only *not* solved the problem of anti-Semitism, he writes, but rather has intensified it, giving rise to a new wave of hatred for Jews, now labeled anti-Zionism.[3]

These strong words were written during the difficult period of Israel's international isolation and anti-Israel incitement, and their great weakness lies in the fact that they relate to circumstances that were soon to change. Rabbi Jakobovits represents the Jewish world-view, and therefore it is only natural for him to utterly reject the solutions offered by secular Zionism. It is astounding, however, to what extent this idea was received by secular Israeli thinkers and philosophers. One of these, author Aharon Megged, considers hatred for Jews, which in his opinion is now focused on hatred for their state, "an irrational and mystical" phenomenon, another link in the singular Jewish history:

> And what increasingly astounds us here in Israel—the more deeply rooted here we become—is that Zionism has changed nothing in this irrational pattern. Zionism, which believed that it would do away with the "reasons" for this disease, thus completely eradicating it; that it would "restore the nation to take its place in history," that is, rational history! No, unlike all of Pinsker's and Herzl's predictions—it did not do away with the hatred, nor did it even decrease it; it only changed its color and designation.[4]

It was possible to refute these extreme comments even at the time they were written; today, after we have been given a taste of the beginnings of the peace process during the Rabin government, they sound completely hollow. Israel did not abolish anti-Semitism, nor did it claim this as one of its aspirations; yet the Jewish state not only changed the status of Jews, granting them new pride, but also changed the way Jews are perceived. Israel's existence changed something fundamental in the relationship between Jews and non-Jews.

Dr. David Hartman, an Orthodox rabbi and lecturer in philosophy at the Hebrew University in Jerusalem, elucidated this point:

---

3. Immanuel Jakobovits, *The Holocaust, Contemporary Jewry, Zionism Today—A Call for Reappraisal* (London: Office of the Chief Rabbi, 1979), 6–7.
4. *Davar* (21 September 1979).

The profound sense of isolation and spiritual loneliness experienced by the Jewish people in the Diaspora stemmed from our not being heard in the way we hear ourselves. Christianity saw us as an anachronism, as a pariah in history. Because the intimate relationship between peoplehood and spirituality in Judaism was incomprehensible to others, we found ourselves put into a straitjacket, not able to make ourselves and our relationship to God intelligible to others. . . . Now Israel stands before the world and announces publicly that peoplehood, nationhood, and spirituality are inextricably bound with each other, that Judaism cannot be understood without recognizing its peoplehood aspirations. In this sense, Israel has healed anti-Semitism by forcing the world to listen to us and hear us as we hear ourselves, and not in alien categories. . . . Israel's existence has liberated both Christians and Jews to listen with profound sensitivity to each other's particularity.[5]

Israel has put an end to this situation. It epitomizes both aspects of Judaism, the particular and the nonparticular: a combination of land, nationality, culture, and an ancient religious tradition; a normal nation, living in a normal country. Thus, says Hartman, Israel has provided a partial cure for the scourge of anti-Semitism, in forcing the world to "hear us in the way we hear ourselves." This new ability to listen opens the door to a fruitful and effective dialogue between Jews and Christians, who can now be aware of the particularity and difference between them without forcing an artificial similarity. It is no coincidence that Jewish communities are far more confident today—totally integrated politically, academically, and economically—than at any period in the past. As mentioned previously, Israel's flourishing and thriving in the wake of the Oslo agreements and the launching of the peace process during the Rabin administration provide overwhelming proof of the flimsiness of those apocalyptic theories that made traditional anti-Semitism analogous with opposition to Israel. The events of the 1990s have clearly demonstrated that the realization of the Zionist ideal is difficult and

5. David Hartman, *Ami* (Journal of the world union of progressive Judaism) 11 (Purim, 1970), 10.

requires formidable political compromises, but it is not dependent on occult or arcane factors that lie beyond or outside the laws of history. This awareness, accompanied by the tolerant and open atmosphere prevailing in democratic countries, where Jews can flourish and thrive, has completely changed the status of Jews and their own self-image and the image of Judaism in our time.

Even the alleged failures attributed to Zionism are not failures at all. The ostensible failure of the Sabra, the "super-Jew," supposedly symbolizing the enormous change Zionism brought to Judaism, is not a Zionist failure. Israeli reality has proved that a perception of the super-Sabra as the negative image or the antithesis of the inferior Diaspora Jew was artificial from the outset. Today this is all the more apparent, for alongside Israel there exists a flourishing Diaspora Jewry, sure of itself and its position, its image as remote as can be imagined from the classic one of the ghetto Jew.

The failure of the Labor movement to create a model society, and a source of inspiration—a light—unto the nations, must also be viewed soberly. The magnitude of the failure stems from the magnitude of the utopian aspiration: to do what no other nation or society had ever done; to translate the Messianic concepts and millennial vision of religious tradition into a political and economic reality; to turn a persecuted people into an ideal, egalitarian, just society. The Labor movement failed in this, but its failure requires a balanced appraisal, not only because of the grandiosity of its vision, but also because of the transmutation of the basic premises on which it was founded. The founders of the Zionist-socialist doctrine could not have foreseen the full significance of the external and internal circumstances in which they would have to build the new Jewish society. The socialistic utopia included a pacifist ideal and a burning faith in the ability to overcome Arab hostility by means of its universal vision. In 1922, the *Gdud Ha'avoda* (Labor corps) newspaper published its vision of Ein Harod, one of the first kibbutzim, after one hundred years. The writer depicts a flourishing, prosperous Ein Harod, with its "Oriental"-style houses and the monument located at its center: two people, a Jewish and an Arab worker, sitting on a stone holding a banner with the words "Equality, fraternity and freedom" emblazoned on it. A teacher relates the history of the rebirth of the Jewish people to his class "in the modern period, after the regime of the oppressors and the oppressed has come to an end, and with the foundation of the common working family of all humanity."[6] Today in Ein Harod, we can find the Sturman House, built to commemorate three generations of the Sturman family who fell in Arab-Israeli wars.

Like all the founders of the Labor movement, the architects of the Labor corps did not foresee the depth and magnitude of Arab hostility. Nor did they anticipate the dominant phenomenon that was to change the face of Israeli society after the establishment of the state: the mass immigration of Jews from Muslim countries, which brought a new urban proletariat to Israel, with whose problems the Labor movement was unequipped to deal. The absorption of this immigration, and the disparities that still characterize its second and third generations, adversely affect Israel's achievements. And yet, if the education system carries on the comprehensive reform started during the Rabin administration, and if other corresponding steps are taken, this wound will eventually heal as well.

Alongside its inability to put a total end to anti-Semitism, to be absorbed into the family of Middle Eastern nations, and to establish a model society, this sober vision of Zionist history can present a list of Israel's accomplishments. The list is impressive, particularly because the State of Israel was forced to arise and develop under the shadow of endless Arab-Israeli conflict and the burden of the absorption of mass immigration. Despite all its shortcomings and faults, Israel has succeed in maintaining civil freedoms, a democratic government, the supremacy of the courts, and freedom of speech, even in times of siege and war. The Ingathering of the Exiles and the mending of their wounds were undertaken under the most difficult of circumstances. Under successive governments of Israel, especially during the Rabin administration, Arabs in Israel attained economic prosperity and advancement in the area of education, although complete equality is still a long way off.

Despite economic failure in the early years, an impressive industrial substructure was established. There were exciting accomplishments in agriculture and technology, and Israel became a prosperous country with a very impressive rate of growth. The immigration from the Commonwealth Independent States and Ethiopia, on a

---

6. *Mehayenu* (Journal of the Labor corps) 11 (November 1922); republished by the Labor archive in 1971.

scale unrivaled except by the previous mass immigrations in Israel's early years, not only strengthened Israel but also gave added validity to the Zionist ethos: If not for the existence of the Jewish state, entire communities of Jews—especially in Arab countries—would still be living in a state of economic and political inferiority, devoid of civil rights or the ability to realize the potential they embodied.

From this aspect, it can be stated that indeed Zionism has won and that its victory must touch the imagination of any objective observer. But a new and destructive Israeli reality threatens the classic Zionist perception based on the philosophy of the founding fathers of Zionism. The threat comes from two directions. The first is the danger of religious and haredi Judaism becoming the spearhead of nationalism in its most repulsive forms; the second is the threat to the essence of Judaism and the introduction of unenlightened elements into it. Rabin's assassination was no accident. In the words of Rabbi Aharon Soleveichik, "This is the greatest catastrophe we have brought upon ourselves since the destruction of the Second Temple."[7] The assassination must be considered along with everything that preceded and followed it—the latent and not inconsiderable support the assassin enjoyed, the absence of haredim from the funeral, and the repeated attempts to desecrate the grave—from the Jewish historic perspective. Jewish communities lived in the Diaspora for many generations, and they took on both virtuous and negative characteristics, but ideological murder, murder in God's name, was not one of them. And here, within the national home, of all places—in direct contravention to everything Zionism stands for—has arisen a considerable force that champions, both in word and action, murderous and destructive ideas against Arabs and Jewish "traitors"—all in the name of the Torah. This force is actively threatening Israeli democracy and uses violence routinely to protest against decisions that are not to its liking. One has to pinch

---

7. A quote from comments made by Professor Avi Ravitzki at a roundtable discussion on the subject "Yitzchak Rabin—A Self-Examination" which took place at the Democracy Institute on September 18, 1996, published by the Institute, page 2. Ravitzki quotes from his notes additional comments made by Rabbi Soleveichik: "I also failed in that I did not protest with the required force against those who sought a dispensation for the murder. Therefore we cannot say that our hands did not spill this blood." But in the discussion itself, Ravitzki added, "I think he has calmed down a bit since then." It is characteristic that even this lone and courageous voice is not to be found written anywhere, but is available only in the (reliable) testimony of Ravitzki.

oneself when recalling that on the eve of the Six-Day War, the National Religious Party ministers opposed the conquest of the West Bank and East Jerusalem. Their political offspring have undergone a political mutation. One has to remind oneself that haredi rabbis were always afraid to "provoke the Gentiles," and because of the law of *pikuach nefesh*—the risk to human life—they were always at the forefront of the opposition to Jewish nationalism. This caution has been replaced by a kind of haredi nationalism that does not participate in the national defense effort, but demands the implementation of an antipeace policy, which may increase the danger of war.

The danger to Judaism itself is also apparent. The humanistic and anti-idolatry tradition that Judaism bequeathed to the world is being worn down by two types of objectionable rituals: one, practiced by those who exalt the ancestral tombs in order to hold on to all of the land of Israel, and the other practiced by those who exalt the tombs of rabbis for the purpose of healing, blessings, vows, amulets, or simple commercialism.

In the period that preceded the Six-Day War, the leaders of religious Zionism sought to find a synthesis between adherence to tradition and enlightened progress, between Torah and Labor; instead, it produced a synthesis between dark malediction and idol worship. This reality was completely unforeseen by the founders of Zionism, both of the Right and the Left. It is distressing to large sectors of the population, including right-wing and nonsecular people, to whom this phenomenon is completely alien. Tommy Lapid, a journalist never associated with the Left, writes:

> Where does it come to them, these Jews? This confidence in a Messianic vocation, coming from the barrel of a gun? How, in one generation, did they turn hundreds of years of Jewish humanism into a doctrine of sanctimonious aggression? What type of primordial Judaism do they represent? Is this Judaism? Are they Jews? Is this how Jews behave?
>
> Religious Judaism is making a fatal mistake: the haredi brand, which transported the Diaspora to this country, and the nationalist brand, which left behind in the Diaspora the humanistic sides of Judaism. A wave inspired by an evil wind is sweeping over us, and we are drowning in the mire, grasping at straws. You don't have to be a Leftist or a bleeding

heart—it's enough to be a secular liberal to wonder: Do I have any idea what country I'm talking about?[8]

But this reality takes on even more severe implications because of the fact that the majority of Jews—especially those who originate from North America and western Europe—no longer live in misery and deprivation in the Diaspora, but rather in a democratic, tolerant and open society. Thus, the Diaspora—which was once negated by Zionism—suddenly becomes an equal, a parallel community abroad, sometimes a source of envy for those Israeli Jews who consider themselves part of a democratic and humanistic family. And, indeed, in many aspects that community abroad becomes a model that many Israelis aspire to reach: The Jewish communities abroad are free of the burden of the combination of religion and politics, of religious coercion and the Orthodox monopoly; they exist and flourish on the basis of pluralistic tolerance. This coexistence persevered until Israel began exporting its own problems to the Diaspora, introducing strife and contention in its vain and unsuccessful attempt to confine Judaism within the bounds of the halachic-Orthodox version. The responsibility Israel must bear in this matter, because of its divisive policies and the capitulation to the demands of Orthodoxy, is indeed grave. Zionism today must contend with the question of the continued collective existence of the Jewish people with all its various divisions and factions. Professor Joseph Gorney writes that the current divisive trend among American Jews, especially between the Orthodox movement and the non-Orthodox groups—a consequence of the "Who is a Jew?" issue and Israel's refusal to recognize the existence and legitimacy of these movements—is liable to gain momentum if no effort is exerted from above to check it: "The halting of this process is a Zionist mission, because there is no other idea or ethos, save Zionism, which can unify most of the different movements and shades in the Jewish people."[9] This link with the Diaspora is indeed Israel's greatest achievement, as well as its great failure: without it there is no real common denominator; with it, the common denominator is weakened and endangered.

---

8. *Ma'ariv* (Hebrew daily) (Tel Aviv), 27 December 1996.
9. *Ha'aretz*, (Hebrew daily) (Tel Aviv), 1 August 1997.

But it is not only the distress of Jews living abroad that is involved. Israeli Jews who are not observant of Jewish law have also come to realize that it is easier for them to preserve their bond to Jewishness while they are abroad: There they can send their children to Jewish schools, visit the local Jewish community center, go with the family to synagogue, and get married, without any of these activities becoming embroiled or implicated in Israeli politics or the great debates dividing Israeli society.

The religious-haredi-nationalistic assault has rent asunder the delicate fabric that enabled Zionism and Israel to mend the rifts, incorporating both the national and halachic element in it. This assault endangers the use both worldviews have made of each other over the years, the mutual benefit both perceptions have derived from each other. It eclipses the other, magnificent, and exceptional achievements made by the Jewish national revival movement. Classic Zionism is sustained by two mutually opposing but complementary theories: that of Ahad Ha'am, who considers the religious manifestation an incarnation of the national spirit, and that of religious Zionism, which considers the national-secular manifestation an authentic Jewish incarnation. Worst of all, this assault not only imperils the political compromise between two Jewish forces, but also damages the true and complex view of the Jewish experience.

Secular Judaism must recognize the complexity of the Jewish experience, its historical-religious foundations, and the unique character of its culture and history. A perusal of the history of the Jewish people cannot but arouse amazement and admiration at its remarkable survival, its enormous store of talent, and its inability—even when a considerable number of those among it are interested in doing so—to lose its particular identity. The same can be said for the responsibility of halachic Judaism to recognize the complexity of the Jewish state and its duty to preserve the rules of democracy and grant full equality to all its citizens, including the right of its Arab citizens to take part in deciding its future. Torah Judaism must also realize that there is no point or purpose to a Jewish state that is not democratic. The soul-searching that the leadership of religious-Zionist and religious-haredi Judaism must perform should have taken place following the series of traumatic acts of violence and murder, which reached its height with the assassination of Prime Minister Yitzhak Rabin. But this soul-searching never took place, and the little that was begun was swept away by the jubilation at the election victory achieved by these two camps in the 1996 elections when Netanyahu was elected prime minister.

The two extreme views—that which ignores Jewish heritage and that which would eradicate the moral and universal foundations of Judaism—harm the delicate balance between Israel, which values its connection with Jewish communities abroad, and the communities themselves, for whom Israel is the focus of interest. The religious and haredi nationalism is taking Judaism back to the ghetto—this time armed to the teeth with the latest in state-of-the-art weaponry, but still a ghetto—from which it desired to escape. This ghetto is twofold: It is closed off from the "goyim," and it is a ghetto within the Jewish world, the vast majority of which rejects the new fundamentalism.

It could, of course, be claimed that classic Zionism tried to evade the choice between two opposing Jewish views, and that the national and folkloristic attitude toward halachic Judaism is tainted by hypocrisy. But there was a lot of useful charm in this "hypocrisy," which tried not to exhaust all these disparities while retaining both a semblance of mutual affinity and a nebulous desire to preserve the old-time traditions. Herzl, who was called to the Torah to recite the Torah blessings in the Synagogue in Basel on the eve of the first Zionist Congress, was no mere political maneuverer. He was expressing a broad popular yearning to unite the people on an as yet unclear foundation, based on their almost instinctive need to work together. What did the Zionists ultimately want?

When one surveys the history of Zionist thought, one must be impressed by the duality that inheres in the very concept of normalization. On one hand, there are the lofty ideals and the impressive deeds, in seeking to turn the Jewish state into a model state, a leader of nations, a pacesetter on the road to progress; on the other hand, one is also struck by a certain spiritual shallowness of the vision itself. Secular Messianism may have sounded like an apt term—and the semireligious revolutionary fervor was certainly there—but Zionist thinking is bereft of true religiosity. Those who gave expression to the Zionist idea and made it come true did not see in Jewish nationalism a means of spiritual salvation. They wanted to establish a progressive Jewish society, but they did not seek to give the Jews new tablets of the Law. Theirs was a down-to-earth wish: to give the

Jews a home—a house, not a Temple—so that they would be able to live in it in decency, preserve old traditions, develop their old-new language, create their new culture, continue their quarrels, and serve as a welcoming shelter to their suffering brethren. They wanted the new dwellers of the old, forsaken home to become new liberated Jews and to act as orderly good neighbors among the older members of the family of nations. Herzl and his followers needed neither a new Temple nor an alternative to old altars. It was not a cultural void or a spiritual need that drove them to the newly espoused idea. The claim to the Land of Israel, neglected and partially unpossessed, was made not because of its religious sanctity, but because this was the only home that Jews had ever known, from which they had been ejected, and to whose memory they have always clung. It was, in short, the only house they could call their home. The early Zionists were not conscious of the fury with which the Arab occupants would reject the return of the old owners. But this rejection, as well as the boycott of the whole neighborhood, cannot alter the nature of the house that Zionism has built: a home and not a temple, a secular nation and not a sacred tribe, a good neighbor waiting for feuds to subside and not a recluse destined and willing to reside alone. Now that the heroic period has ended, now that Israel has proven how strong it is despite its exposure to so many dangers; now that it has matured over the years and gained much experience, the time has come to reformulate the goals of the Jewish state. It will be a home—yes, but it will be a common home, in the full sense of the word: no longer will Israeli society force on its members one exclusive model or mold. Israel is the common state to so many different ethnic groups, religions, and cultures. In recent years we have witnessed a new trend. On one hand, we recognize the right of these groups to be different, their right to preserve their distinct cultures, traditions, and, as far as immigrants are concerned, their languages as well, without being forced to lose any of their unique characteristics within a common melting pot. This new understanding stems from the lessons drawn from the tribulations experienced by the immigrants in the early 1950s, as well as a more mature awareness of Israel's character and special attraction. Israel must be able to offer its citizens a diverse society with multitraditions; the special flavor of such a society springs from its unique blend of cultures, each preserving its own particularity. This particularity, however, is also the source of friction, both on the national level—between Jews and Arabs, and on the religious level—between Jews and Jews. Indeed, the recognition of the right to retain and preserve the unique qualities and features of each ethic group has become dominant. Yet an antithetical trend has developed as well, one that claims that these differences should be bridged by stressing the common values that all Israelis share and by imbuing Israeli citizenship with a meaning and substance of its own. This new sense of citizenship is particularly relevant to the status of Israel's Arab minority.

The new attitude was especially evident when Rabin was prime minister. A new path was marked out under this government: peace with the Palestinians and the Arab countries and equal rights for Israel's Arab citizens. In 1995, the Ministry of Education adopted a new civics curriculum to be used by all secular state schools, Jewish and Arab, and the ministry also took a number of additional steps to emphasize the principle of equal rights. This turning point in Israel's history, which was evident in many different areas, as well as in the very fact that the government coalition depended on Arab parties for the first time, was of great consequence, but many did not fully comprehend its implications. Suddenly, it appeared as if the old vision of abolishment of the hostility been Jews and their immediate surrounding—the Arabs, and their more remote surroundings—the international community, could perhaps be realized. A new agenda was about to be presented for relations between Jews and Arabs in Israel, and for the first time, since the establishment of the state, the seeds of a shared destiny by Israel's Arab citizens and the state began to germinate. When Rabin was assassinated, a spontaneous mourning erupted, embracing the vast majority of Israel's Arabs, attended by fear lest the assassination put an end to this new vision.[10] The perception of Israel as a society pulling in two contradictory directions—pluralism, on one hand, and full civic participation, on the other—is bound up in the preservation of Israel's dual framework, which merges and defines Israel as a *Jewish* and *democratic* state. This definition, which is included in two of Israel's basic laws outlining the civic rights of citizens of the State of Israel—Basic Law:

---

10. Shlomo Fisher claimed that the fact that "the Labor government attempted to enhance the civic nature of the State of Israel, both on the symbolic as well as on the practical level" was one of the main causes of the significant turnabout in the haredi community. *Meimad*, 9 (June–July 1997): 16.

Human Dignity, and Liberty and Basic Law: Freedom of Occupation—has been agreed upon by the Knesset and by the Supreme Court. A political compromise, advanced by this writer, lies at the foundation of the basic laws, enabling a fusion of both definitions to satisfy both desires: the desire of the religious-haredi camp to see the state described as a Jewish state, and the desire of the liberal-Left camp to see the values of the State of Israel as a democratic state anchored in a constitution-like document. In actual fact, the necessity of this dual definition encountered almost no opposition, and it enabled the passage of two basic laws that safeguard human rights for the first time in Israel's history. This definition pertains to the existing, as well as the desirable, situation. Israel is a Jewish country—the majority of its population is Jewish; it retains an inalienable bond to Jews all over the world; its official holidays are Jewish, as are its symbols and conventions. But everyone who resides within its borders—Jew and Arab alike—is entitled to all the rights enjoyed by citizens of democratic countries. The fundamental idea is that as a democratic country, Israel belongs to all its citizens, and all its citizens belong to it; its Jewish ties do not, and must not, controvert this commitment. Everything that makes it uniquely Jewish must be subject to democratic principles, and anything that cannot meet this requirement cannot be part of the common home, the laws, or the norms of Israeli society.

We do not have a precise definition that can provide criteria by which Israel's "Jewishness" can be measured. But one thing is eminently clear: What is involved is a general heritage, not the characterization of Israel as a state whose legal system is prescribed Jewish religious law. Justice Menachem Alon, an observant Jew who served as deputy chief justice of the Supreme Court, defined Israel's values according to the basic laws as deriving "from the values of Israel's heritage, and Jewish tradition and from the values of democracy of a freedom-seeking country."[11] But what is this heritage, this tradition? Chief Justice of the Supreme Court Aharon Barak responds to Alon's comments:

> To the extent to which Justice Alon considers the values of the State of Israel to be Jewish . . . having an exclusively

---

11. *Suissa v. the State of Israel,* Piskei Din (19), vol. 46 no. 3, 338 at 343.

halachic nature, I cannot concur with his position. But to the extent to which he considers the values of the State of Israel to be a range of values, including some having a religious-halachic nature (Jewish tradition) and others having a universal-Zionist nature (Jewish heritage), I fully concur with his view.[12]

Basing his survey on the Declaration of Israel's Independence, Justice Barak gives a general outline of global Jewish values, which in his opinion reflect general national and parliamentary consensus:

> A Jewish state is, therefore, the state of the Jewish people . . . to which every Jew has the right to immigrate, and of which the ingathering of the exiles is a fundamental value . . . whose history is intertwined and fused with the history of the Jewish people, whose language is Hebrew, and whose holidays reflect the national revival . . . which perpetuates the memory of Jews who were slaughtered in the holocaust, and which has been designated to be, in the words of Israel's Declaration of Independence, "the solution to the problem of a homeless Jewish people lacking independence, through the renewal of the Jewish state in the land of Israel" . . . for whom the values of freedom, justice, integrity and peace of the Jewish heritage are its values . . . whose values are derived from its religious tradition, for which the Bible is the most basic of its books, and the prophets of Israel are the foundation of its morality . . . in which Jewish law plays an important role, and where matters of marriage and divorce of Jews are decided according to the laws of the Torah.[13]

Indeed, in Justice Barak's opinion, Jewish values must be viewed in a Zionist context: "In this manner, for example, the right of every Jew to immigrate to Israel—as promised by the Law of Return—participates in the shaping of the values of the State of Israel as a Jewish state, and this influences human rights. This is a reflection of the Jewish-Zionist character of the state."

---

12. Aharon Barak, *Parshanut baMishpat* (Constitutional interpretation) vol. 3, 334.
13. Ibid., 332.

What happens when there seems to be a conflict between Jewish values and democratic values? Justices Barak and Alon express an accepted position on the matter: It is advisable to aspire to finding a common denominator between the two parts of the definition. In other words, an interpretation that can avoid a conflict between Jewish tradition and democratic principles should be found. This type of interpretation is a Zionist tradition. Justice Barak, expressing a well-established Zionist tradition, says:

> Indeed, the country is Jewish, but not in the halachic-religious sense, but rather in the sense that Jews have the right to immigrate to it, and their Jewish essence is the essence of the state. . . . I am referring to humanitarianism, the sanctity of life, social justice, following the true and honest path, preservation of the dignity of humankind, the rule of law, and all the other values that Judaism has imparted to the whole world. The invocation of these values must be on the most abstract, universal level, consistent with the democratic character of the state. Consequently, the values of the State of Israel as a Jewish state must not be identified with Jewish law. We cannot lose site of the fact that a large non-Jewish minority lives in Israel as well. Indeed, the values of the State of Israel as a Jewish state are the same universal values common to all members of democratic societies, which developed out Jewish tradition and history.[14]

Justice Barak adds that when a conflict arises between Judaism and democracy, despite the attempt to find a compromise, priority must be given to those laws that serve the goals of the basic laws—the protection of human rights, and the instructions included in both laws that determine that basic rights are founded on the recognition of the value of humankind, the sanctity of human life, and the right of all men and women to be free.

All these interpretations reflect a social and political aim: to maintain a comprehensive common framework in which the Zionist perception along with the belief in the rights of minorities and the

---

14. Barak, *Parshanut baMishpat,* 342, quoting from his article "The Constitutional Revolution: Protected Human Rights," *Law and Government,* vol. 1, 9 at 30.

individual are preserved. Let us not forget that those who interpret Jewish tradition other than according to the minutiae of halacha—rules that were formulated when the Jewish people were subservient to other nations—have no problem finding a solution to the apparent contradiction:

> Even those who support the supremacy of democracy must realize that religious and national values per se are do not conflict with democratic values. Moreover, the sources of the values according to which human rights and the idea of a covenant that would shape the democratic constitution can be found in the Jewish religion and Jewish nationalism.[15]

Hence, the expression "Judaism and democracy" has a twofold meaning. First, the two terms must be interpreted in such a manner so as not to contradict each other; in particular, the idea of Jewish identity cannot be interpreted so that it conflicts with the principle of equal rights for all residents and citizens of the country. Second, Jewish identity itself is perceived as a democratic concept, inasmuch as it is made up of various Jewish and Zionist perceptions, not of one monolithic, predetermined perception. Moreover, the decisions concerning the controversial "gray" areas are themselves subject to democratic rules and can only be made by the state institutions—the legislature or the judiciary.

In truth, Israel would not be able to exist without this type of pluralistic view. The overwhelming majority of Israel's Jews want to maintain their Jewishness and want their children, and their children's children, to continue to be Jewish. They express this desire in their lifestyle and even by continuing to observe those religious ceremonies that involve no coercion by law. It is curious to note that virtually all Israeli Jews have their sons undergo ritual circumcision, perform bar mitzvah ceremonies, are called up to the Torah, place a *mezuzah* at the entrance to their homes, and have Jewish burial services. The same cannot be said for marriage. Because of the legally sanctioned coercion, the disqualification of certain people from marrying each other, and the resented prohibitions of a coercive

---

15. Eliezer Schweid, *Hatsiyonut Aharei Hatsiyonut* (Zionism beyond Zionism) (Jerusalem, 1996), 117.

rabbinate, the number of couples who are opting to marry outside the rabbinate is on the rise.[16] Non-Orthodox Judaism—a more accurate term than "secular Judaism"—lives an instinctively Jewish life. The State of Israel brought into the world a new brand of Judaism: effortless Judaism, in which children grow up as Jews and celebrate Jewish holidays and speak Hebrew, without having to make any conscious personal decision as to their Jewish identity. And in truth, this freer Judaism has created a new Hebrew culture—one that is vibrant, critical, innovative—which has acquired an international reputation. Its poetry, literature, music, historical and archaeological research—all these are the components of an Israeli Judaism, as relevant to the self-awareness of the non-Orthodox population as the halachic bookcase is to the observant. This community, which does not even know how to exploit its political power, is not prepared to limit the concept of Judaism to the halachic civilization, even if it is respectful of its depth and ability to survive. These Israelis consider everything that happens to Jews and everything that Jews create—including the works of Heine, Kafka, and Freud—as part of their own civilization.

This relaxed and undemanding Judaism has forgone what is known as *Kulturkampf*. It is a one-sided war: The attack always comes from the same direction against the so-called promiscuous, hedonist majority. Indeed, the non-Orthodox public, which also contains a large number of traditional elements, is seen by Orthodox Jews through the distorted lens of vulgarity, obscene language, and quasi-pornography, characteristic of some sectors in the media. Thus, this very large public is often misrepresented as mere pleasure-seekers, "living for the moment." But the truth is entirely different. It is this population that forms the creative and dynamic nucleus of Israeli society, in the arts, in science and industry. Without this creative element, Israel's society would be poorer in every sense, including materially and spiritually. Despite this, the non-Orthodox public does not return ideological fire. There is no longer any contemporary echo to Herzl's demand "to prevent any theocratic tendencies

---

16. In 1974, 28,568 couples married in the rabbinate; twenty years later, after the Jewish population of Israel had risen by 52.7 percent, from 2.9 million to 4.44 million, and despite the large rise in population among the religious and haredi sectors, only 26,680 couples married in the rabbinate in 1994. All the others opted to marry outside the official rabbinate of Israel.

from coming to the fore on the part of our priesthood" or to his promise that "we shall keep our priests within the confines of their temples in the same way or we shall keep our professional army within the confines of their barracks."[17] It is hard to outdo the bluntness and boldness of Jabotinsky's comments, unqualifiedly rejecting Judaism as if it implied "the interference of religion in life, a woman in a wig, with whom a strange man cannot shake hands" that Jabotinsky refuses to consider part of "the organic essence of Judaism."[18] What has happened to the "Maskilim"—the eighteenth-century rebels—defying their parents' and grandparents' traditions? Gone are all the antireligious ideologists of yesteryear, the apostates for spite, the old firebrands. The non-Orthodox want only one thing: to be left alone to preserve their own lifestyle and the pluralistic character of their state and society. This is their war of defense, and because of their own nonbelligerent and individualistic nature, there is no real war.

This nonbelligerent camp has resigned itself to the basic asymmetry that exists between it and the two more belligerent camps—the haredi and the religious-nationalist—mobilized on the other side. The state-religious education system, to say nothing of the hermetically isolated haredi education system, will not allow entry to any nonobservant person in any capacity, not even to teach neutral subjects such as mathematics, languages, or natural sciences, whereas the regular school system is open to all. Religious proselytizers are permitted to do their work in non-Orthodox neighborhoods, but the opposite is inconceivable. Religious-nationalist settlers may defy the will of the Knesset and the government, but everyone else must be completely law-abiding.

Despite all this, despite this passivity on the part of the non-Orthodox population, religion has become the number one issue in the country today, the subject of intense controversy. Indeed, this is the source of the great paradox: It is now, at a time when the great and thorny controversies that characterized the Jewish world before the Holocaust have disappeared, when an undemanding atmosphere of laissez-faire, of live-and-let-live, has developed among the non-Orthodox population, that the dispute has so intensified. But the

---

17. Theodor Herzl, *The Jewish State* (New York: Dover Publications, 1988), 146.
18. Ze'ev (Vladimir) Jabotinsky, *Reshimot* (Notes) (Tel Aviv, n.d.), 281–282.

reasons for this stem exclusively from the attempt to enforce norms in Israel—both in regard to political issues, as well as in matters of lifestyle—which the vast majority of the general public, despite its passivity, rebels against.

Indeed, these distressing circumstances can only dictate one solution: The Jewish democratic state must be like an apartment complex whose individual units belong to the tenants, as in a condominium—so common in Israel. But this is not just one more building on the block; this is the Jewish national home, the place where all Jews will feel at home.

This is the home, and it is not the sanctified home of the zealots and sicarii of the Second Temple. Yes, the Holy Temple is preserved in the hearts of observant Jews, and their prayer for generations has been that "the Temple be rebuilt in our time"; but Zionism, including religious Zionism until its fanatical fringe took hold of it, never considered this prayer to be a realistic political blueprint for action. Religious Zionism believed that a time would come when "[God's] house shall be called a house of prayer for all people." Yet in 1967, its representatives in the government opposed the conquest of the Temple Mount and East Jerusalem and supported the prohibition against Jewish prayer—for halachic as well as political reasons—in the place that had become a holy site to Islam. The building of the Third Temple was not part of the National Religious Party's political program.

Indeed, Israel should be involved in the construction of a different type of house—in the meanwhile, until the Messiah comes, the believer would say; building a place to live, the home of Jews who will share it, in equality, with other Jews and non-Jews; and it will be a place of refuge for Jews who wish to find shelter in it, and to feel that it is their home. This common home symbolizes Israel's two components: unity and particularity—that is, a common citizenship, with a variety of cultures and religions; common property side by side with individually owned separate cultural apartments.

This book has shown that Zionism did not want to relinquish the unique characteristics of the new Jew—his old and new language, the treasures of his tradition, his ancestry, the values of his unique culture. But the fathers of Zionism did want—consciously and deliberately—to relinquish the idea of the Jewish people's separateness from all the nations of the world. They aspired to release the Jewish people from its traditional position in which it stood outside of history, waiting for the coming of the Messiah. Put simply, the question is: Will Israel now return to the foundations of its pre-Zionist Jewish existence? But this question pertains not only to Israel's external relations, but also to everything involving the psychological relationship of Israel and its Jews to its non-Jewish citizens. During its pre-Zionist period of self-isolation, Judaism had to protect and defend itself from its vulnerability to attack and persecution from the Gentile world by developing extreme anti-Gentile laws.

A delightful little utopia, written in 1898 by an Algerian Jew, Jacques Behar, made the same point through a grotesque parable. Entitled "Anti-Gentileness in Zion," the short tale appeared in *Die Welt* while the Dreyfus affair was raging, its ramifications reaching the shores of North Africa. Behar, who represented the Algerian Jews in the First Zionist Congress and depicted there the plight of his brethren, described in his piece the Jewish state in 1997, the one-hundredth anniversary of the Basel Congress.

In that year, his story goes, the Jewish state witnesses an inverted Dreyfus case. A Jew is brought to trial because of an anti-Gentile article he has published in which he inveighs against the plots hatched by foreigners and non-Jews. The trial is a Dreyfus mirror image except for one aspect: "While in Europe, the masses sided with the bigots . . . the inhabitants of Jerusalem demonstrated the hatred they felt for him . . . as well as for the small, but agile, anti-gentile party." And why? Because in their state, "all the distinctions pertaining to religion, race and creed were obliterated and one law was promulgated for Jew and non-Jew alike. This law brought to the Jewish state a stream of non-Jewish immigrants, who have benefited the land and who intermarried with the indigenous Jews."

Who are these anti-Gentile groups? The words are scathing:

> They are always the ones to use lofty phrases—pretending to be the meek and righteous of the earth—to stress the importance of sublime principles; but they fulfill not even one of those principles. And while the whole country highly esteems the great benefits these foreigners have brought to our country, they cast aspersions on the entire country, accusing it of being anti-patriotic, advocating a brutal and parochial form of nationalism.

The accused defends his libelous article in court: "I am a Jew, a native of Eretz Israel. Born on this sacred Canaanite land, in Hebron, site of the resting place of the Patriarch Abraham, man of God, and therefore I am tied to our land through stronger links than those cosmopolitans." But the prosecutor responds to this anti-goyish tirade by reaffirming the nation's concepts of its tolerant, pluralistic nature and demands, "in the name of Herzl and Nordau," a severe sentence. This request having been granted, the masses rush to the streets to celebrate the victory of tolerance and "congratulate each other upon the demise of anti-Gentileness."

Indeed, religious chauvinism in Israel also ignores problems created within a strict Orthodox tradition. Their attitude to the non-Jew, both within and outside Israel, invokes sayings and rules from the Halachah that date back to the very origins of Judaic law. Theirs, so they claim, is the true interpretation governing relations between the People of the Convenant and the rest of the world. Their interpretation of Mosaic sources is rejected by many religious sages and thinkers within Israel and, needless to say, finds no receptive ears in non-Orthodox Jewish communities in the Diaspora. But the very issue that they have raised should be examined and exposed to a frank discussion.

Judaism was forged in a desperate battle against paganism; it was an island of monotheism in an idol-worshiping civilization. The central themes of Mosaic Law and biblical admonitions—chosenness, sanctity, the Convenant—were the issues on which this battle was joined. By the time other monotheistic creeds came into being, the Jews had lost their independence and were fragmented into subservience and persecution. Jewish laws pertaining to the pagans, the worshipers of idols, were thus instinctively applied to the new oppressors—Christians as well as Muslims—with an understandable vengeance. This application served a dual function: preserving the separate entity of the endangered creed and providing a kind of psychological relief from, and a sublimated retribution for, the humiliation and suffering inflicted upon them. As the persecution of the Jews in the Middle Ages grew to horrific proportions, so did the anti-Gentile streak acquire a more explicit, if merely academic, nature. There had always been theological elements justifying such an attitude, but the growth of persecution drenched these elements in blood and the fires of the Inquisition charred them beyond recognition. How pathetic was this Jewish response to the blood libels, the stakes, the pogroms.

The Jews scribbled on papers their claim to superiority, corroborating in the rabbinical *responsa* the inferior nature of the heathen non-Jew, elaborating on his state of rightlessness, adumbrating the injunctions against lending him assistance or credibility. While they scribbled these impotent dicta, Jews were being expelled, burned at the stake, beaten to death, and massacred en masse. In this uneven contest, Christian anti-Semitism scourged the Jews with physical violence while the Jews had to content themselves with a paper revenge, inveighing against the Gentiles with their Talmudic scholarism, drawing a direct analogy between the Christians and the idolators against whom the prophets rained their fury. Until the Age of Enlightment, the Jews had virtually no legal rights in Christian Europe, but in their literature they denied such rights, in thir powerless rabbinical courts, to Gentile witnesses.

That this paper vehemence against the non-Jew was directly related to the state of the Jews cannot be doubted. Theological considerations were influenced not only by dogma, which by its very nature lends itself to various interpretations, but by the actual relations between Jew and non-Jew. Professor Jacob Katz of the Hebrew University, in a series of studies, demonstrated this link between the factual position of the Jewish communities and their scholastic attitude toward the Christians. From the Middle Ages, when the very act of *kiddush hashem,* the voluntary sacrifice of the Jewish martyrs, sought to demonstrate the moral superiority of their faith over that of their oppressors, Jewish religious writings moved to an intermediate stage in the sixteenth and seventeenth centuries: The Christian neighbor acquired a new status, and the common basis of Judaism and Christianity was gradually admitted. The new tolerance by Christians in the seventeenth and eighteenth centuries gave rise to a new type of enlightened Jew, the Maskil; its impact was not lost even on the Orthodox rabbis.

Two of the most renowned sages of the time, Rabbi Yair Chaim Bachrach (1638–1702) and Rabbi Yaacov Emden (1697–1776) reacted to the new tolerance by emphasizing the common religious tradition of the two great monotheistic creeds, and the latter went even further by claiming that Jesus did not intend to deny the binding power of the Torah but only aspired to spread the basic tenets of

Judaism among the Gentiles. The brutal conflict between Christians and Jews was thus seen as but the tragic outcome of a historical misunderstanding. With the rise of rationalism, this trend acquired greater influence—especially in such tolerant countries as Germany, France, and Holland—and became manifest in the humanistic and universalist approach of Moses Mendelssohn and, later, of the founders of Reform Judaism. By 1807, when Napoleon convened the famous Sanhedrin, a council of Jewish scholars and sages from France, Italy, and Germany, to respond to his questions about the nature of Judaism, the Jewish consensus had shifted toward an emphasis on the universalist nature of the Jewish tradition and on the commandment to treat the Christian citizens with brotherly love. The members of the Napoleonic Sanhedrin wrote:

> This sentiment was at first aroused in us by the mere grant of toleration. It has been increased, these eighteen years, by the Government's new favors to such a degree that now our fate is irrevocably united with the common fate of all Frenchmen. . . . It is impossible that a Jew should treat a Frenchman, not of his religion, in any other manner than he would treat one of his Israelitish brethren.[19]

Indeed, by the end of the nineteenth century, Western Jewry was so engrossed in this new ecumenical spirit that many were appalled by the tauntings of the new anti-Semites citing, as they did, the embarrassing old quotations from forgotten pre-emancipation days.

The reaction of the early Zionists to these old allegations of the new anti-Semites was to cut through this maze of accusations, apologetic rebuttals, and counteraccusations and to turn thir backs on the two history-laden traditions. The Zionists' response was forthright: their wish to transplant the newly born Jewish concept of true equality for all races from the alien soil of Christian Europe to the promising land of Israel. There, in Zion, will the new tolerance really thrive, because the Jews, having been the victims of prejudice and bigotry, will create a new political climate, a true enlightened environment, where the non-Jews will enjoy the rights that Jews

---

19. Quoted in Jacob Katz, *Exclusiveness and Tolerance* (New York: Modern Times Press, 1962), 185, 187–188.

sought in vain. The new land—Herzl's *Altneuland* is merely one instance of this aspiration—is therefore the utopian mirror image of the Christian society that the Jews desired. The Jews, having gained their sovereignty, will do unto others what they wanted others to do unto them.

This mirror-image concept dominates much of early Zionist literature and fills many pages in Herzl's utopia. Yet Herzl is not blind to the dangers of a new Jewish chauvinism. In *Altneuland,* this mirror-image anti-Semitism is personified by a character named Geyer, who appeals to the mob by flaunting his anti-Gentile slogans. But Herzl inveighs against such view:

> Hold fast to the things that have made us great: liberality, tolerance, love of mankind. Only then is Zion truly Zion. . . . We stand and fall by the principle that whoever has given two years' service to the New Society as prescribed by our rules, and has conducted himself properly, is eligible to membership no matter what his race or creed.[20]

To Herzl, who named his Zionist periodical not *Zion* but *Die Welt,* it was clear that Geyer's anti-Gentile view would be soundly defeated by the enlightened Jewish majority.

It is clear how the Orthodox rabbinical establishment—and not only the rabbis of Gush Emunim—responded to the Zionist revolution. They took the anti-Gentile halachic injunctions and sometimes applied them, with even greater intensity, in the state where the Jews represent the majority of the population. They have refused to learn the ever so meaningful lesson of the Zionist revolution and the obligations imposed by the entry of Israel into the family of nations. Jacques Behar's utopia takes the authentic Zionist path, seeking to learn the lesson of Jewish suffering: that it should lead to a humanistic universalist approach emphasizing the dangers of intolerance and racism. This is the lesson embodied in the oft-repeated biblical reminders that the Jews were brought "out of the land of Egypt, out of the house of bondage," and that, consequently, they were enjoined, "Love therefore the stranger, for ye were strangers in the

---

20. Theodor Herzl, *Old-New Land,* tr. L. Levensohn (New York: Markus Wiener, 1960), 139.

land of Egypt." The nationalistic-religious front of today, on the other hand, takes the diametrically opposed route, pursuing revenge for past sufferings, beckoning the Jews, now that they have their state, to hunt with the wolves and—invoking the biblical injunction to remember the Amalekites—seeks to apply rules of exclusiveness laid down in totally different circumstances. Some seek not only to mimic the Gentiles of the past, but also to imitate the behavior of the worst elements among them. For Behar, as for Herzl, his mentor, the Jews in their country would not behave as the Gentiles had behaved toward them. In this lay the uniqueness of the Jewish people. Since then the situation in the world has changed dramatically: The majority of the Jews in the world live as equal citizens in democratic countries, where human rights are respected. But in their own country, Jews are being forced to fight to maintain a democratic system in an atmosphere of soaring nationalism.

The Rabin assassination was the climax of this extremism. The assassination itself was no mere accident, but rather a station on a road paved by an utter distortion of Judaism and Zionism. The question now is, What next? Is this assassination the last stop on an extremist-religious-nationalist slope? Or is it just one of many? Can Israel return to authentic original Zionism—the practical, broad, and tolerant Zionism of Herzl and the fathers of Zionism? Is it possible to navigate the ship of state among the rocks of violent nationalism and bring it to a safe haven, where it can again fulfill its traditional role—to be a bulwark of democracy and relative justice, enjoying broad international support?

This book has outlined the rise and fall of the original authentic Zionist vision, which aspired, above all, to turn the Jewish people into a nation like all the nations of the world without relinquishing its particularity or uniqueness. Indeed, many stumbling blocks obstructed the path Zionism sought to travel; unexpected hurdles and obstacles turned the road from a highway into an uphill trail filled with tears and tragedy. But there is no other road. Only by returning to original Zionism can Israel continue to exist as the state of the Jews, as the leader of the Jewish people, as an independent nation residing in security in its homeland, and as a nation that wishes and can attain peace with its neighbors.

Is this possible? Does Israeli society have the inner strength to pull itself out of the mire? Yes, Israel goes onward. But does "onward" mean moving forward—or, perhaps, backward? Are the Israelis going to sacrifice themselves on the graves of their forefathers—or are they going to heed the heritage of the fathers of Zionism?

One hundred years after that momentous event in Basel, it is difficult to give unequivocal answers to these questions.

This uncertainty remains unaffected by the results of the 1999 elections. True, in these elections, Ehud Barak, representing the Labor Party and declared disciple of the assassinated Rabin, won an impressive 56 percent of the popular vote, and Benjamin Netanyahu lost the elections and resigned from the Knesset. Nevertheless, the results of the separate elections to the Knesset indicated quite clearly that there was no electoral *volte-face*. The bloc consisting of the right wing and the religious parties did not diminish in power. Though the prospects of peace have been enhanced through the election of Barak, the jury is still out on the major ideological issues discussed in this book.

INDEX

Amnon Rubinstein's brilliant political career spans more than a quarter of a century. In 1974, he founded and led the "Shinui" party, which became part of the Democratic Movement for Change ("Dash"). From 1974 to 1984, he served as a member of the Knesset (Israel's Parliament), and in 1984 was appointed Minister of Communications. From 1987 to 1992, he sat on the Constitution, Law and Justice Committee, the House Committee, and was Chair of the Ethics Committee. During that time he initiated Israel's only legislation providing Constitutional protection for Human Rights: Basic Law for Human Dignity and Liberty and Basic Law for Freedom of Occupation. In 1992, he served as both Minister of Energy and Minister of Science and Technology. From 1993 to 1996, he held the post of Minister of Education, Culture, and Sports. He is currently a member of the Knesset and Chairman of the Constitution, Law and Justice Committee.

In earlier years, before Professor Rubinstein entered government service, he was Dean of the Tel Aviv Law School. He has also authored many articles and books, including *The Zionist Dream Revisited* (Schocken, New York, 1984) and *The Constitutional of Israel, Fifth Edition* (Schocken, Tel Aviv, 1997).

Amnon Rubinstein resides in Tel Aviv with his wife and their two children.